T0318437

Memory
as a
Moral
Decision

Memory as a Moral Decision

The Role of Ethics in Organizational Culture

Steven P. Feldman

Routledge
Taylor & Francis Group

LONDON AND NEW YORK

First published 2002 by Transaction Publishers

2 Park Square, Milton Park, Abingdon, Oxfordshire OX14 4RN
605 Third Avenue, New York, NY 10017

Routledge is an imprint of the Taylor & Francis Group, an informa business

First issued in paperback 2020

Copyright © 2002 Taylor & Francis

Library of Congress Catalog Number: 2002017989

Library of Congress Cataloging-in-Publication Data

Feldman, Steven P. (Steven Paul), 1954-
    Memory as a moral decision : the role of ethics in organizational culture /
Steven P. Feldman.
        p. cm.
    Includes bibliographical references and index.
    ISBN 0-7658-0586-3 (alk. paper)
        1. Business ethics. 2. Corporate culture—Moral and ethical aspects.
        I. Title.

HF5387 .F445 2002
174'.4—dc21   2002017989

ISBN 13: 978-0-7658-0586-7 (pbk)
ISBN 13: 978-0-7658-0105-0 (hbk)

To Philip Rieff

Contents

Preface

The study of management and organization is not known for its
remembrance of things past. In the structure of time—that is, past–
present–future—the past is generally forgotten. Managing the present
and mastering the future receive the lion's share of attention. Objects
of the past, like yesterday's technology or the stories of the old and
retired, are relegated to the status of museum pieces. In the study of
management and organization, of a piece with modern culture generally, the chain of memory has been broken. Perhaps nowhere in management has this resulted in more destructive loss than in the area of
ethics. Without the thread of continuity between the past, present, and
future, moral ideals have decayed; moral commitments have become
vague and shallow.

I address this loss in the field of management and organization
studies by developing a theory of *moral tradition*. The theory of moral
tradition is designed to investigate the historical and cultural context
of moral commitment. It is based on the sociology of culture and the
sociology of religion literature. It focuses on the relations between
moral culture, the individual, and the past. I apply this framework to
theories of organizational culture to investigate their moral assumptions and moral implications, that is, to explicate and understand the
moral life they imply. Theories of organizational culture, an increasingly important part of management and organization studies, are intimately related to ethics because they address the symbolic resources
men/women use to create a working environment of cooperation, purpose, and, more or less, trust.

Theories of organizational culture, although developed over the past
seventy years for different purposes by writers with different backgrounds and personalities, all turn their back on the past as a founda-

tion for moral direction. From one side or another, they incorporate the central oppositions in modern culture—for example, a hyper, secular rationalism, or irrational reactions against it; the pursuit of individual well–being, or a concern to overcome excessive individualism; and a distrust of or wish to rebuild internal moral and cognitive controls. In a series of seven critical essays, I analyze the main theories of organizational culture to investigate the moral quality of modern culture as it is found in the field of management and organization studies. For each theory, I identify explicit and implicit moral assumptions, discuss their implications for society, organizations, and the individual, and provide a historical and cultural evaluation in terms of the theory of moral tradition.

My wife, the anthropologist Regina M. Feldman, has been a partner in this endeavor. More than generous with her support, she edited each chapter in the book, often times pointing our theoretical ambiguities and weaknesses in the interpretive argument. To her I owe the most, a debt unpayable.

I have been lucky since the beginning of my career to have senior colleagues impressively knowledgeable and generous with their time and insight. For two decades John Van Maanen has commented on my manuscripts and advised my intellectual efforts. Chris Argyris and Edgar Schein have also been very kind in their help. Special appreciation goes to David K. Hart who taught me something about what an academic career should be.

Friends and colleagues from the psychoanalytic study of organizations group have also been part of my intellectual community for many years. I would like to express appreciation to Michael Diamond, Larry Hirschhorn, and Howard Schwartz.

More recently, I have benefited from conversations with and reading the works of Richard Nielsen and Mike Reed. From Nielsen I learned something about the intimate relationship between ethics and politics. I also benefited from Reed's important work analyzing organization theory in terms of the history of ideas.

I would also like to express appreciation to three editors: Clay Alderfer of the *Journal of Applied Behavioral Science*, Karen Legge of the *Journal of Management Studies*, and Ray Loveridge of *Human Relations*. Their hard work, dedication, and professionalism are most admired.

I would like to thank colleagues from the Society for Business Ethics for their support, encouragement, and for the important work they have done in creating an environment where ethics and management can be seriously discussed and debated. In a "culture" of endless change this is no small accomplishment.

I would like to say a word about the person to whom this book is dedicated, Philip Rieff. As a student, I took two seminars on textual analysis with Professor Rieff in 1981 at the University of Pennsylvania. I have spent much of the two decades since working to explore, grasp, and apply to management what he taught. This book is an interim report on this journey.

Special thanks go to my department chairman, Leonard Lynn, for his support in the writing of this book.

Finally, I would like to thank Teresa Kabat for her expertise and professionalism in typing and bringing together this manuscript.

Acknowledgments

The author gratefully acknowledges the following publishers and publications for permission to use previously published material:

Chapter 2, originally published in somewhat different form under the same title in *Journal of Management History* 2 (4):34—47, (1996).

Chapter 3, originally published in somewhat different form as "The Ethics of Shifting Ties: Management Theory and the Breakdown of Culture in Modernity," *Journal of Management Studies* 23 (2):283–300, (1996).

Chapter 4, originally published with minor differences under the same title in *Business Ethics Quarterly* 10 (3):623–43, (2000).

Chapter 5, originally published in somewhat different form under the same title in *Journal of Applied Behavioral Sciences* 36 (4):474–90, (2000).

Chapter 6, originally published with minor differences under the same title in *Human Relations* 50 (8):937–55, (1997).

Chapter 7, originally published with minor differences under the same title in *Journal of Management Studies* 35 (1):59–79, (1998).

Chapter 8, originally published with minor differences under the same title in *Journal of Applied Behavioral Science* 35 (2):228–44, (1999).

"The impulse to pray is a necessary consequence of the fact that whilst the innermost of the empirical selves of a man is a Self of the social sort, it yet can find its only adequate Socius in an ideal world.

All progress in the social self is the substitution of higher tribunals for lower; this ideal tribunal is the highest; and most men, either continually or occasionally, carry a reference to it in their breast. . . . for most of us, a world with no such inner refuge when the outer self failed and dropped from us would be the abyss of horror."

William James, *Principles of Psychology,* Vol. I, 1890: 316

Part 1

Introduction

1

The Chain of Memory: On the Relations Between Moral Culture, the Individual, and the Past

Studies of organizational culture are a central part of management and organization research. Yet the ethical aspects of organizational culture have received only minimal attention, and even less relative to moral psychology. In this chapter, I develop a theory of culture that will be used throughout the book to analyze the literature on organizational culture in terms of its ethical assumptions and implications. My goal is to increase interest in and understanding of the importance of ethics in organization life. The theory of culture I develop will focus on the relationship between individual moral development and cultural context. This will include a discussion of the role of the past in the present; that is, the role moral tradition plays in maintaining the integrity of both moral culture and character. Examples from telecommunications, electronic, medical, and educational organizations will be used to ground and develop the theoretical framework.

In the twentieth century, modern culture evolved to the point where the individual's private sense of well–being has split off from his/her sense of social responsibility (Rieff 1987). The essential fact in what amounts to a moral revolution is the breakdown in the tension between the inner feelings and outer values of man/woman. The revolution was stimulated by not only the central cultural change of our time, the growing importance of the idea of the individual (Dumont 1986), but also by the exciting social, economic, and political opportunities, and the fascinating technologies available in the external world. As in primitive culture, our focus has once again passed into things, our symbols have grown increasingly concrete (Rieff 1990). Science now stands where once stood religion. Our spiritual selves are a shrunken version of their former piety.

By breaking the tension between inner commitment and external action, men/women left behind what they shared most, their systems of belief. It was here, in their shared beliefs, that moral ideals and images were maintained, developed, and cherished. With the decline in systems of shared belief, the inner life has taken its revenge: On one hand, the search for "community" is mouthed by politicians and the need for organizational "culture" is pursued by managers; on the other hand, a selfish individualism destructive of community, culture, and the natural environment is proclaimed as the hallmark of freedom and maintains a broad following. Politicians, managers, and professionals of every stripe now control huge organizations where the concentration of power is greater than ever before. The ethical foundation of these organizations, however, like the society of which they are a part, remains confused and disoriented.

My purpose in this essay is to develop a theory of culture that can be used to investigate the breakdown of the tension between inner commitment and outer life, both individual and collective. I will give special attention to the role of memory in maintaining moral culture because it was the destruction of the memory of the past by rationalist forces in modern culture that struck the near deathblow to the moral traditions that had kept man/woman's sense of social responsibility alive and vigorous. The theory of culture developed in this chapter will be applied in the following chapters to analyze and critique both theoretical formulations of and empirical studies in organizational culture in regard to their moral assumptions and implications. In this way, it is hoped, a contribution can be made toward reforming the way in which we think about our moral responsibilities in organizations.

I define culture in terms of two main moral functions: First, culture organizes the moral demands men/women make upon themselves into a system of symbols that make men/women intelligible and trustworthy to each other, thus also rendering the world intelligible and trustworthy; second, culture organizes the expressive remissions by which men/women release themselves—to some degree—from the strain of conforming to the controlling symbolic, internalized variant readings of culture that constitute individual character (Rieff 1987). The system of symbols men/women use to organize and regulate their relations is not only shared among them, it is also shared with ancestors and other predecessors (Shils 1981). Hence, moral culture, as well as being internalized in the individual, has depth in time. It is this depth, the reenactment of the past in the present, cultivated over generations in traditions through a chain of memory, that gives culture its wisdom and moral weight.

In the following section I develop a theory of moral culture, indebted to the work of the sociologist Philip Rieff (1979; 1985; 1987). Rieff's work concerns the democratization of culture and its effect on moral restraint. An essential part of Rieff's work is his reformulation of Freud's theory of repression. Within this reformulated theory of repression, I focus on how moral values are established and maintained in the individual. In the third section, I develop a theory of moral tradition, building an understanding of collective memory as the basis of moral culture. The works of Hannah Arendt (1968), Michael Polanyi (1958), and Edward Shils (1981) are used extensively in this section. Throughout the two theoretical sections I will introduce examples from my own research and experience in organizations to demonstrate my argument. I will utilize data I collected during fieldwork in a telephone company (Feldman 1985; 1986a; 1986b; 1986c; 1988b), an electronics company (1988a; 1989a; 1989b; 1990), and a children's hospital (unpublished). I will also include examples from classroom experience and university administration. Finally, concluding remarks relate moral tradition to moral culture and the cultivation of individual responsibility.

A Theory of Moral Culture

The choice of duty over self-interest or impulse, of the normatively desirable over the actually desired, was defined by Kant as the essence of moral conduct (Wrong 1994). Morality is basically a discipline (Durkheim 1925). It promotes a certain regularity in peoples' conduct, answering to whatever is recurrent and enduring in men/women's relationships with one another. As such, morality is inseparable from culture. What is moral becomes and remains self-evident only within a powerful and profoundly compelling system of culture (Rieff 1987). Morality is the generative principle of culture; it integrates the symbolic world within which the individual socially functions, thus committing the individual to the group. In so doing, moral culture deprives the individual of an almost endless array of possible actions, narrowing his/her behavior in line with ideals that represent the meaning of core commitments in that culture. Only through the idealization of values and ideas does moral culture remain vital for us.

An example of a moral ideal from my fieldwork in Telephone Company is represented by the integrating symbol "the little old lady in tennis shoes." Telephone Company employees prided themselves on their ability to deliver telephone service to the public no matter what technical or natural catastrophe struck their system. The symbol "the little old lady in tennis shoes" imagined the customer as a poor grandmotherly figure who was dependent on Telephone Company for her lifeline. During floods, storms, and other disasters, Telephone Company employees went to extreme lengths and personal sacrifices to reestablish telephone service. The "little old lady" symbolized moral duty at the center of Telephone Company culture.

In my view of culture, human nature is enormously complex, containing social, asocial, and anti-social aspects (Wrong 1994). In Durkheim's (1925, 42) words, the individual is filled with a "multitude of human passions," giving man/woman the capacity to do anything and everything (Rieff 1985). Indeed, in a company as big as Telephone Company a vast variety of behaviors occurred. For example, just referring to the category "company vehicles," the following incidents were recorded: a high–level, married executive wrecked his car late one night under the influence of alcohol and with another woman in the car; another high–level executive damaged the underneath of his company car by driving it through the fields on his farm; and a telephone repairman, in an attempt to use the ladder from his truck to save a drowning boy in a flooding river, drowned himself.

In the Freudian view, the passions or emotions cannot be known directly, but can only be grasped once they enter into a cultural form, that is, once they are clothed in a representation (Rieff 1979). Furthermore, the emotions are prevented from being expressed directly by a self-canceling relation among the emotions themselves, expressed as ambivalence. Ambivalence is the primary psychological modality inside culture (Rieff 1985). Since human passions are eternally in conflict, any commitment, any belief is always under pressure for reversal. This irremovable openness to changing one's feelings points to the fragility of all human commitment. It is both a problem and a source of hope.

Hence, underneath the integrative symbol "the little old lady in tennis shoes," signifying the culture of service at Telephone Company, was the culture of control. The culture of control did not have such an altruistic face. On the managerial level of the company, it was characterized by intense competition for rewards and promotions not always resulting in what was best for the customer. Managers sometimes withheld cooperation from peers to damage their service evaluation, thus improving their own chances for rewards and promotions.

The psychological centrality of ambivalence is a second reason human action must be restricted so peace and harmony can be brought to social life (Rieff 1954). Culture provides compensatory pleasures for its insistence that the individual must restrain his/her actions. Restriction of choices, for example, offers a more rational design for action with more effective and fruitful results (Santayana 1905). Given that the alternative—complete expression of one's contradictory impulses—would lead to disaster, the sacrifice of self appears less oppressive.

At Children's Hospital, for example, a central integrating cultural symbol was the Nike slogan "Just do it." This symbol points to the physical skill and prowess needed to manage the punishing physical demands required in resident medical training. After countless sleepless hours of work and faced with feelings of ambivalence toward treating yet another patient, the Nike slogan offers the resident a self-understanding dressed as athletic achievement and competitive superiority. This assists the resident in maintaining his/her focus and fighting off distracting feelings of fatigue and resentment, thus contributing to his/her rational effectiveness.

The process of socialization by which the individual develops a specific social self involves the individual's imaginative participation in social interaction (Mead, in Wrong 1994). Through the use of systems of symbols, including language, the individual learns to take the role of the other because in addressing the other the individual arouses in him/herself the same tendency to respond that he/she is attempting to elicit from the other. In making sense out of the response of the other, he/she is able to grasp the other's experience and look back on him/herself, the stimulus to the other's response, as he/she appears to the other. Out of this perception of the perceptions of other, the individual imagines his/her *self*. Eventually this process is interiorized in the mind by the development of the institutions of the "I" and "Me." The self becomes split between a perceiving "I" and a perceived "Me." This allows the self to become an object of experience, enabling it to reflect on itself: upon rational reflection, he/she can change him/herself. This is the basis of selfhood and consciousness of kind which makes both imitation and identification possible, two fundamental forms of social attachment.

Under stress, the dialogue between "I" and "Me," a mirror of the relation between self and other, can break down. At the end of a shift, the tired first year residents would all be talking at the same time as they dressed to leave the hospital, no one listening to the others. This resulted partly from the intense demands for performance throughout the day under the watchful eyes of their many levels of superiors. By being so focused on their own performance and the observation of this performance by superiors, the normal process of listening to peers (and patients) is exhausted. The doctor-in-training's self thus develops blocking mechanisms to avoid identifications with competitors or patients who can distract him/her from his/her goals of developing skills and winning the support of powerful superiors. As this process is interiorized in the doctor's self, the doctor develops a highly selective capacity to ignore the emotional demands of others, thus maintaining the boundaries of his/her skill-based identifications and the ability to concentrate on implementing them.

Given that the individual is faced with an array of representations for defining and directing his/her life amid the diversity of his/her own impulses, the self has no choice but to negate some representations and impulses and embrace others in an effort to establish itself in reality (James 1890). Without this process of selection and rejection, the self would be swamped by confusion and contradiction. Thus, the mind is ever striving to produce some sort of unification or harmony in its experience (Cooley 1922). Feelings, thoughts, and representations are attached a value and allotted a position in a hierarchical structure of the mind. Cooley (1922, 372) refers to this order as the "moral sense" because it is the law of our mental integrity. To lose it would result in insanity, a random or socially unacceptable pattern of thought. The way the socially acceptable individual integrates all the materials of the inner and outer worlds is the basis of his/her individuality. Moral character is a personal accomplishment.

Hence, the doctor-in-training who focuses too much on patient care and does not complete his/her assignments inevitably runs into trouble with the dominant culture. Cultures are systems of hierarchically established values. In the process of socialization, the initiate has choices to make about how much to conform to the dominant values. These choices determine both the basis of his/her individuality and his/her "fit" with the dominant culture and its powerful representatives. The doctor-in-training, by insisting on more personalized patient care at the expense of productivity, might be, according to external value systems, exercising a higher level of moral character, but in the training hospital culture he/she is certain to run afoul of the organizational authorities. This tension is typical in modern professional training.

The fact that the individual makes cultural choices assumes the exclusiveness of his/her personal authority to choose (Rieff 1991). It also implies, therefore, a sense of responsibility: authority means responsibility (Rieff 1985). Authority/responsibility requires distance from the social world for its development (Dumont 1986). One must justify one's position ideally because only in an ideal world can the good be reflected on and worshipped, its value brought into contact with the heart, and its aesthetic form used to cultivate the self that grasps it (Santayana 1905).

At Telephone Company, a well-liked young executive was offered a major promotion, but turned it down because it would have required that he spend less time with his family. Turning down a major promotion was extremely unusual for a high-level executive because getting to a high level had already required a great commitment to career and company. His refusal to accept the promotion highlights his personal authority to choose. This authority, his personal authority, was inseparable from his responsibility to himself, his family, and the company. In carefully thinking through the decision, he concluded that his responsibility to his children was most important.

Initially, the individual's moral decisions are not so reflective. Moral character originates in family life in the process of *identification* (Freud 1936). The small child identifies with (internalizes) the moral qualities of parents and other figures of authority, making their characteristics and opinions his/her own. Failure to live by these internalized values results in painful self-criticism.

The mechanism by which the family induces the individual to accept its values is love (Freud 1930). Parental love provides the incentive for the child to sacrifice his/her private inclinations, replacing them with identifications with the parents. However, family relations suffer the same ambivalence characteristic of all human feelings. Families are competitive and conflict-laden. Even love, in the best of cases, is touched with ambivalence. Nonetheless, it is here, in the narrow confines of family tension that moral character begins to emerge. In families without love, where the child has little incentive to internalize parental values, moral character does not develop and the individual can direct his/her whole aggressiveness outward.

In addition to living up to one's own values, receiving the approval of one's peers also leads to pride and self-respect (Sullivan 1950). The individual who is rejected and criticized by his/her peers, is subject to anxiety. Anxiety is the painful feeling of self-rejection, sometimes referred to as shame, guilt, or self-doubt (Wrong 1994). Hence, since we cannot escape the presence of others, managing how others treat us is unavoidable. We try to ensure others think well of us as a preventive strategy to avoid anxiety. Indeed, our "preventive strategy" can go so far as simply denying or forgetting anything that would lead us to be rejected, including moral demands.

At Children's Hospital, a group of doctors/supervisors were discussing the performance of a resident. One group was complaining that the performance was poor and recommended that a letter be put in the resident's file noting it as such. Another group was arguing for a less severe sanction. In the end, the former group won out. However, the latter group was actually in control of the administrative process and after the former group left the meeting, the administrators ripped up the letter. It was the administrators who bore the brunt of resident morale, so by tearing up the letter they avoided having to deal with an angry resident. The fact that they forgot or denied the organization's consensus policies and their own administrative responsibilities went unremarked by all.

Denial and forgetting can have a positive function too. They are signs of *repression* in the relationship between culture and the individual (Freud 1930). Repression is a function of the individual's ego. The individual employs repression to mediate between his/her own emotions and the demands of the social environment. Feelings or impulses that are unacceptable to cultural norms (that is, unacceptable to the super-ego, the representative of culture inside the individual) are repressed. The essence of repression is a turning away from direct and conscious expression of everything that is before praise and blame (Rieff 1979). A culture without repressions could not exist because everything thought or felt would be done instantly. By standing between individual desire and its object, culture represents the moral regulation of the individual. This shows the positive function of the repressive process and its necessity for the preservation of collective life.

The repressive process vital to organizational culture can even extend into employees' private lives, and, in turn, reinforce the organizational culture. At Telephone Company, the culture of control demanded strict deference to superiors. One group of influential executives on the middle management level had to act within the culture of control, yet simultaneously function within the halls of power. They accomplished this by a slow and careful balancing act. I was quite astonished when I heard that three of these powerful men had taken up the hobby of growing rare flowers in their spare time. The patience, attention to detail, and careful planning required for this hobby is a good analogy for their political behavior. In the culture of control all impulses toward disobedience and efforts to overpower opponents were out of the question. These tendencies were repressed. For many employees these repressions marked the end of their political efforts. But for others, like the gardeners, the repressed impulses, tamed and tempered, found their way back into organizational life. The gardeners pursued their own interests, but they did so carefully, secretly, and over long time horizons.

Human experience thus derives from the recurrent splitting motion by which human passion is evaluated and transformed into culturally acceptable thought (Rieff 1979). Culture functions as both the achievement of unconscious repression and, indirectly, conscious expression through the process of substitution; that is, culture splits human impulses, repressing one part while allowing another part to enter into consciousness through attachment to publicly accepted symbols or cultural forms. In the culture of control at the Telephone Company, the gardeners were just such an example of the dynamics of culture: They simultaneously repressed their rebellious urges and expressed them through acts of subvert manipulation. Hence, repression points to the double life of each individual in the dynamics of culture.

The two sides of repression, immediate to every issue in life, interpenetrate (Rieff 1979). They come to resemble one another, inseparable as long as the repression remains in force. Cultural controls, in command of the repressed contents, thus rest on an unstable foundation (Rieff 1981). If the controls are not constantly renewed by attaching them to fresh impulses (for example, aggression), the repressed impulses will overrun their boundaries and destroy the controls. In this perspective, the moral quality of character is a measure of how well one manages the dividing line between internalized moral ideals and the impulses that contradict them. Knowing this much about the structure of moral character, we can perhaps better tolerate its ambiguities.

Not all managers at the Telephone Company were gardeners. One highly competitive vice president who had excelled at sports in high school was known to blow his cool at the company. Once at an office party, after losing a game of Ping–Pong, he threw his paddle into the table and forced a subordinate to continue playing until he himself won. Abusive treatment of subordinates was reported in his department. In this case, the culture of control rested on a shaky foundation often overrun by the vice president's outbursts of anger, aggression, and competitiveness.

For Rieff (1979, 368), the repressive nature of culture is the "spiritual rule of life." Culture divides each of us against ourselves in the process of splitting evil and good. This process originates in the unalterable craving of the mind for connecting oppositions, oppositions it hierarchically values (Dumont 1980). The differentiation of good from evil is involuntary; it is required by the rule of *incompossibility* (total incompatibility): What cannot be true together must be denied (Rieff 1979); it is required by the need to live in a meaningful world. The repressive authority of culture creates cognitive and social order by dividing what *is* from what *is not*. Thus purposeful action becomes possible, on the surface of life.

Connecting oppositions, though necessary, are not always fully functional in relation to company goals. Despite excellence in product technology, Electronics Company had a long history of weakness in their marketing function, notwithstanding continuous efforts to the contrary. One reason they were not able to strengthen their marketing function while maintaining their emphasis on technological quality was that technology/marketing was constructed as a connecting opposition in the corporate culture. The engineers' understanding of and focus on technology was scientific, that is, impersonal. Marketing required a focus on the customer and his/her personal perceptions and needs. The corporate culture had developed in such a way that the technological function of the product precluded and denied the person who actually used it.

Through the differentiation of "good" and "evil," the individual finds his/her way to self-respect. Self-respect is derived from a respect for cultural ideals that makes possible a distance within the individual between what is good and what is not. These ideals are the ground on which man/woman claims freedom and respect, and on which he/she receives freedom and respect from those who share the same ideals (Polanyi 1959). This process of sharing commitments to the same ideals stabilizes culture and supports the individual's psychological integrity (Homans 1989).

At Telephone Company, the angry vice president was seen as being obsessed with competitive superiority and in violation of the service image the publicly regulated telephone company wanted to portray. The other vice presidents rejected the angry vice president's openly competitive behavior by relentlessly teasing him. One form the teasing took was that the other vice presidents would park in his parking space in the vice presidents' private lot just to pique his anger and then shared their laughter as they watched him from their office windows storm into the office building. This vice president's open expression of his own emotional needs was seen as undignified in the culture of control.

In practice, cultural ideals occupy one end of the *range* of cultural authority (Rieff 1987). In addition to organizing the moral demands men/women make upon themselves, culture also organizes the expressive *remissions* by which men/women release themselves—to some degree—from the strain of conforming to ideal standards. For example, at Electronics Company honest reporting of financial information was expected. However, in the case of projected future profits for a newly developed product, top management usually did not criticize rosy projections that offered no realistic justifications. The ideal of honesty was relaxed in this case out of fear that a too strict enforcement of it would squash the always fragile motivation for innovation. Over time as new products went to market and financial results became known, top managers adjusted their willingness to grant remissions from realistic profit expectations based on the innovator's track record.

Rieff (1985) refers to the range of cultural authority—from ideal demands to release from these demands—as an "interdictory-remissive" complex. He sees this complex as the inescapable moral structure of cultural life. The individual, his/her personality stretched across this structure, must act, in obedience or revolt, within the range of cultural authority. Outside of this structure there is only meaninglessness.

Interdicts, communicated through cultural representations, reveal the "thou shalt nots" or taboos of a culture (Rieff 1987). It is from the interdicts that repressions gather their energy. Interdicts, then, are gifts of self-concealment, allowing the individual to repress one part of self in order to identify with cultural ideals with another part (Rieff 1985). As Weber (1918b) noted, few of these gifts are recognized as such now, given that they are obscured or overwhelmed by the cult of personality. Nevertheless, behind the illusion of our unique individuality, we are "free" to choose among authority relations within multiform cults, once called gods, that is, within the interior flexibility of interdictory-remissive complexes.

An example from my teaching experience can serve as a concrete example of this theoretical point. When using short stories to teach ethics to master of business administration (MBA) students, it is typically the case that the students ignore the story's plot and context and focus solely on evaluating the actions of the main characters. The students identify the characters immediately as autonomous personalities and judge them as such. The moral values used for these judgments remain mostly implicit. Hence, the students' dependence on their own socialization in a historical-cultural era remains unrecognized as does their responsibility for the choices they made from the options available in that era. Recognizing the exaggerated individualism of the present age is, I think, an important challenge in teaching ethics to professional students.

Within the interdictory-remissive motifs which constitute moral order, the remissive mode is our typical place of residence. The message of self-deprivation in interdictory contents always stimulates anxiety; the more demanding the interdict, the more intense the anxiety; the more intense the anxiety, the stronger the intellectual equivocation (Rieff 1987). The remissive middle between interdict and transgression, where what is not to be done yet done, is the safest place to hide out from what is above and below (Rieff 1985).

Given the dominance of the remissive middle in moral life, especially in practical affairs, there is a danger that we can loose our sense of the difference between right and wrong. Sometimes in teaching ethics to business students, it appears that the meaning of being ethical is reduced to not getting caught breaking the law or offending a large portion of the public at the cost of hurting one's business. Hiding out in the middle runs the risk of moral minimalism.

Remissions either subserve or subvert the interdicts. Clearly, given the Freudian view of human nature which posits man/woman as having a voracious, acquisitive appetite, the interdicts face constant backsliding. Hence, the remissions play a central role in moral behavior. They can vex or soothe, corrupt or purify, exalt or debase, barbarize or refine us, according to whether they aid the interdicts or destroy them. Since most of us spend most of our time shuffling between the anxiety-producing demands of an ideal life and the guilt-producing transgressions, the remissions, through a steady, uniform, insensible operation, carve out the character we become. In great measure, the interdicts are dependent upon the remissions.

There is much concern among academic administrators about the lack of research productivity among tenured faculty members. Tenure is seen as leading to remissive behavior that undermines academic ideals. Because of this problem, one academic organization created policies whereby tenured faculty could be rewarded for increased service to make up for their research shortfall. The result of the implementation of these policies was that the remissive culture undermining research was transferred to the area of service. "Service" became tinged with either passive administrative conformity or political intrigue. In either case, academic ideals were not strengthened; a weak research environment was made weaker by the increased power of administrative interests and the substitution of customer service to students for academic standards. The plan was discussed in ideal terms, but its implementation was inevitably in remissive ones. The original problem was not simply a lack of research, but a remissive culture that undermined ideal standards.

However, because we all live in the remissive middle, stretched to the breaking point between good and evil, culture is always and everywhere the scene of struggle. Indeed, modern culture, for the first time in Western history, has reversed the relationship between interdicts and remissions (Rieff 1987). The remissive imagination is now dominant. This is why much of our culture has become incoherent, as seen, for example, in Melville's (1853) story, *Bartelby the Scrivener*, about the manager who compulsively shifts between charitable concern for his employees and ruthless demands for efficiency. For the remissions to be productive of cultural order, they must subserve the interdicts. With this relationship destroyed, the remissive imagination is like a boat without a rudder. Hence, we live in a period of endless cultural transition. When a culture can no longer maintain itself as an established span of moral demands, it opens itself up to destructive levels of aggression.

Even the most established organizational cultures can find their legitimacy suddenly questioned. At one point in the history of Electronics Company, the company founder had a stroke and left the company for several months. The paternalistic culture he had established, run consistently for two decades with the assistance of the president, the founder's trusted aide, fell apart. Severe conflicts broke out between the vice presidents and between one particularly powerful vice president and the president. It was each man for himself. The company started losing customers and inevitably significant amounts of money. Despite the threat to the company, these individuals were unable to put the company before their own interests and settle their differences. Not until the founder's return and several high-level firings did behavior return to a level of self-constraint.

The key to regaining a moral culture more evenly balanced between self-interest and collective good, is the feeling of guilt (Rieff 1979). The feeling of guilt originally arises in the individual from his/her wish to reject the rules and values of his/her parents. As the child grows into an adult, community values take the place of parental rules. The individual's natural wish for freedom and power inevitably comes into conflict with community values. As was noted above in the discussion of repression, these impulses are turned back upon the individual in the process of internalizing these values. The feeling of guilt is the mechanism for ensuring these values are obeyed.

I will illustrate this point with an example from my hospital fieldwork. A third year resident was the only doctor working in the emergency room at a small rural hospital one weekend. A twelve-year-old boy was brought in by his mother with a cough that had developed suddenly and would not subside. After examining the boy and being unable to determine the cause of the problem, the resident left the room to telephone her superior for a consultation. This was a mistake. With this type of respiratory symptom, the resident should not have left the child's side. A nurse could have made the telephone call. While the resident was out, the child worsened and was unable to breathe. The resident rushed back in, but was unable to stop the deterioration, and the child died. The resident was stricken with guilt. She felt she was unfit to be a doctor and wanted to quit the profession. The senior emergency room doctor at the main teaching hospital where the resident was in training while not denying the mistake, assured the resident that she would be a fine doctor. She now runs a large emergency room in a major urban center. Her strong guilt reaction to her mistake was a healthy and productive response to the situation.

In less extreme situations, the feeling of guilt is primarily unconscious because it does not refer to any act of rebellion the individual actually commits, but only to the *wish* to rebel (Freud 1930). The super-ego is aware of the wish to rebel. Thus, the feeling of guilt comes about even though the wish was renounced and repressed from the beginning. Because that part of ourselves that gives rise to our own self-centered desires is irremovable, the conflict with culture is also irremovable and results in an "unconscious need for punishment" (Freud 1930). The individual experiences the "need for punishment" as anxiety, that is, fear of the super-ego.

Ironically, some managers experience anxiety not out of frustration for missing their goals but from their successes (Freud 1916). One talented manager at Telephone Company attracted the support of a powerful vice president which led to a major promotion. Instead of reacting with pride and pleasure at her well-earned good fortune, she became depressed and was afflicted with feelings of inferiority. In this case, her unconscious feelings of guilt arose from her past. Early in her life, she had internalized feelings of guilt for wishes she felt were wrong. When her wish for a promotion in adult life actually materialized, it became associated with the earlier forbidden wishes thus triggering the painful feelings of guilt. This example shows the power of the past as the prototype for the individual's relation to the present.

In Freudian theory, the entire edifice of morality (and religion) arises to appease the feeling of guilt (Freud 1913). But by elaborating and ritualizing guilt, morality perpetuates it. This reinforcement of the feeling of guilt is the spine of moral authority. While morality is based partly on the necessities of collective life, its deeper foundation in the human soul is the expiation it offers to the feeling of guilt, the cross man/woman must bear for living both an individual and collective life.

The neurotic manager who responded with guilt to receiving a promotion also demonstrates the morally difficult situation the individual experiences having been socialized into a cultural order. In her case, she was one of the first women to be promoted to middle management in Telephone Company history. Since she was backed by a powerful male vice president, rumors circulated that her promotion was based on sexual favors. Here, we see social change—that is, the promotion of women—running into resistance from established mores, that is,

management is a man's world. Though here morality misses its mark—
the just and the fair—it does demonstrate the mechanism of guilt
performing its morality enforcing function. Many of the first women
breaking into management did face both their own unconscious guilt
and the unconscious guilt of others (in this case projected and distorted into rumors about sexual favors) as they established new social
relations.

For each man/woman the feeling of guilt is mandatory, a motor for
the driving in of social demand thus rendered moral (Rieff 1990).
Within the moral lifeplan of each cultural order, the individual finds
his/her self-esteem, the feeling of guilt a painful reminder not to stray
too far and thus lose the source of one's self-respect. Granted a working balance of self-esteem and guilt, each man/woman, collecting him/
herself from elements of the social order, experiences the pleasures
and pains, the supreme self-confidence and the depths of despair of
his/her drift through social existence.

The motor now, like the one on the apparatus for punishment in
Kafka's (1914) penal colony, is sputtering and unreliable. The idea
that our moral ideals should be clear and unambiguous is widely ridiculed. Our moral traditions are but vaguely remembered.

A Theory of Moral Tradition

The phenomenon of self and that of memory are merely two sides
of the same fact (J.S. Mill in James 1890): the individual knows him/
herself through an uninterrupted succession of past feelings, going
back as far the memory reaches and forward terminating in the present
moment. Memory is thus the basis of the individual's identity, the way
we know ourselves different from other. Certainly we change over
time, but at our core we possess the same memories (James 1890).
Importantly, when the *chain* of memory is severed, our sense of responsibility is also lost because we can no longer feel or ascend to the
issue in question. Moral responsibility requires some connection to
one's identity, that is, to the chain of memory out of which identity is
constructed.

Lack of memory is most easily discerned in lack of historical knowledge, and with it comes a socially irresponsible erasure of differences.
In discussing racial discrimination issues with MBA students, it is not
uncommon for some white students to argue that their grandparents

faced discrimination earlier in the century upon their arrival to the United States from Europe. These students go on to argue that their grandparents picked themselves up by their bootstraps and made a better life for themselves and their children. The students use this argument to criticize portions of the African American community who they feel lack the necessary work ethic to make economic progress. In discussions with these students, it is clear that they have little knowledge of the history of the African American community in the United States and indeed little knowledge of slavery. Without this historical memory, they have little understanding of the experience of the African American community, and merely equate them with other immigrant groups in the United States.

Our memories do not register our experience as it actually happened; memory synthesizes experience and, in a sense, raises it above time (Santayana 1905). Memory is ideal. It detaches us from the world of flux and thus from ourselves and our path through life. By taking us out of the temporal nature of existence, it plunges us into the depths of time where eternal values such as love, justice, trust, loyalty, and generosity can be contemplated. These values provide a picture from which a heightened vitality might flow. Without them, improvement could be neither remembered nor measured nor desired. Mere change would be all. With them, the self grows like the ideal which it conceives.

The ideal nature of memory can be seen in the case method used to teach residents at Children's Hospital. Part of the pedagogical rationale for the case method is that over a three-year period the resident will see numerous occurrences of a particular disease and thus learn how to treat the disease through recurring experiences with it. However, in speaking with residents another aspect of case learning becomes apparent. Residents have memories of *particular* experiences, for example, of a particular patient or a particular treatment of a patient. In other words, a particular memory is pulled out of the stream of experience and some of its components are given heightened importance. These components absorb and come to represent a much broader array of experiences that have retreated into the subconscious. The remembered event or activity becomes a sort of sign marker for knowledge in the area. More exactly, it becomes an ideal, rich in tacit meaning and reflective potential.

Given the importance of memory for moral responsibility, it follows that *forgetting* is also morally significant. Perhaps nowhere is the morality of forgetting explored in such depth as in Freud's work (Rieff 1979). Freud (1901) expanded the concept of memory to include the unconscious. Motives and events too disturbing to the ego to be remembered are repressed. In this view, forgetting is not passive, it is active; one chooses what to remember and forget. Repression thus becomes an infallible record of ethical import. What is too imperative to be remembered suffers the privilege of being forgotten. Indeed, once forgotten, the importance of the repressed is actually heightened because the effort needed to maintain the repression is a decisive determinant of the structure of personality. Hence, what defines the impact of memory is one's reaction to it, against it.

Speaking with employees at Electronics Company in 1985 about the disastrous period in 1981 surrounding the founder's stroke, their stories demonstrate an interesting example of forgetting. After the founder's departure, the stories explain that the weak-willed president showed his dependency on the founder by making a series of poor decisions driving the company toward the abyss. After many trials and tribulations, the founder returns, the stories continue, saves the day, and all is as it was in the beginning. The president is reunited with the founder and is a much improved manager having learned from the harrowing experience. Nevertheless, there is no evidence in the stories demonstrating the president's improved management skill. Indeed, the stories end on a happy note, suggesting that the employees were happy to have the founder return and the founder and the president were happy to be reunited. Neither the employees nor the founder and the president were inclined to address the psychological issues in the founder/president relationship. So all involved forgot about the president's inability to manage autonomously. This forgetting ensured that this problem and all its implications for the organizational culture would continue as it had in the past.

As was noted in the previous section, the process of repression, the motor for the driving in of moral demands, originates in an act of submission on the part of the child. Importantly, the parallel process that continues throughout adult life is responsible for the transfer of knowledge between generations. The relation of apprentice to master, student to teacher, or popular audiences to distinguished speakers all work only when a previous act of affiliation is made by the novice (Polanyi 1958). By assuming there is something to learn, appreciating its value, striving to act by its standards, and, above all, by placing trust in authoritative persons, the apprentice places him/herself into a (moral) tradition. Hence, the transmission of knowledge—practical, moral, and scientific—from one generation to the next takes place.

Telephone System (of which Telephone Company was a wholly-owned subsidiary) had always chosen a president for Telephone Company from within the company's own ranks, but because of a wish for the company to make major changes, they brought in an outsider. The new man, though still from Telephone System, was not from the East Coast but from the West Coast. The past presidents had all been similar compared to the new president. He wanted to implement a participative management style instead of the strict hierarchy the company had always known. His officer group, however, was unable to make the act of affiliation to him or his ideas, and the attempt at organizational change failed. The officers did not see his ideas as worth learning, appreciate their value, or strive to act by their standards. Not only was there no transfer of knowledge, but the old hierarchical system broke down into conflict as well, since the new president did not play his role in it. The transmission of traditions is a delicate process but without it social stability is impossible.

Most human beings, to some degree, seek contact with what they see as good or of crucial importance (Taylor 1989). Indeed, if they did not, they could not become functional human agents, having neither reaped the rewards nor avoided the dangers life has to offer (James 1890). Another reason individuals seek the good in human communities is to transcend themselves as individuals (Shils 1981). Only in this way can they share in a common identity with others. This creates the gravitation to the shared past which is a characteristic of all cultures. It at once stabilizes and enriches individual and social experience. To be sure, most adherents to any tradition are fair-weather friends. Most people follow traditions to avoid offending group opinion and receiving the animus of their peers.

Family-dominated Electronics Company illustrates my argument. New employees knew they were not coming to work in an open environment where entrepreneurial impulses would be given a free hand. On the contrary, the founder was committed to employee job security and benefits. Employees with long employment at the company were sometimes referred to by their number in the original group of hires, for example, "Joe" was known as "six" because he was the sixth employee to be hired thirty years earlier. Some employees came to the company for this paternalistic environment; they sought to be part of an organizational family. To be sure, other employees came for other reasons. But the paternalistic traditions were maintained partly because a core group of people were committed to them and partly because almost everyone else conformed.

To be carried forward, the past does not have to be remembered by all who reenact it; it is carried forward by a continuing chain of transmissions and receptions (Shils 1981). Clearly, the individual is often the unaware vehicle of traditional ideas and sentiments. According to Shils (1981), most human beings do not have enough imagination to think up an alternative to what is given. It requires little thought or effort to do what one has seen others do. It permits life to move along lines set and anticipated from past experience, and thus subtly converts the anticipated into the inevitable and the inevitable into the acceptable. Furthermore, imitation is encouraged by primitive sentiments of fellowship; conviviality is in man/woman's nature and imperceptibly stimulates the transmission of specific experiences, for example, sympathy at the sight of another's suffering (Polanyi 1958). Finally, many traditions are functional; they have been handed down over generations to address particular problems and they appear to "work." This leads to their becoming unquestioned habits. Traditions are not merely functional, of course; they also have moral implications. There are "good" and "bad" traditions; in either case, habit joins them to man/woman's nature.

In teaching MBA students, one notices a strong pattern in student comments insisting on the obvious self-interest and autonomy of the individual. Historically, the root of this idea lies in Christianity, with much of its modern meaning established during the Protestant Reformation, becoming secularized in the Enlightenment, and continuing to develop along with capitalism (Tawney 1926; Dumont 1986). For the students, it is simply part of reality. In other words, for them it is an unconscious tradition, a transmission they accept without much conscious reflection on its social, let alone historical, formulation. Importantly, the unconsciousness of the tradition allows the students to ignore the unavoidable collective aspects of social reality and the dependency relations that that entails. In this context, the tradition of modern individualism shouts out economic freedom while repressing the reality of bureaucratic and political oppression in organization and society.

Whether one likes it or not, tradition is a dominant force in life. There is so much knowledge maintained in a living culture, it is not in the power of any single generation to replace most of what it is given (Shils 1981). Traditions enter into action by defining the ends and standards and even the means. Traditions stand around the boundaries of the field in which deliberate and passionate actions are taken. They remain tacit, implicitly prefiguring "rational", moral, cognitive, and even emotional behavior.

This can be seen in the tradition of individualism as it manifests itself in the activities of some MBA students. It is taken for granted by many students that upon graduation they are entering a "market" where they must function as self-interested competitors. Their relations to the employers who hire them are also seen as one where both parties are self-interested. This leads to a great deal of "negotiations" and "bluffing" where the students attempt to present themselves as highly attractive and sought after by other employers in order to maximize their prospective salaries. Much of the information exchanged is not truthful, but is seen as legitimate because of the assumption that the relationship is between self-interested competitors.

Tradition must dominate social life because knowledge is primarily tacit (Polanyi 1966). For example, in the act of analyzing the theory of tradition, I use a language whose rules I do not consciously acknowledge and words the meaning of which I do not explicitly define. I pursue some lines of inquiry and drop others for reasons I do not completely reflect upon. If I took the time to fully understand these choices, I would have no time left to carry them out. In addition, I accept some conclusions as true in view of their bearing on a reality beyond them, a reality which may produce unsuspected manifestations at any time. The transmission of knowledge from one generation to the next must be predominantly tacit, because the application of knowledge cannot be explicitly taught in total and its apprehension cannot be absolutely verified (Polanyi 1969).

This facet of learning was commented on earlier in connection with the act of affiliation that the learner must make to authoritative persons or authoritative traditions. As was also noted, the cultures of management schools are centered around traditions of individualism and, it may be added, innovation, entrepreneurship, and organizational change. This leaves the educational programs and organizational cultures of many management schools exaggerating change and underestimating continuity. It not only leaves them vulnerable to fads—is "reengineering" or "total quality management" really different from previous management behaviors?—but also makes them neglectful of management ethics. Ethics, to be worthy of respect, must be stable.

Since no one transcends his/her formative milieu very far and for the most part must rely on it uncritically, it forms the matrix of our thought and determines our personal calling (Polanyi 1969). In so doing, it provides the foreknowledge we use to seek the truth while limiting our responsibility for the conclusions we reach. To be sure, one is responsible to apply this heritage afresh, within the context of contemporary controversies which perhaps challenge the inheritance and raise novel questions of principle. The use of our heritage, the way we interpret it, and the conclusions we reach with it can only be our responsibility in the present. Hence, our relationship to the past is paradoxical. When we conform to it, we still change it because we interpret it in our own terms; when we dissent from it, we still partially accept it because we are reacting to it and communicating our differences, to ourselves and others, in terms of it (Polanyi 1958). We see here the irresolvable tension between past and present within which the most radical minds are but modest variations of central cultural forces.

As was noted, an exaggerated valuation of the present (and future) undermines the ethical base of professional practice. In an academic organization, it was decided that traditional values were no longer productive or in line with community (market) demand and thus a major organizational change effort was called for. Traditional ideas of research, teaching, and service were all redefined. For example, research was renamed "discovery;" service was renamed the "scholarship of service." After a few years the result was considerable confusion as to what any of the terms meant and what standards applied to them. Even though it was not clear a new culture had been created, it was clear the old culture had been destroyed. In the confusion, individuals and groups pursued their own interests. Without continuity with the past, the range of possible behavior, for good *and* bad, is infinitely increased.

The key issue in our relationship to the past is that of moral responsibility. Tradition is a process of selection (Arendt 1968). By following a tradition, we are making choices in the present about what is valuable in the past and should be continued. Our choice is an act of remembering. Through memory an objective deposit is left in tradition (Shils 1981). We have a moral responsibility to remember, that is, to preserve and hand down what is good and just in tradition. Indeed, we have a responsibility to reflect upon it, correct it from our own experience, and pass it on strengthened. These choices are moral choices because they affect how we act towards others, past, present, and future.

In my previous example, the replacement of the word "research" with the word "discovery" was perceived as being inconsequential by the faculty who approved it. But the word "research" represented a tradition, that is, it had a historical existence, related to previous events such as faculty training, publication experience, teaching, and evaluations. The details of these past events had become tacit, that is, implicit in present acts of perception and judgement. In other words, the word "research" is like an old tree that had developed an extensive root system. The effort to reengineer the history that gave meaning to "research" by transferring it to "discovery" is an uncertain endeavor at best. Of course, we must change and adapt to new circumstances, but to do so without a careful review of the past and one's commitments to what is good in the past and should be continued, runs the risk of worsening the current situation.

Memory of moral values is particularly important because moral values affect our lives more deeply than intellectual values (Polanyi 1958). A man/woman, for example, may be very intelligent, capable of making great scientific or organizational contributions, but be vain, envious, spiteful, or a sycophant. A person is ultimately valued by their moral force, that is, what effect their moral striving has on their whole person. Hence, our moral character, the internalized moral values by which we evaluate our own action and the action of others, controls our whole selves, not merely our intellectual faculties. To live by these values, to follow the tradition that provides them, is to live by them in a comprehensive sense involving a deeply personal commitment. Memory of moral traditions, then, is a moral decision that determines the ultimate moral value and character of the individual.

Personal moral commitments have a direct impact on organizational life. The founder of Electronics Company provided pension benefits to his employees starting in the early 1960s. This was quite unusual for a small firm at that time. He was willing to face strong opposition from powerful members of the board of directors because he believed the company should assist employees with their basic financial needs. His decision was not primarily intellectual but moral; he felt a moral commitment to his employees' welfare. The founder was well-liked and respected by most of his employees because he was perceived as being fair and caring. He felt and understood the importance of these values and followed them all his life.

Without memory of the moral accomplishments of the past, the individual has little capacity for a radical criticism of the present (Rieff 1979). In this situation, the individual tends to follow the preferences of dominant members in his/her immediate social circle (Mill 1838). The inhibiting art of memory, on the contrary, is a brake on the remarkable potential of human beings to do and become anything. Moral traditions can instruct respect for and knowledge of what has already happened, the suffering that is past, passing, and to come (Rieff 1985). Human action is fundamentally tragic; its effects may be both good and evil. The individual must fuse his/her own interests and desires with enough moral ideals to keep him/herself in what Charles Horton Cooley (1922) called the "middle-road" of civility and self-respect where men/women can communicate and disagree—yet work and live together peacefully.

At Telephone Company, one young executive felt wining and dining regulators was a great way of winning more generous rate increases from them. He argued that generous treatment of public officials was routinely practiced in the private sector, so it could be equally beneficial in the quasi-public world of the telephone monopoly. Upon his promotion to vice president of regulation, the young executive took a few elected members of the regulatory commission to an exclusive private golf course. Someone, however, on his staff or the commissioners' staff was incensed that the memory of the tradition of a strictly professional relationship between the company and the commission created to regulate it had been disregarded. An anonymous caller notified the local newspaper. Promptly, a photographer with a telescopic lens was put in the bushes abutting the golf course. The picture of the executive and the commissioners on the putting green made the front page of the newspaper the following day. Both the company and the commission were publicly embarrassed and public mistrust increased, raising doubts about further rate increases. Without the inhibiting art of memory, self-interest swells to fill the whole decision-making calculus. At first the risks look small to the decision-maker in comparison to his/her potential rewards, but this is only because the risks to others have been left out of the equation.

Modern man/woman, however, having thrown off the "burden" of the past, rejects the limitations of tradition as a constraint on his/her personal freedom (Shils 1981). But without a stable cultural space within which to reside, he/she wanders from place to place, always uneasy, always alone (Santayana 1905). His/her criticisms express no ideal; his/her experience is without depth, without cumulative development. Indeed, without a secure symbolic, man/woman can hardly bear to know themselves, terrified at their own alienness and the emptiness of the endless choices they face (Rieff 1987). The result is a "minimal self," characterized by a restriction of perspective to the immediate demands of daily survival, without any overview of life or any emotional investment in it (Lasch 1984).

Some business students have argued in class that they would market a product they knew would kill a small percentage of its users if their job depended on it and if to do so was not illegal. These students have restricted their sense of responsibility to a minimum level. Organizational life to them is a harsh competitive world and they believe they have a right to "survive." They have little or no moral overview of their work and certainly no emotional investment in it. They argue that "no product is perfectly safe" or "one could get killed just crossing the street." Indeed, these statements have some truth but in this context they represent a minimal self, justifying a moral withdrawal from the world.

The traditions we have lost have not disappeared without a trace, but, like the repressions of the individual, live on as potential in the unconscious memory of the community (Rieff 1953). Carl Jung (1959) argued that the repression of our religious and moral traditions has disconnected us from our emotional depths, leaving us without the energy needed to justify moral belief. The replacement of moral traditions in modern culture by scientific rationality has left us psychologically and morally impoverished. Indeed, the twentieth century saw the rise of the perverse "religions" of German fascism and Russian communism. These forms of totalitarian organization arose partly because traditional values had been so weakened they were unable to provide resistance to what previous generations would have considered unspeakable evil (Arendt 1950).

To be sure, it was populations of atomized individuals lost in a downward spiral of self-interest and exclusive concern for their own security who eagerly accepted totalitarian propaganda in order to escape the inner chaos and outer violence of a seemingly meaningless world. The central problem of loss of moral tradition and the dangers associated with it persist. Typically, each year I teach courses in business ethics not only to MBA students but to undergraduate students as well. The undergraduates are of course younger and, mostly having had only part-time work experience, are more under the sway of their family's values than the older MBA students. In general, the undergraduates are more motivated by ideals and are more sensitive to ethical issues, than MBA students. The MBA students I teach are mostly night students with two or more years of full-time work experience. These students are much more oriented to and influenced by the organizations in which they work. The ideals of the undergraduates have been mostly replaced by concerns for efficiency and competitiveness in the MBA students. Sensitivity to and knowledge about legal issues has also significantly increased. Importantly, many of these students do not consider the organizations they work for to be ethical (see Badaracco and Webb [1995] for similar conclusions from survey data). Their desire in an ethics course is that they be taught "skills" or be given "tools" for solving ethical problems. Hence, moral traditions are at best fading memories to these students. But without historically developed, socially maintained, and individually internalized moral traditions, will these students care enough about moral values to go through the trouble of living their life by them?

Moral traditions, continuously developed over generations, cannot be replaced by the decision-making capacities of organizational leaders because these traditions are constructed by a practical infinity of experiences (Chapman 1967). Only against these experiences can a tradition be evaluated. To organizational leaders who are rightfully attempting to correct abuses in their organizations, each stage of correction seems legitimate. But if the internal meaning and outer structure of tradition are so corrected that they lose their transmissive efficacy, the broader society runs the risk of lapsing into the state of *bellum omnium contra omnes* ("war of all against all," Hobbes 1651) followed by the system worship that naturally arises out of it (Shils 1981). To be cut off from a shared past is as disordering to a society as being cut off from the present. Similar to their responsibility to the natural environment, organizations have a responsibility to not destroy the shared past.

Changes in moral values proceed best from the pressure of particular reasons of particular men/women, drawing eventually and collectively on a comparable vastness of experience (Chapman 1967). Change takes place over generations because only over time can an adaptation of the contending experiences of a people be carried out. Only time can produce the compromises that make social life tolerable and cultural life worthy of our respect.

The hyper-rationalism of the business and professional worlds has of yet not found a substitute for the traditional values that they have helped destroy. The pieces that are left of these traditions are carried in the lonely hearts of isolated individuals. But the importance of ethical values to society is too great to rely on the long shot that these isolated moral individuals will make their way into leadership positions. In any case, few of these individuals can develop an integrated set of moral values in a morally fragmented social world. Moral leadership requires institutional supports for both leader and led to be effective.

Conclusion

The theory of moral culture and the theory of moral tradition are related. The dynamics of culture work through the mechanism of repression to create a socialized individual, that is, the individual, in a unique way, internalizes the values of his/her family/community/society. As parents and other figures of authority relax the demands they make on children and initiates, the internalizations become less consistent, systematic, and strict. Perhaps this relaxation of cultural repression was needed in earlier centuries when religious ideals reached fanatical levels of enforcement. However, the problem now is not so much excessive repression as excessive openness. The moral treasures of our defining traditions are being lost through an indifference to the past and what it has to offer.

Openness to experience is now encouraged, as if diversity of experience is in itself good, independent of any standards by which to judge it. Moral traditions define and maintain our standards of judgment. With their decline, we arrive at the problem of meaninglessness, the central problem of our time. Our standards of judgment have taken on a looseness that is easily exploited by our rationalizing (manipulative) tendencies. At its worst, it atomizes individuals leaving them desperate for any consistent meaning, including totalitarian systems of meaning. More commonly, it leaves the individual empty, focused on mere superficialities as a means to displace the boredom from having an infinite number of choices with little reason for making any one in particular; or the individual joins a competitive frenzy, attempting to find a meaningful identity in acts of superiority, in "winning." Behind these types of social practice is an empty interior, an attempt to live life in the immediate present where hollow men/women mistake their rootlessness for freedom.

The loss of appreciation for moral traditions is a tragedy because these traditions conserve our most noble ideals, studied, refined, and deepened continuously by past generations. The past offers a way to evaluate the present, to gain distance from its seductiveness of power and pleasure. Today, the God of Rationalism rules, only to be challenged by its opposite, Irrationalism, both leaving us open to endless possibility, pregnant with excess. Tradition, on the contrary, offers an arrestment, a theory of truth, where the mind can cultivate long treasured ideals in its own personal way, receiving a basis for individuality. Within this heritage, the individual's authorization to choose holds the individual responsible for the choices made. Only inside these limits can responsibility be found.

The theory of moral tradition will be used in the remainder of the book to analyze the ethical and cultural aspects of approaches to the study of organizational culture. The main body of the book is divided into three sections: analyses of classic works, works by ethical rationalists, and works by ethical relativists. This sequence is used because it thematically follows the historical development of the field. In Part 2, I begin with analyses of two classic texts, Chester Barnard's (1938) general theory of management, *The Functions of the Executive* (chapter 2), and Melville Dalton's (1959) ethnographic study of American managers, *Men Who Manage* (chapter 3). These two authors were chosen because they deal explicitly with ethics and they represent original themes in the field of organizational culture research. All of the approaches analyzed in this book reject tradition as the basis of morality and as the source of ethical insight.

Barnard is an ethical rationalist, arguing that organizational life is permeated with "moral complexity." Because "moral complexity" requires superior rational abilities to resolve, Barnard argues that rationally superior executives should be put in control of it. He posits society as socially and morally "nebulous," instead of recognizing the

disruptive effects the Enlightenment had on moral belief, thereby further justifying his preference for executive control over moral decision-making. Developing his theoretical analysis independent of historical context is a key means Barnard uses to justify executive moral
superiority. Barnard's executive has superior rationality because he/
she is capable of resolving "moral conflict" through "moral creativity." In replacing moral continuity with moral creativity, Barnard replaces society with the individual as the source of moral truth. Barnard's
discussion is practically void of specific moral values. The reader is
simply asked to put his/her faith in the superior rationality of the
executive. The Protestant tendency to collapse authority into power is
apparent, leaving ethics, at best, vague and abstract, without any resistance to immediacy. The theme of ethical rationality carries on in
contemporary approaches to the study of organizational culture in different forms. In Part 3, ethical rationalism is analyzed in critical organization theory (chapter 4) and the "new institutionalism" (chapter 5).

Dalton is an ethical relativist, arguing that the extreme individualism in his ethnographic data is justified by the economic productivity
and individual creativity that result from it and, in any case, he states,
it is "natural" and inevitable. He takes the cult of the individual a step
further than Barnard by developing the idea of manager as "social
lion." The social lion, a powerhouse of creativity and leadership, continually organizes and reorganizes social relationships to advance his
own and his followers' interests. Built into Dalton's theory of infor-
mal/formal organization, the social lion is a master of playing one type
of organization against the other, creating and exploiting "uncertainty."
The reference to "uncertainty" points to the latent rationalism underlying the obviously exaggerated individualism (and worship of power)
in the notion of the social lion. Dalton's work, unlike Barnard's, is
peppered with historical references, but nonetheless lacks a general
theory of history. Historical references are decontextualized tidbits,
used to justify the moral relativism inevitably resulting from the social
lion's competitive drive. On the surface, Dalton justifies his argument
in terms of democratic individualism, but ultimately its justification
rests on the values of organizational creativity and economic effectiveness. To these ends, he willingly sacrifices moral ideals. In somewhat
different forms, the theme of ethical relativism appears in contemporary approaches. In Part 4, it is analyzed in postmodern organization
theory (chapters 6, 7, and 8).

Part 3 begins with an analysis of critical organization theory (COT). COT sees the world as not rational enough. Following the German philosopher Jürgen Habermas, whose own work has been burdened with the special problems of memory in German culture (see, for example, Habermas 1994), COT advocates the use of "perpetual criticism" to ensure individual autonomy from various forms of cultural domination. COT relies on an exaggerated confidence in rationality in general and the rational capacities of individuals in particular. By one-sidedly pursuing the autonomous power of individual rationality, COT ignores the importance of the past for providing stability and continuity in moral and cultural life. Advocating criticism over commitment can only fan the fires of nihilism, leaving the individual homeless and dependent, the exact opposite of what COT seeks.

Diane Vaughan's (1996) use of the "new institutionalism" to analyze NASA's organizational culture and its relation to the *Challenger* disaster, presents another form of moral rationalism. In this chapter, however, I do not carry out a textual analysis of Vaughan's work. Instead, I develop my own conceptual framework and primarily focus on reinterpreting her data on NASA culture. I do note that Vaughan's use of the "new institutionalism" posits culture as "pre-rational" and "pre-conscious." This leads her to conclude that macro forces (institutions) created a cognitive context that incapacitated rational decision-making at NASA. Hence, for Vaughan, institutional bias, not individual responsibility, was at the root of the *Challenger* disaster. I argue, however, that Vaughan's framework over-structuralizes culture and thus exaggerates cultural homogeneity. I demonstrate in an analysis of the Flight Readiness Review that the exercise of power and the reaction to it was an important part of the context of decision at NASA. Managers and engineers did make conscious decisions about their own interests and participation. I argue that these individuals are morally responsible for the decisions they made.

Part 4 focuses on the moral relativism of postmodern organization theory (POT). Instead of seeing the world as not rational enough, POT sees it as too rational, that is, as dominated by invisible systems of power that function to control individuals and organizations according to their own inhuman logic. Like COT, POT also advocates perpetual criticism, not to achieve rationality, but to undermine rational systems. By rejecting the seductiveness of belief, the individual takes some control over his/her own thoughts. Hence, also like COT, POT is concerned with the failure of Enlightenment rationalism, but unlike COT, POT seeks the solution by throwing a dose of irrationality into the rational machinery, instead of trying to put man/woman back at the controls. In this sense, POT is the flip side of COT. Back to back, rational/irrational, they both seek to rest on the island of individual freedom, neither of them having any love of submission, which, I argue, is the only way to find truth, beauty, and justice in an otherwise meaningless world.

The first analysis in this Part focuses on the Foucauldian concept of power/knowledge. POT posits power and knowledge as coterminous, that is, the individual's knowledge is seen as an alien form of power used to oppress him/her. The POT concept of power/knowledge assumes a "natural" individual that is somehow coherent and capable of self-consciousness independent of cultural order. This Enlightenment assumption underwrites the concept of power/knowledge. I show the impossibility of such an existence independent of time and place. Man/woman, to exist at all, must exist as specific social beings in specific social and historical contexts. POT misunderstands the individual because its view of history begins in the eighteenth century, limited to the tragedy of Enlightenment individualism. By absurdly characterizing all previous religious history as merely forms of "power/knowledge," they are blind to the profound sources of freedom and resistance in belief.

The next analysis focuses on the method of deconstruction. In deconstruction, POT seeks to dismantle all cultural authority by uncovering the repressed component in cultural meaning. The purpose of "unmasking" culture is to free repressed meaning and thus suppressed voices. Deconstruction is shown to be basically nihilistic because culture requires repression in the process of forming meaning. By releasing the repressed opposite, deconstruction destroys the boundary between what *is* and what *is not*. Instead of freedom, deconstruction achieves meaninglessness. Freedom requires authority, which simultaneously limits *and* protects freedom's borders. I argue that only by remembering, evaluating, and cultivating our moral heritage can rights and freedom be stabilized and safeguarded.

The last chapter in this section focuses on POT's goal of cultural egalitarianism. Again, POT uses the concept of power/knowledge to confront the powers of subjection inherent in knowledge. This time, however, instead of focusing on the tool of criticism, it develops the idea of egalitarian forms of self-knowledge, that is, carefully managing one's commitments to avoid being taken under the spell of any particular one. Continuous ideational movement is advocated. Using data from electronic, telecommunication, and academic organizations, I argue that cultural egalitarianism destroys the basis of moral culture. If all values are equal, how does one tell the difference between right and wrong? Hence, we see underneath POT's moral relativism an unreasonable confidence in rationalism: man/woman can somehow avoid commitments, yet recognize the difference between good and evil. POT, like its first cousin COT, wishes to somehow reject cultural values and have them too.

Finally, in Part 5, the Conclusion, a few general observations are presented. I note that all the theories of organizational culture analyzed in this book assume one or more of three fundamental values: rationalism, individualism, and democracy. I review the relationships to these values in each theory and compare and contrast the theories and their implications for organizational ethics. I argue that all the theories can be seen as attempts to provide secular leadership for moral questions, given the criticisms of modern culture and society that they present. Each in its own way attempts to provide a moral sanctuary against the modern world. They all do so, however, without (nay, against) the moral accomplishments of the past. It is this tension, between a present moving into the future and a present moving into the future while committed to and cultivating the past, that underlies the intellectual journey presented in this book.

Part 2

Establishing Traditions

2

The Disinheritance of Management Ethics: Rational Individualism in Barnard's *The Functions of the Executive*

Chester Barnard's classic work in management theory, The Functions of the Executive, includes one of the first systematic discussions of management ethics. It is an attempt to create a new justification for executive control and organization freedom. The literature reviewing Barnard's effort has focused on the various arguments he uses to justify these ends. I argue that the key to understanding Barnard's work on management ethics is that he broke with any historical continuity of (traditional) moral belief. Barnard attempts to replace traditional moral beliefs with a rational process of moral conflict resolution controlled by the executive. He develops a complex system of dichotomies, assumptions, and concepts geared to incorporate the individual into the organization and demonstrate the moral superiority of the executive leader. This theoretical effort is shown to be based on a contradictory reversal of the definitions in the individual-organization dichotomy. The reversal supports Barnard's objectification of organization which enables him to reduce morality to a functional role within the organization. The argument is based on the dubious ambition that only organizations, not society, can provide an integrated moral whole. Barnard's justification fails in that rational individualism cannot provide a stable or legitimate moral system.

In 1904 Barnard wrote of "my conversion to the Lord Jesus Christ" (Scott 1992, 62); in 1946 he wrote "Christian ethics had developed in agricultural, pastoral, and nomadic societies and were chiefly expressed in terms intelligible to the people of such societies" (Scott 1992, 147), thereby implying that Christian ethics was not applicable to modern society. Thus, somewhere between these two dates Barnard broke ranks with the traditions of his faith. I contend that this departure from tradition is the key to understanding Barnard's theory of management ethics. Once a stable moral truth was no longer accepted, a radically different—in other words contingent—ethics had to be developed. The new ethics required a new theoretical justification and it is to this justification that Barnard (1938) turned in the last substantive chapter in *The Functions of the Executive*. In this chapter I will analyze Barnard's new justification for management ethics to explicate its basic assumptions, social implications, and claims to legitimacy.

Nowhere in *The Functions of the Executive* does Barnard clearly state the moral basis for the new management ethics. As with so many aspects of Barnard's writing, multiple interpretations are possible, and four different bases for Barnard's management ethics have been identified in the literature. Golembiewski and Kuhnert (1994, 1223) wrote, "The measure of organizational morality, after all, is pure persistence and that in turn is defined in terms of a continuing ability to mobilize incentives." Barnard uses such words as "endurance," "maintenance," and "survival" as the ultimate moral value. Perrow (1972) and Scott and Mitchell (1987) focus on cooperation as the ultimate moral value because it is based on shared goals. Godfrey (1994) stresses that the moral justification for management in Barnard's work is expertise or rational superiority. Executives have a special capacity for complex reasoning which justifies their moral leadership. Finally, Smith (1994) argues that "responsibility" is the key moral ingredient in management.

In this chapter, I will analyze the role that all four moral justifications play in Barnard's management ethics as well as several other key assumptions. I will show that there are themes central to all of Barnard's attempts to create a new justification for management ethics. Barnard's new ethics is an attempt to replace the moral authority of the Judeo-Christian tradition with a belief system based on the rational superiority of the individual executive. But despite his labors to create a new management ethics, Barnard says little about specific ethical values. Instead, he presents an abstract discussion on how executives resolve moral conflicts – for example, they use "moral creativity." There are no established moral standards, only the continuously mobile effort of executives to synthesize conflicting moral codes.

Scott (1992) was right to conclude that Barnard was a social contractarian in that Barnard's assumption of the calculating individual and his faith in the problem-solving power of rational thinking are reminiscent of eighteenth century political and economic theory. The point I want to stress is that Barnard breaks the moral linkage to the past. His whole effort to create a new theoretical justification for management ethics is based on removing organizations from the social history that produced them and investing them with the twin prides of the modern era: an exaggerated confidence in individual autonomy and rational calculation.

It is true that Barnard explicitly warns of the exaggerated importance of rationality in modern life (Wolf 1994). It is also true, however, that Barnard is not a clear writer; it is often difficult to understand what he means (Scott 1982; Mitchell and Scott 1985). Indeed, several writers have found more than a hint of contradiction in his work (Wells 1963; Strother 1976; Golembiewski and Kuhnert 1994). I will demonstrate that once the wide range of Barnard's statements are considered, it will be clear that he replaces the idea of a moral heritage with a new faith in rational individualism as the foundation for management ethics. Furthermore, I will show that this new theoretical justification is achieved through a contradictory use of key concepts. In the end, Barnard's theory will be shown to fail as a basis for management ethics.

The Individual-Organization Dichotomy

The individual-organization dichotomy is, as it is for everything else in Barnard's work, the root of his management ethics. Barnard develops three separate dichotomous frameworks in regard to the individual: the person-individual dichotomy, the individual-society dichotomy, and the organization personality-individual personality dichotomy. I will begin with the person-individual split. Barnard (1938, 16) writes,

In this book persons as *participants in specific coöperative systems* are regarded in their purely functional aspects, as phases of cooperation. Their efforts are depersonalized, or, conversely, are socialized, so far as these efforts are coöperative. . . . Second, as outside any specific organization, a person is regarded as a unique individualization of physical, biological, and social factors, possessing in limited degree a power of choice. These two aspects are not alternative in time; that is, an individual is not regarded as a function at one time, as a person at another. Rather they are alternative aspects which may simultaneously be present. *Both are always present in coöperative systems.* The selection of one or the other of these aspects is determined by the field of inquiry. When we are considering coöperation as a functioning system of activities of two or more persons, the functional or processive aspect of the person is relevant. When we are considering the person as the *object* of the coöperative functions or process, the second aspect, that of individualization, is most convenient.

This split between "person" and "individual" presents immediate problems for management ethics. It enables Barnard to make ethics secondary in the study of cooperation; that is, ethics becomes a part instead of the whole. The dichotomy is clearly biased in favor of the organization. (Even the concept of the "individual" looks at the individual "as the *object* of the coöperative functions"). Indeed, the concept of the "person" alters the moral integrity of the individual because moral choice is the responsibility of the whole individual (Rieff 1979). Barnard defines the functioning of the "person" within an organization as "depersonalized" or "socialized" by which he means nonindividual and personally non-responsible. He destroys the moral autonomy of the "person" by subsuming him/her into a purely functional role. Personal autonomy, however, is a basic element of morality (Durkheim 1925). Barnard's functional definition of the "person" shifts the moral responsibility from the individual to the organization. This loss of individual autonomy undermines the development of the personal sense of duty or dedication which is the inner nature of morality (Hennis 1988). When relationships are "depersonalized," the basis for personal dedication is destroyed.

It is noteworthy that Barnard refers to this impersonalization of relationships as "socialized." It exposes the moral relativism underlying his framework. Since the "functional aspects" of work can be easily modified by changes in the system of functions, the "person" can be resocialized through the same rational restructuring process. Thus, "socialized" means little more than "role-playing." One role is as good as another depending on the needs of the system. There is no abiding social system in the sense of cultural and personal identity. Identity is changed along with the functional system. The enduring beliefs of society are redefined so that they can be manipulated to meet the functional needs of the organization. The organizational "person" is the new functional component in the new moral system: organization as society. Rational-functional organization replaces psychohistorical society.

This overly rationalized definition of "person" could perhaps be offset by a deep socialization of the "individual," but in Barnard's framework the "individual" is a utilitarian rationalist. Barnard (1938, 85) writes, "willingness to cooperate, positive or negative, is the expression of the net satisfactions or dissatisfactions experienced or anticipated by each individual." Thus, Barnard's "individual" makes de-

cisions based on calculated self-interest. Even if the individual's perception of his/her self-interest are affected by "values," as Barnard
assumes they are, the "individual" is still primarily self-centered. Indeed, Barnard (1938, 139) writes, "egotistical motives of self-preser-
vation and of self-satisfaction are dominating forces." Hence, both
"person" and "individual" are based on rational processes—organizational and individual—and neither assumes an autonomous moral capacity.

The individual-society dichotomy further distances the individual
from a social and moral whole. Barnard (1938, 97) defines society as a
" . . . complex of informal organizations . . . ." He (1938, 115) writes,

> By informal organization I mean the aggregate of the personal contacts and inter-
> actions and the associated groupings of people. . . . Though common or joint pur-
> poses are excluded by definition, common or joint results of important character
> nevertheless come from such organization.
>
> Now it is evident from this description that informal organization is indefinite
> and rather structureless, and has no definite subdivision. It may be regarded as a
> shapeless mass of quite varied densities . . . .

Thus, the individual belongs to neither a social or cultural whole by
which to peg his/her identity. The multiplicity of "informal organizations" leads to social uniqueness in every individual because of the
diversity of associations. Importantly, Barnard has little to say about
ideational systems or what is usually referred to as culture. His social
theory is grounded in "organization" and culture is only transmitted
through organization. This underestimates the partial autonomy of culture (Geertz 1973): the ideational and symbolic nature of culture can
be communicated and experienced independently of organizational affiliation. One's interpretation of a novel or a painting, for example,
can hardly be reduced to (or deduced from) one's membership in
certain "informal organizations." Barnard's individual-society dichotomy therefore underestimates the social nature of the individual
by burying nonorganizational culture in a concept of societal fragmentation.

The organization personality-individual personality dichotomy is
based on the person-individual dichotomy: "organization personality"
means that the individual makes decisions in reference to the cooperative process as a whole, "individual personality" reflects the individual's
self-interest. There is, however, one important difference: *the organization personality-individual personality dichotomy is not applied iden-*

tically to all organization personnel. Executives have an organization personality by definition; it is the essence of "organization" and the means of executive control. Non-executives do not have an organization personality. It is the central task of the former to see to it that the latter adopt one. Hence, executives are more organizational and less individualistic than non-executive personnel. Their morality, then, is organizationally based. Barnard never states what this morality is, other than the survival of the organization.

Barnard is stressing psychological control over other forms of organization control by selectively applying the concept of organization personality, and by defining the central task of executives as indoctrinating non-executive personnel into the organization personality. Barnard (1938, 220) writes, "The most important single contribution required of the executive, certainly the most universal qualification, is loyalty, domination by the organization personality." Hence, despite the overly individualized bias in Barnard's definition of the individual, ultimately it is all nullified by the domination of executives by the organization personality and the executive's indoctrination of other personnel into the organization personality. Barnard is thus a collectivist in that the core of his theory of management is the organization personality. He undermines moral character, since he undermines the autonomy needed for moral choice.

Barnard never exactly defines what "organization personality" signifies. Similar to his concept of "objective purpose," organization personality assumes an objectivity that is never clearly demonstrated (1938, 87)[1]. At best, it functions empirically as an ideal. He (1938, 223) alludes to its meaning through the use of physical or physiological metaphors such as referring to an organization as an "organic whole." The problem with assuming that the organization functions as an objective whole is that the political basis of organization is concealed. Weber (1946, 220) was lucid on this point: "the sure instincts of the bureaucracy for the conditions of maintaining its power . . . are inseparably fused with the canonization of the abstract and 'objective' idea." Hence, Barnard's objectification of the concept of "organization personality" conceals his political intention: the controlling of organization personnel for the purpose of accomplishing ends chosen by executive personnel. This political end is the hidden irrational value in Barnard's objectification of organization.

Perrow (1972) is certainly correct to note that Barnard presents a reified conception of organization. Barnard (1938, 79) writes that he regards organizations as "social creatures 'alive,' just as I regard an individual human being." This anthropomorphization of the abstraction "organization" allows Barnard to exaggerate the integrity and self-sufficiency of organizations. Thus, he also exaggerates the independence organizations have from the societies in which they are created and the individuals who create them. In this way, Barnard claims an autonomy for organizations that frees them of any kind of political control or even social responsibility. Scott and Mitchell (1989) are right to claim that Barnard holds management accountable only to itself.

It is this political end—management is accountable to itself—that is the irrational terminal point towards which all of Barnard's discussion is directed. The dichotomies—person-individual, individual-society, and organization personality-individual personality—work to justify the end of managerial autonomy. Even though the dichotomies are formulated in value-free terms, they all function to legitimate the value of executive control. Wolf (1994) and Pye (1994) are right to claim Barnard uses the dichotomous polarities to set up a field of analysis. However, they miss the key point that the rational formulation of the dichotomies and the rationalized analysis they make possible, conceal Barnard's strenuous effort to justify executive control by making executives the embodiment of rationality. The presumed objectification of "organization personality" is the moral fountainhead which invisibly justifies and directs the rational instrument of executive control. It is the canonization of the idea of "organization personality" on which Barnard's management ethics rests.

The Instrumentalization of Morality

By objectifying "organization," Barnard (1938, 201) reduces morality to a component: morality becomes the "moral element." As an element, it takes on a supportive function in Barnard's canonized "organization." Morality functions as the " . . . spirit that overcomes the centrifugal forces of individual interests . . . " (Barnard 1938, 283). Hence, its importance for Barnard is the function it has in controlling organization personnel. It controls them by creating "faith." Faith persuades and inspires individuals to commit to the organization.

However, for Barnard, working with the "moral element" to create faith is a daunting task. Barnard (1938, 207) writes,

The developments of processes, tools, and men are not equal in all directions. They are not equally good in respect to the various elements of the environmental situation. Every such situation to which the purpose of man applies always involves in some degree physical, chemical, biological, physiological, psychological, economic, political, social, and moral elements. The powers of discrimination are most developed in some such order as that in which I have named these elements; so that there is inevitably an unbalance in the perception of the various elements of the total environment to which *as a whole* every decision relates. Therefore, the precision of decision is greater in the same order.

Note that Barnard puts morality on the lowest rung of a hierarchical continuum conceived in terms of *scientific* knowledge. By making morality a form of scientific knowledge, he makes it an instrument of action. It thus fits appropriately into the executive's bag of skills. As we will see, the executive is not so much a protector of moral codes as a solver of moral "problems." In this way, morality functions to support the objectification of organization rather than to evaluate it. Hence, in Barnard, the "moral element" is a means of political control.

Perhaps nothing demonstrates the implications of Barnard's instrumentalization of morality more clearly than how he treats the past. In a chapter on decision making he (1938, 209) writes, "The legitimate significance of the past is not in the present objective environment, but in the moral aspect of the formulation of new purpose." The fact that morality is made an "aspect" of purpose demonstrates the despiritualization of purpose. The fact that morality is made an aspect of "new" purpose, demonstrates the abstractness (and ambiguity) of morality in Barnard's management ethics. Indeed, by taking morality out of the "objective" environment, morality is reduced to a mere subjective phenomenon. Furthermore, by taking morality out of the "present," Barnard is breaking the moral linkage between past-present-future (Arendt 1968). In this way, Barnard breaks the historical spine of morality. This enables him to subjugate morality for the purposes of "organization."

The change of morality from a continuous tradition to an abstract "element" changes the scope of morality from an objective moral constraint to a subjective moral influence. Its priestly authority is lost. Morality becomes a team player. The weight of social and communal obligations is significantly lightened as morality competes with other "elements" inside organization purpose. In comparison with Christian social ethics, for example, morality ceases to be the central social priority.

From a historical point of view, Barnard was a transition writer (Stewart 1989). Christianity had been in decline since the eighteenth century (Rieff 1987). The great restlessness and commotion of American democratic culture that Tocqueville (1850) commented on in the 1830s was struggling with the new harness of bureaucratic authority in the 1930s. Barnard, in the midst of this transition, wanted to justify the new form of social control, but in attempting to give executives the greatest possible freedom, he cut them loose from the shared past as a stable anchor for moral character. Instead, Barnard pinned his faith on executive "rationality."

The Rationalization of Ethics

The fundamental assumption in Barnard's (1938, 275) theory of management ethics is that morality is characterized by "complexity." Barnard (1938, 262) writes,

> Morals arise from forces external to the individual as a person. Some are believed by many to be directly of supernatural origin; some of them derive from the social environment, including general, political, religious, and economic environments; some of them arise from experience of the physical environment, and from biological properties and phylogenetic history; some from technological practice or habit. . . . What has just been said about the origin of morals suggests the convenience of postulating several sets of general propensities or codes in the same person, arising from different sources of influence and related to several quite diverse types of activities.

Since morality is derived from different sources, each individual develops "several private moral codes" (Barnard 1938, 262). Having "several private moral codes" will inevitably result in moral conflict, both within the individual and between individuals.

Barnard's position appears to be arrived at logically by inferring from experience. He cites no references for his conclusions. Max Weber (1946) considered this ethical stance to be characteristic of modern civilization. He believed that developments of the last several hundred years—for example, science, capitalism, and the expanding division of labor—have all challenged the dominance of Christian social ethics that had dominated Western civilization for the previous millennium. Today, in Weber's (1918b, 149) words, "many old gods ascend from their graves" and "resume their eternal struggle with one another." Hence, by defining morality abstractly and independent of historical context and positing it as naturally conflictual, Barnard legitimates as much as describes morality in our epoch. Indeed, he gives a logical rationalization for the cultural fragmentation of modern society. "Several private moral codes" is a social, cultural, and historical development which Barnard grasps only in terms of individual experience. Thus, Barnard's work on ethics is reductionist.

The sharp individualism in Barnard's theory of management ethics is continued in his discussion of how moral conflict is resolved. The individual executive must exercise "ability" to resolve moral conflict. Barnard (1938, 271–72) writes,

> The dilemmas which result from numerous conflicts imply in general at least one of the following consequences: either general moral deterioration, beginning in frustration and indecisiveness; or diminution of the general sense of responsibility . . . or the development of the ability to construct alternative measures that satisfy immediate desires or requirements without violating any codes. When the last alternative is taken it undoubtedly increases the general sense of responsibility and perhaps usually the moral status of the individual; but it requires resourcefulness, energy, imagination, general ability.

Hence, for Barnard moral "ability" implies and requires mental superiority on the part of the individual executive. By moral superiority, he means having the capacity to resolve moral conflict. He bypasses immoral resolution of moral conflict with the aside that nothing will be sensed by subordinates quicker than "insincerity" (1938, 282). Thus, individual executives are the ultimate source of morality. There are organization codes, but the executive rises above these in his/her role as resolver of conflicts between different organization codes and between the codes of individuals and the organization. As Scott (1982, 199) states, the executive has the final judgment about "what is "good" or "bad" *for the organization* . . . ."

Several authors have noted a similarity between Barnard's theory of management ethics and totalitarianism. Since the environment is characterized by "moral complexity," the organization is free of an external moral order (Golembiewski and Kuhnert 1994, 1223). This leaves organizations "sovereign unto themselves" (Scott 1982, 199). Following this criterion, Godfrey (1994, 1077) concludes that the "Gestapo" qualifies as a moral organization, since it "acted in accord with its stated objectives." The problem is that by objectifying the organization, a totalizing schema is created. For Barnard, however, this is precisely the solution to the problem of "moral complexity." By resolving moral conflict in terms of a consensus on organization purpose, executives create a moral whole out of moral complexity. Indeed, for Barnard (1938), this is the origin of morality in modern society, but the problem of totalitarianism remains. Barnard's solution to the problem of organization control is similar to that of Lenin's (Wolin 1960): An autonomous body of moral belief is replaced by the totalizing abstraction of the "organic whole."

Giving organizations a monopoly on morality has three problematic theoretical implications in addition to the totalitarian-political ones. First, Barnard (1938, 119) assumes that organizations are "the poles around which personal associations are given sufficient consistency" and thus best equipped to overcome moral complexity. This is not true, however: history is filled with examples of individuals and societies overcoming the diversity of their experience through commitment to non-organizational belief systems (Weber 1922), for example, Protestantism and Buddhism. These systems are rationally structured to the same extent as organization purpose. Barnard's preference for organization purpose as a moral whole is based only on his political wish to have society controlled by formal organizations.

Second, a society composed of morally self-sustaining organizations has no way to regulate the moral relations between organizations other than societal laws. However, laws could never completely regulate the complex interactions between organizations. Without a societal moral consensus, the letter of the law would soon be overwhelmed by the imaginative power of individuals trying to advance their own and their organization's interests (Durkheim 1957). Indeed, in any case, this is a natural pressure in all societies.

Third, Barnard (1938, 79) has to split the individual—that is, organization personality-individual personality—to explain how the individual conforms to the moral organization while living in "an informal, indefinite, nebulous, and undirected system usually named a "society"." If society is truly "nebulous," how does it produce morally integrated individuals who become executives and create moral organizations? The contradiction is severe but Barnard never addresses the issue. Perhaps, as Godfrey (1994) points out, Barnard is using the moral integrity of the Greek city-state as his model for the organization. The Greek city-state, however, was a social whole; the organization is only a social part. Thus, Barnard's conceptual remedy of the split personality is misleading, because the human being functions as a psychological whole only to the extent that he/she is part of a social whole (Cooley 1922).

Barnard avoids the issue of the cultural fragmentation of American society by developing his theory of management ethics towards a radical individualism. He accomplishes this by splitting morality into two parts: he separates "moral status" from "moral responsibility." Barnard (1938, 263) writes,

> Moral status and responsibility are not identical . . . .The important point here is that persons of high moral status may be weakly controlled by their moral codes, and are then relatively irresponsible; and vice versa.

Later he (1938, 270) adds,

> Those who have a strong attachment to the organization, however it comes about, are likely to have a code or codes derived from it if their connection has existed long; but whether they appear responsible with respect to such codes depends upon the general capacity for responsibility and upon their place in the spectrum of personal codes.

Hence, "responsibility" becomes a "general capacity" existing without any content. The individual picks from his/her inventory of moral codes determining his/her moral status those toward which he/she will exercise responsibility.

Barnard is forced to make this split because his assumption of "moral complexity" would otherwise turn each individual into a confused collection of contradictory moral codes. The individual has the choice of being morally responsible to some of his/her moral codes and not others, thereby having the capacity to be morally rational. This freedom of choice, however, institutionalizes an extreme split between self and society. Indeed, as was shown, for Barnard society does not exist as an organized moral system; there is only "moral complexity." Hence, there is no way to explain why individuals are responsible to particular moral codes and not others (Douglas 1990). More importantly, there is no way to explain why executives choose to be dominated by the organization personality. Barnard not only does not explain, but cannot because his split between moral status and moral responsibility removes any historical or sociological influences from the decision. Yet, this unexplained choice is the foundation of Barnard's management ethics.

Smith (1994) tries to explain Barnard's concept of responsibility by arguing that it is the natural result of individuals joining a cooperative effort. Individuals choose to be responsible to the organization as part of their decision to join the organization to enhance their productivity. Like Barnard, however, Smith assumes a stable *culture* of utilitarians. This assumption is hardly consistent with each individual starting with a socially empty capacity for responsibility and developing morally only through their own unique experiences. Moreover, even if all individuals became utilitarians, it in no way precludes, and might even encourage, what Williamson (1985, 47) has called "self-interest seeking with guile."

Thus there is no way to explain how Barnard's individual makes moral choices with an abstract capacity for responsibility. The reader must simply jump the unbridgeable gap to the "organization personality." Once this end is accepted, Barnard has little to say about morality. He is basically a moral relativist: His framework clearly stresses an abstract "responsibility" over "whatever morality" the individual chooses to be responsible to (1938, 67). Scott and Mitchell (1989, 304) are wrong to argue that Barnard's stress on the "spirit that shapes ends . . . [are] . . . the words of religious conviction." Religion requires commitment to sacred beliefs that are distinct from profane needs (Durkheim 1915). Barnard's "organization" is neither perceived to be sacred nor independent of profane needs. Indeed, Scott and Mitchell (1987, 54) themselves conclude that ultimately Barnard's organization is based on "mutual interests." "Mutual interests" are not a basis for religion. This is why Barnard can work with "whatever morality."

When Barnard gives examples to demonstrate moral behavior, he is not so much trying to demonstrate religious conviction as he is trying to replace society with organization as the locus of the individual's moral attachment. He feels that "public codes . . . [or those] . . . most professed publicly" are of little importance (1938, 265). On the contrary, organization commitments are central. He (1938, 267–68) makes up a story to demonstrate his point:

Mr. A, a citizen of Massachusetts, a member of the Baptist Church, having a father and mother living, and a wife and two children, is an expert machinist employed at a pump station of an important water system. . . . We impute to him several moral codes: Christian ethics, the patriotic code of the citizen, a code of family obligations, a code as an expert machinist, a code derived from the organization. . . . if pressed, what he might say probably would indicate that his religious code is first in importance. . . . [But] for his children he will kill, steal, cheat the government, rob the church, leave the water plant at a critical time, botch the job by hurrying. If his children are not directly at stake, he will sacrifice money, health, time, comfort, convenience, jury duty, church obligations, in order to keep the water plant running; except for this children and the water plant, he cannot be induced to do a botch mechanical job—wouldn't know how; to take care of this parents, he will lie, steal, or do anything else contrary to his code as a citizen or his religious code...

Hence, God and country are pushed to the end of the list. Oddly, though, organization loyalty and work ethic not only come before country, they also are put before parents. In fact, Barnard (1938, 269) gives another example of a switchboard operator whose behavior he praises as "moral courage" for staying at her post as she watches her house burning down with her bedridden mother inside from an office window at work.

Barnard's examples demonstrate that he is trying to weaken all social bonds, excluding only those needed for biological reproduction (notice that love of the marital partner is not mentioned), that could interfere with organizational commitment. It seems reasonable to suggest he is taking aim at the Christian ethic of brotherly love. The Christian ethic is universal and spiritual and thus presents a problem for Barnard's goal of organizational supremacy.

"Mr. A"—as in Mr. America—is similar to the individualist Tocqueville (1850, 506) discovered in American society who is disposed " . . . to isolate himself from the mass of his fellows and withdrawn into the circle of family and friends; with this little society formed to his taste, he gladly leaves the greater society to look after itself." Barnard, however, makes a not so subtle change: "Mr. A" builds his "little society" out of children and organization. Hence, in Barnard, Tocqueville's image of the American individualist is transformed into the committed organization man. The withdrawn individual becomes the loyal employee. It is not the religious language of self-submission that Barnard uses, but the organizational mythology of totalitarian domination.

The indispensable fulminator Barnard uses to create the totalitarian organization is executive leadership. A "distinguishing characteristic of executive work . . . [is] . . . the function of creating moral conditions" (Barnard 1938, 274). Mitchell and Scott (1985, 254) have described this approach as an "unabashed manipulative perspective." Two problems will be discussed. First, as noted above, morality has been subordinated to organization purpose which undermines moral truth. Second, the executives are in a conflict of interest: they create "moral codes" to accomplish goals they set and for which they are rewarded.

Barnard tries to avoid these problems in two ways. First, he claims that organization action based on cooperation is moral, because the ends being pursued are shared. In this way, Barnard uses an abstract definition to detour questions about organizational morality. Perrow (1972) has pointed out the fallacy in this argument: "organizations" are not persons and cannot be considered moral or immoral. Barnard's abstract conception of organizations as moral because they are based on shared ends is empty of specific moral values. Individuals must be judged in terms of the specific ends, means, and results involved in their cooperative activities. Gestapo henchmen did pursue shared ends, but they are hardly moral.

Second, Barnard (1938, 281) tries to base the moral nature of organization in the moral "conviction" of the executive which he defines as the "identification of personal codes and organization codes." In other words, the ultimate justification for organizational morality is the executive's integration of his private codes with the organization's codes. Barnard (1938, 281) writes,

> The invention of constructions and fictions necessary to secure the preservation of morale is a severe test of both responsibility and ability, for to be sound they must be "just" in the view of the executive, that is, really consonant with the morality of the whole; as well as acceptable, that is, really consonant with the morality of the part, of the individual.

Importantly, the "morality of the whole" exists in the "view of the executive." Barnard moves beyond the postulated morality of the reified organization to a dynamic morality originating in the integrative abilities of the individual executive. However, as was shown, the fundamental characteristic of the executive is his/her commitment to "organization personality." So we are right back where we started. The fact that the executive leader must be consonant with the morality of the individual is also circular, because the individual's natural "moral complexity" means he/she only develops a fully focused morality under the sway of organizational commitment.

A deeper problem with the creative-executive-basis for organization morality is its instability and ambiguity. Ultimately, Barnard does not have an organization morality, because it is continuously changing to meet the non-moral requirements of the organization. To maintain social respect and achieve psychological depth, however, moral codes must be stable, though not inflexible, over time, since morality assumes a standard of justice, and since justice will have no integrity if it is continuously open to change for pragmatic reasons. In Barnard's formulation, on the contrary, only the needs of power-holders will be pursued. Instead of being an autonomous standard by which to evaluate worldly goals, morality becomes a tool to achieve these goals. In the quote from Barnard above, the fact that "just" is put in quotation marks demonstrates again the underlying moral relativism in Barnard's ethics. Barnard requires moral relativism because moral codes must continuously change to justify continuously changing organizational goals.

Barnard (1938, 284) ends the chapter on management ethics with the phrase, "out of the void comes the spirit that shapes the ends of men." This summarizes the underlying rationalism and individualism in Barnard's moral theory: the "void" implies a lack of historical memory or societal beliefs, only the executive leader creates the spirit out of nothing. Indeed, the fact that the "creative aspect of executive responsibility is the highest exemplification of responsibility," demonstrates the primacy of creativity over continuity (Barnard 1938, 281). At one point, Barnard (1938, 281) even suggests that a "few" can create moral codes "objectively." Objective creation of moral codes shows the ideal of rational instrumentality at the base of Barnard's ethical theory.

Scott (1992, 150), however, using Pincoffs's (1986) "quandary ethics," argues that "conscientiousness" is central to Barnard's moral philosophy. Quandary ethics states that where no rule applies to a particular decision, a person must create a new rule that "is consistent with other rules that he accepts" (Scott 1992, 150). However, Scott (1992) misses the point that Barnard's theory does not state *any* moral rules. In Barnard, one finds references to "loyalty," "sincerity," "honesty," "persistence," and "responsibility," but these are only stated in terms of accomplishing organization goals. They are not ends in themselves. This formulation begs the question concerning conflicts between organization goals and moral rules. Hence, one can add conscientiousness to the list, but it also refers only to accomplishing organization goals. In Barnard's theory, quandary ethics, similar to moral creativity, can only function to rationalize conflicting demands in the pursuit of organization goals.

Conclusion

In this chapter, I have argued that Barnard's theory of management ethics has no clear and stable moral position, but ambiguously relies on the rational problem-solving "abilities" of individual executives. Barnard (1938, 261) himself seemed confused about his position on management ethics, because despite the primary emphasis on executive rationality in his discussion, he defined morality as "a matter of emotion." This split between rational thought and emotional sentiment is typical of eighteenth century social thought (Rieff 1979). Within this tradition, Barnard employs the split with an overriding bias towards the rationalization of the moral process. This is why he splits morality into status and responsibility in his discussion of moral codes, enabling him to tie commitment more closely to creativity (rationality), separate from nonrational questions of status or belief in any particular historical period.

The focus on the moral process rather than moral belief exposes Barnard's rationalizing intentions. Morality is not primarily viewed as a system of belief, but as a *process* of conflict resolution. Moral creativity, his main symbol in this effort, whether defined variously as the inventing, substituting, justifying, redefining, or refining of moral codes, always originates as a rationalization of moral conflict. Importantly, Barnard is not trying to rationalize a specific moral system. On the contrary, he is trying to replace moral belief with the process of rationalization itself. By replacing content with form, Barnard is creating a system of control that can never become obsolete: it simply rationalizes all moral conflict to its own advantage. In a society that he implicitly assumes to be in a state of moral fragmentation, Barnard provides a technology to achieve control. In so doing, he replaces morality with politics.

Underwriting Barnard's whole effort is the individual-organization dichotomy. Interestingly, Barnard utilizes two versions of the individual-organization dichotomy to achieve his theoretical results. Generally, individuals are egoistic, but special individuals, executives, are dominated by the "organization personality." This selective application of the concept of individual is needed for Barnard to arrive at the distribution of power he desires.

Executives, dominated by the "organization personality," are synonymous with organization control. The "organization personality" expresses the reification of the organization. Executives are simply the loyal automatons of this system. Barnard hardly mentions hierarchy or power because "organization personality" acts as a substitute for them. Likewise, since the organization personality is legitimate by definition, and since non-executive personnel are egoistic by definition, there are no competing purposes for the organization. It is simply a matter of persuading non-executive personnel to give up their selfish ways. Thus, the double definition of the concept of the individual magically avoids the ancient problem of organization legitimacy.

Legitimate or not, Barnard still has the problem of conflict between individual moral codes and the organization personality. This requires more conceptual magic: in the chapter on management ethics, Barnard reverses his selective application of the concept of the individual. In the process of persuasion, the non-executive individual is incorporated into the organization personality. The executive, however, in resolving the conflict between individual and organization, rises above the organization personality and creates new moral codes. Thus, in the end, Barnard's theory of management ethics rests on the rational superiority of the individual executive. The fact that he must reverse the definitions of executive and non-executive in the individual-organization dichotomy to accomplish this end, demonstrates the contradictory dichotomy in Barnard's theorizing and the contradiction at the base of his theory of management ethics. It also lays bare the seed of Barnard's effort, that is, the false idealization of the executive as mentally and morally superior.

Ultimately, Barnard's attempt to replace the declining system of moral belief in American society with a rational process to resolve moral conflicts in organizations further undermines moral belief. The continuous use of "moral creativity" is sure to weaken the capacity for commitment as moral character is continuously uprooted and repainted with new "moral codes." The robust confidence Barnard places in the rationality and "responsibility" of the individual executive also seems misplaced. Even if we accept the dubious assumption that executives usually have these qualifications, it in no way guarantees they will be used for morally good purposes. Indeed, this is my major criticism of Barnard's management ethics: it fails to establish a stable moral position by which human activities can be judged.

Note

1. Barnard (1938, 87) uses an image of "detached observers" observing from a "special position" to portray the objective use of purpose.

3

The Ethics of Shifting Ties: Moral Relativism in Melville Dalton's *Men Who Manage*

Despite a long tradition of documenting unethical practices in organizations, the sociology of organization literature has seldom addressed the question of management ethics. One early work in the field, Melville Dalton's Men Who Manage *(1959), did develop a contingent approach to ethics that is seen as a precursor to contemporary discussions in modern and postmodern organization theory. In this chapter, I analyze Dalton's work using a non-modern or hierarchical understanding of morality. It is concluded that Dalton created a powerful but false intellectual rationale for the historic decline in moral commitment found in modern culture. By replacing moral commitment with the cult of the individual, morality, in effect, is reduced to politics.*

Over the last five decades detailed sociological studies of management and organization have documented acts of aggression, blatantly selfish behavior, sexism, racism, and destructive political intrigues. It is surprising that questions of management ethics have not received more explicit attention. The predominance of researchers studying organizational culture have limited their conceptual concerns to issues of individual psychology (Jaques 1951), organizational structure (Kanter 1977), politics and history (Pettigrew 1985; Smith, Child, and Rowlinson 1990), and social interaction (Kunda 1992).

One of the earliest studies, Melville Dalton's (1959) *Men Who Manage*, did try to come to terms with the moral aspects of management behavior. Dalton's work engages in a moral debate with the likes of Whyte (1956), Riesman (1950), Orwell (1949), and others that argue organizations exercise excessive control over people and thwart their moral development. Dalton attempts to show that a healthy individualism is still alive inside the organization and that it is a benefit to the organization.

The patterns in Dalton's field data are nearly identical to what are found in many recent studies. The themes of managerial politics—cliques, power, leadership, compromise—that are central to Dalton's account, run through the work of Pettigrew (1985) and Smith, Child, and Rowlinson (1990). The importance of secrecy, or what Dalton (1959) calls "protective coloration," is almost identical to discussions of "chameleonic adaptability" in the work of Jackall (1988). Indeed, Dalton's work is considered a classic today and has broad-ranging influence (Kanter 1977; Van Maanen 1988; Kunda 1992; Clegg 1994).

For these reasons, it seems timely to revisit Dalton's work to carry out a detailed textual analysis to examine how he evaluated the moral aspects of management behavior, what conceptual tools he used, and whether his work provides an adequate model for moral analysis in management. In this way, the moral aspects of management, within the sociology of organization literature, can be reconsidered and a discussion can be initiated on questions of theoretical orientations and philosophical positions.

The approach Dalton develops for analyzing the moral aspects of management is based on a modern attitude toward moral prohibitions. For example, during his fieldwork he discovers that 15 percent of all the firm's materials are unaccounted for every year. He (1959, 283) mentions in the "Appendix on Method" that he repeatedly moralized over this issue and for more than a year saw it "purely as theft." However, "after long reflection on the web of incidents which bound [his close informants] to others . . . I saw the oversimplification I was making and shifted from an interpretation of [his] too rigid and exclusive categories to a more realistic judgment about the whole" (Dalton 1959, 283). This led Dalton to replace the category of "pure theft" with what he calls "unofficial rewards"—rewards forbidden by company policy—which he considers legitimate because they are tacitly approved by executives as "essential maintenance of the social mechanism" (1959, 214). Indeed, he goes on to argue that "pure theft" is not problematic if the costs do not exceed the cost of an alternative incentive system.

It is this "realistic judgment about the whole," which opens up the "too rigid and exclusive categories" of traditional morality, that is the central characteristic of Dalton's moral analysis. This "opening of meaning" is also a common theme in the work of critical theorists (Alvesson and Willmott 1992) and post-modernists (Burrell 1988; Cooper 1989). In other words, Dalton is a forerunner to current views in modern and post-modern organization theory. In order to gain conceptual distance from Dalton's framework, I will use a distinctly different framework which is centered on the idea of an enduring *moral tradition* (Arendt 1968; Rieff 1987; MacIntyre 1984). By contrasting the two frameworks, I will isolate Dalton's moral framework and identify its basic assumptions.

The idea of tradition has been defined as that "which selects and names, which hands down and preserves, which indicates where the treasures are and what their worth is" (Arendt 1968, 5). Tradition provides a social group with a stable set of beliefs and commitments by which to define itself as a group and preserve itself over time. Moral beliefs are the core of tradition because they limit individual behavior, integrating the individual into the group (Rieff 1987). The crucial point from this perspective is that without a moral tradition there cannot be consistent and stable moral behavior because moral belief would be open to continuous challenge. Rieff refers to this type of openness as a "negative community" (1987, 53), because the challenges or negations "are never final" (1991, 322). Critical organization theory, for example, represents a nearly pure type of negative community because no moral statement remains unchallenged. No moral statement except, of course, the principle of criticism, which is left uncriticized (MacIntyre 1984).

Dalton, as we saw, provides a critical analysis of the concept of "pure theft" and opens up its meaning until he arrives at what he feels to be the contextually valid concept of "unofficial rewards." From the point of view of the theory of moral tradition this is a breakdown in morality. Dalton's reformulation of the traditional prohibition against theft exposes his contingent or modern approach to morals. MacIntyre (1984) argues that openness to moral rules is actually a disregard for morality because it leaves morality vulnerable to continuous change. This disregard originates in the replacement of traditional moral authority with the ends of technical effectiveness and individual self-interest. Indeed, as will be shown, this is what Dalton means by "a more realistic judgment of the whole:" economic payoff for the organization and freedom and gain for the individual.

The theory of moral tradition takes the position that morality must be predicated on an agreement as to what is the good in human life taken as a unity (MacIntyre 1984). The good is contextually interpreted, but it cannot be contextually determined without respect for the past. When moral goods are determined in the continuously changing world of practice, then a "subversive arbitrariness will invade the moral life" which leads to the destruction of morality (MacIntyre 1984, 203). This is what is at stake in Dalton's contingent approach to morality and in other contemporary contingency frameworks. Thus, a textual analysis of Dalton's work offers the opportunity to examine its interpretive dynamics and moral judgments to evaluate their implications for our understanding and practice of morality in management.

The Concept of American Culture

Dalton begins his analysis with a discussion of the American cultural context. He believes that the central American cultural category of "equality" has a paradoxical effect on American business. On the one hand, it simply means that Americans have a "great dislike of superiors that behave as superiors" (Dalton 1959, 265). This especially affects rewards and promotions because it leads to the "ideal in American business and industry that measurable contributions and reward should clearly match in all cases" (Dalton 1959, 173). On the other hand, the belief in equality leads to a robust individualism. Each American believes, according to Dalton (1959, 264), that he is "as good as the best and better than most." This over-confident individualism gives American society a "loose and shifting nature" as each individual seeks self-advantage (Dalton 1959, 191). In organizations, however, this "weakens existing formal means" (Dalton 1959, 191). Hence, not only does this contradict the formal system needed to match "measurable contributions and reward," but it also represents a contradiction within American business culture itself.

Dalton's grasp of this paradox leads to his most important contribution to the study of management: the theory of "informal organization." Dalton grounds this concept deep in American social structure: the American begins to learn about "informal organization" in high school and gets advanced training in college. The college student trying to succeed in campus politics, have an active social life, and get good grades learns to "move in and out of cliques and organizations with minimum frictions" (Dalton 1959, 164). To accomplish all his/her goals, he/she uses his/her contacts and social skills to minimize studying for examinations. Ultimately, however, he/she is left on his/

her own to pass difficult examinations while pursuing his/her other varied interests. Dalton (1959, 165) writes about the essence of the student's college experience,

> He becomes sensitive to intangibles, and learns to live with the elusive and ambiguous. This unofficial training teaches him to get in his own claims and gracefully escape those of others that he must. He learns to appear sophisticated and to adjust quickly to endless new situations and personalities.

Dalton does not even mention the classes the student takes as of any importance for the future executive. The key is "competition as an *experience*" (Dalton 1959, 163). Apparently, the American learns little about the problem of social order, the role of law in society, and the intrinsic value of his/her society, only how to manipulate them and advance his/her interests.

Some classes, however, do change his view of family and neighborhood. "He may lose some dogmas about what is worthwhile, what is good and bad, and about the virtue of fixed ways of doing things" (Dalton 1959, 165). Hence, after polishing external conformity and sharpening competitive drive, college loosens traditional values, while substituting relativism. This experience lays the foundation for the core executive skill of "compromise." After undergoing this self-centered de-education in traditional values, the college graduate enters business where moral constraints amount to little more than "preserving the organization" (Dalton 1959, 167).

In Dalton's (1959, 167) view, American society has become so "complex" that the old "morality of fixity" is no longer viable. People belong to many organizations, each with a different moral code. This calls for more "surface conformity" than ever, since people will have to work with others who hold greatly diverse beliefs. So no matter what one believes, one will have to publicly conform to a locally accepted behavior, while privately calculating one's own strategies to advantage. Deception is both socially functional and individually advantageous. People cannot commit to the whole, because one does not exist. As will be shown, these perceptions establish the ground upon which Dalton builds his theory of management.

Dalton (1959, 108) is quite clear on the amorality of American business organization: "our society . . . sees all divisions of labor as career paths first and moral obligations second." There is a problem, however. The old "ethical tradition of fixity" is still half alive requiring the use of a "public relations front" to conceal the naked power conflicts between business executives (Dalton 1959, 258). Similar to Machiavelli's (1532) attempt to separate the modern prince from the Christian church and rationalize his use of power, Dalton takes it on himself to show that the old moral "fixity" is no longer organization-ally functional for the modern manager: it can put moral roadblocks in front of courses of action that would otherwise be organizationally effective. Hence, Dalton raises organizational effectiveness above mo-rality as the ultimate criteria for managerial action. In MacIntyre's terms, this is the origin of the breakdown in management morality because moral truth is destroyed. In addition to trying to make his case through conceptual argument and empirical analysis, Dalton tries to legitimate organizational effectiveness as the ultimate criteria for mana-gerial action with a complementary picture of "human nature" and through historical example, both of which attempt to demonstrate uni-versal necessity.

It is suspicious, though, that Dalton's view of "human nature" tends to resemble the ambitious American executive. He (1959, 265) writes, "the active seeking nature of man, his ancient and obvious tendency to twist the world to his interests . . . erodes the preaching of parents and superiors." This is a culturally biased characterization of "human na-ture." In an article Dalton quotes on Japanese management, Levine (1955, 63), writes, clearly in contradiction to Dalton's view of "human nature,"

> The employee under this system also felt a moral obligation to accept the employer's decisions. Traditional values which eliminated the notion of individualism and reinforced group conformity underlay this sense of obligation. . . . Self-sacrifice, even to the extreme in some cases, was a *sine qua non* of this type of organization and applied to all members of the enterprise.

Hence, we begin to see a bias in Dalton's presentation of American culture. By positing "human nature" in the form of American indi-vidualism, he justifies (and blocks further analysis of) the role of self-interest in achieving organizational goals. Precisely what is missed by using the universal biological category "human nature"—not to men-tion the ethnocentric formulation—is the specific moral means a particular society uses to regulate and limit individual behavior (Durkheim 1957).

Dalton's use of historical examples shows the same pattern. Each one is used to generalize American behavior. None are used as points of comparison which would at least imply a moral alternative. Surprisingly, since the majority of historical examples are from antiquity and the late Middle Ages, one would think that their origin in the distant past and enormously different cultures would generate a striking contrast with modern managers. For example, Dalton quotes a sixteenth century Italian diplomat advising a prince not to act hastily in seeking revenge, because there will be many opportunities. Dalton (1959, 270) uses this historical example to justify pervasive deception in American business bureaucracies, because he thinks it shows there really are "invisible threats." The great differences between the sixteenth century diplomat and the twentieth century executive are not mentioned: the diplomat had a close personal relation with the prince, not impersonal as is common with executives, sought primarily political not economic goals, and existed in a patriarchal organization, not a bureaucratic one. One is thus left with the feeling that Dalton's use of historical example functions to justify by universalizing instead of analyzing.

Ultimately, Dalton's use of historical generalization is contradictory. On the one hand, he (1959, 258) claims that "the ethical tradition of fixity" is no longer functional in complex society. Change has become the essential feature of business and executives must be open to compromise their beliefs. On the other hand, Dalton's book is peppered with historical examples that attempt to demonstrate modern business behavior is nothing new, for example, dominance of ethnic cliques, subordinates currying favor, conflict leading to productivity. Hence, it appears that the use of historical examples to universalize (thus justify) specific points is done without any overall theory of history. This is a highly questionable method because history becomes an infinite mass of disconnected facts that can in effect be used to justify anything and everything. Thus Dalton's effort to establish organization effectiveness as the ultimate criteria for managerial action by bolstering his one-sided discussion of American culture with ancient examples and a concept of "human nature" fails. Dalton next tries to make his case for the eclipse of traditional morality in terms of the vicissitudes of organization.

The Theory of Management

The central concept in Dalton's theory of management is "informal organization." It is defined through careful discussion of its relations to other concepts and empirical analysis. The key conceptual relationship is with the concept of "formal organization." The formal, which Dalton refers to as a "semantic bulwark" (1959, 234), "precipitates the informal and counter action begins" (1959, 232). Hence, Dalton's theory of management is inherently conflictual. There are many reasons why the formal and informal cannot be in harmony. In discussing the implementation of the "FWD," a formal organization designed to control maintenance costs, Dalton (1959, 51–52) presents a general analysis of conflict:

> Planned changes, such as the FWD, were introduced into an existing system of conflict. That is, in the relations among various departments, ranks, official bodies, etc., there were already ongoing collisions between purpose and surroundings that interfered with direct approaches to goals. Purposes interlocked with cross-purposes. Among factors that variously influence these power struggles are: (1) the inability of higher officers to learn what is going on among subordinates; (2) the practices of executives who know but feign ignorance from fear that action will have uncontrollable repercussions; (3) the opportunity to gain personal or organizational advantages by side-stepping official procedures; (4) the use of change and confusion by some groups to establish footholds for future actions; (5) the resort to expediency as a result of excessive formal demands; (6) deliberate making and continued tolerance of ambiguous rules allowing any interpretation; (7) the claims of friendship, etc.

As can be seen, the opportunities for conflict between formal goals and informal activities are considerable. Why are formal plans introduced into an "existing system of conflict"? Dalton "cannot say" (1959, 52). He simply assumes it as given. It is important to note that out of the seven factors stimulating conflict, five are based on self-interest and/or deception. Only points 5 and 6 are possibly independent of self-interest. Other reasons Dalton (1959, 187) gives for organizational fragmentation are different values among different groups, conflict in one area forcing change in another, and the "democratic situation" forcing executives to use "tacit means" to accomplish their ends. The first and third of these last three causes of conflict are also motivated by self-interest. The important point is that Dalton's data is filled with conflicts that arise from self-interested individuals or groups defying each other or organization directives. Hence, an important purpose for the concept of "informal organization" is to explain self-interested behavior in organization.

The essential difference between self-interested action and organization action is that the latter is based on organization purpose (Barnard

1938). For Dalton, informal action is a hybrid of organization purpose and individual interests. With seven out of ten reasons for conflict between formal organization and informal organization resulting from self-interest, however, the question arises whether this level of self-interest and the conflict it generates can be organizationally justified. Dalton's (1959, 172) concept of "informal organization" tries to justify self-interested behavior by showing how it is inevitable and leads to "gains" for the organization.

Dalton (1959, 166) begins the justification with the assumption that Americans consider "personal success as the major end of life." With this assumed, he points out that the gap between formal directives and informal counter action is inevitable. In fact, this becomes the core of his theory of management: the two colliding systems of action create "confusion" that is the ultimate test for managerial skill (1959, 68). The executive, in devising his/her goals, must reward those who help him/her while avoiding or undermining both formal rules and others with conflicting ambitions. Furthermore, since the "confusion" is the result of two conflicting systems, the ability to act secretly (that is, use "protective coloration") becomes a key determinant of effectiveness (Dalton 1959, 253). The executive who has learned best to conceal and deceive in this competitive struggle and not disrupt the "integrity of the formal" will have an advantage for success (Dalton 1959, 230). Hence, the use of "protective coloration" is both functional and legitimate because it is essential for managing the unavoidable gap between formal protocol and the conflicting goals of self-interested individuals.

To succeed and be promoted in this type of social system, the individual needs to be creative. His/her strategies are usually creative compromises of conflicting pressures. Thus management is highly political. The political, however, is closely related to the dramatic: the executive must be an "actor" in order to deceive and manipulate co-workers (Dalton 1959, 186). The manager must resort to the use of persuasive fictions because, as MacIntyre (1984, 77) points out, without a stable social order moral authority is reduced to a "theater of illusions." Some of Dalton's (1959, 156) informants, however, still cling to the old moral fixity; they complained about the "principles made of rubber" style of management.

A key point, then, in Dalton's concept of "informal organization" is the relationship between change and morality. Managers have to continuously break formal rules to accomplish their goals and satisfy their constituents. Nonetheless, a delicate balance between obeying and dis-regarding formal rules has to be maintained to avoid damaging the organization. Dalton (1959, 166) quotes an executive to justify the balance,

> Cowper . . . emphasized the value of "flexibility" in success. . . . "I'm always will-ing to deviate in clearing up problems. By that I mean to ignore principle for the moment in order to follow it in the long run."

This ability to compromise in order to achieve goals, but to do so while "preserving the organization," defines the moral limit of man-agement. To go to the limit is a strategic advantage in the competition between individuals and groups. The executives most adept at manag-ing at the limit become the leaders of the most powerful factions in the organization.

Dalton calls these factions "cliques." Cliques dominate organization and individual action. They are formed to advance the self-interests and organization goals of their members on an informal basis. They invisibly cut across the formal organization to counter it and each other in the competition for power and rewards. Usually cliques try to collect accurate information and then disseminate both accurate and inaccurate information to their advantage. Passing inaccurate informa-tion is, of course, against the rules, so moral concerns naturally arise. Strong "differences in attitude . . . on the issue of literal or loose inter-pretation of official doctrine" can keep a clique from forming (Dalton 1959, 62). Surprisingly, Dalton's reaction to this range of moral atti-tudes toward compromising formal rules is to warn the reader to see cliques without "moral overtones." He (1959, 52) writes,

> Although the term "clique" *denotes* a small exclusive group of persons with a common interest, it too often *connotes* a group concerned with questionable activ-ity. Without these moral overtones, the term can aptly apply to the initiating nucleus of many group activities in and out of industry. Certainly the negative feeling associated with the term is carried too far, for cliques and secrets are inseparable and essential for group life.

However, by making "loose" attitudes "inseparable and essential," thus universal—he is in effect justifying them. Weber (1946), how-ever, has shown that attitudes to formal rules have varied greatly throughout history. Two prominent examples with little in common with clique behavior are charismatic reversal ("It is written, but I say unto you.") and strict Protestant rule-following ("Honesty is the best policy."). Hence, Dalton's justification of clique activity as universal is exaggerated. It is even more important to note that the universal argument not only justifies clique activity, it allows Dalton to morally ignore what is a morally contested issue in his own data.

Certainly Dalton is not morally disturbed by the nature of the cliques he observed. He (1959, 181) learns that a Catholic elite previously ran the company, but now a "Masonic membership was usually an unofficial requirement for getting up—and for remaining there." This excludes Catholics, since the Catholic Church forbids some Masonic vows. Some managers caught in this dilemma dropped out of the Catholic Church to join the Masons. Other non–organizational requirements for membership in dominant cliques include changing to Anglo-Saxon last names, echoing Republican political views, and joining and working at the "Yacht Club."

Dalton's reaction to promotions based on religious and political beliefs, ethnic make-up, and recreational activities is important. He (1959, 184) quotes Barnard (1938) in arguing that in order for men to work together effectively, criteria for selection may include "race, nationality, faith, politics," etc. This argument is clearly in contradiction with the democratic individualism argument that Dalton uses to justify conflict and competition. Furthermore, the fact that organizational conformity has entered the individual's private relationship with worship and citizenship certainly raises questions about the effect the organization has on the moral character of the individual. Dalton ignores these moral questions and, as we saw, presents a justification based on organization effectiveness.

Dalton (1959, 189) is aware of the criticism that the demand for "yes-men" is nothing more than self-serving protection of the status quo. He (1959, 189) says he is no "apologist." However, he (1959, 189) argues that the phenomenon of yes-men is basically inevitable: yes-men have "always been present in varying degrees in most organizations in the more complex societies." An argument based on inevitability, however, avoids the moral issue. First of all, "most organizations" are not all organizations. A moral comparison can be made, but his universalizing language acts as a substitute for this evaluation. Second, "varying degrees" can have different moral weights. One out of ten is morally different than nine out of ten. Third, given the dominance of conformity and "protective coloration" in his data, there is at least a tension with his praise of the value of individualism. Thus, in regard to his own values a moral problem should arise.

Dalton (1959, 189) continues his argument with another familiar defense. He writes,

> Obviously an industrial firm is fossilizing when selective criteria—as any set of attitudes and characteristics—become ends in themselves. However when concern with social traits is limited to avoidance of what would be blatantly negative items to most members, the threat to the organization is much less than the other extreme of focus on purely formal qualifications.

This implies that selection based on social traits does not have to be an end, but can be merely economic means. However, pervasive patterns of selection based on social traits, as we see in Dalton's data, *are* ends in themselves. The patterns demonstrate an established culture (Schein 1985). Cultures, by their nature, fight to maintain themselves (Larson 1977). By assuming culture can be merely a means and justified in terms of its effectiveness, Dalton ignores the moral implications of promotions based on social traits.

Dalton argues in terms of effectiveness and inevitability on many issues throughout the book. One particularly important area where he uses these arguments concerns "unofficial rewards"—that is, rewards against company policy. Two general points can be made. First, even though both practices—selection by social traits and unofficial rewards—are kept secret, they are so pervasive everyone knows them. This is part of the reason the "informal" dominates the formal: since everyone knows the real criteria for promotions and rewards has little to do with formal standards of fairness, individuals take what they can get when and where they can get it. Dalton misses this point because of his reliance on economic effectiveness and universal inevitability arguments.

Second, the essential reason why the "informal" dominates the formal is because top level executives use the "informal" as their primary means for control—as the requirement for Masonic membership demonstrates. Dalton misses this key point because he does not follow his ethnographic data, but, ironically, restricts his analysis to fleshing out the abstract assumption that "informal" action is unavoidable. He thus avoids recognizing that the behavior of top-level executives is a primary cause of the particular balance between informal and formal in the organizations he studied. Hence, there is a strong conservative bias in Dalton's theory of management, since the concept of "informal organization" ironically functions to justify the maintenance and expansion of top management control.

The Concept of the Individual

Dalton begins his book by presenting a formal organization chart and contrasting it with an informal chart that he says shows the real "authority" structure. "An individual's influence was judged less by the response of subordinates to his officially spoken or written orders than by the relative deference of associates, superiors, and subordinates to his known attitudes, wishes, and informally expressed opinions, and the concern to respect, prefer, or act on them" (Dalton 1959, 20). The key point here is that Dalton focuses only on the group reaction to, not the group construction of, the individual. In discussing the number two man, Hardy, who Dalton (1959, 24) argues actually shares the number one spot, he refers to him, in his own words, as a "social lion."

Deference is a *collective* phenomenon and is apportioned to the individual according to group valuations (Goffman 1967). Dalton's argument demonstrates an exaggerated individualism, because he plants these valuations in individual characteristics. He does not reflect on what they tell us about the group as a whole. His reference to Hardy as a "social lion" is a surprisingly idiosyncratic metaphor whose meaning reflects back on Dalton. In qualitative research, these personal sentiments should be presented as "data" and compared with other types of data (Diesing 1971). The fact that Dalton uses it in the text as an unanalyzed and accurate description shows his excessive attachment to the individual. We now know Dalton values individual power and independence in interpersonal relations.

Dalton's one-sided presentation of the individual can also be seen in his discussion of staff-line relations. He (1959, 107) writes,

Intermeshing staff and line is the impossible problem of wedding change and habit. This natural conflict increases to the extent we are able to perfectly fit men to different functions, for then no one remains to reduce the clash of functions that never interlock automatically or perfectly . . . .However inadequate, some form of the staff-line arrangement is necessary. . . . It is sounder than the other theories of industrial organization. Like them though, it overlooks the complex conditioning of human beings and their varying abilities to escape conditioning, especially when forced to deal with contradictions inside formal limitations.

This formulation of "human" (read individual) variability, assumes a solitary individual, similar to Rousseau's (1755) "noble savage," who Dalton distinguishes by his/her level of natural creativity—"abilities to escape conditioning." However, unlike the "noble savage," who is oppressed by social ties, Dalton's escaping individual could be called the "noble entrepreneur" because of his/her organizational creativity. Indeed, Dalton's language exaggerates the individual's creativity because all creativity is dependent on a vast system of tacit knowledge that is maintained in traditions (Shils 1981). The "escape" could only be trivial compared to the cultural heritage that underlies all knowledge, including new knowledge (Cooley 1922). It can be noted, though, Dalton's escaping individual is very similar to the outdated American ideal self-image of the self-reliant frontiersman (Cochran 1972).

It is interesting that in the chapter where Dalton discusses his most general theory of the individual, he claims a conceptual debt to G.H. Mead's (1934) framework of the "I" and "me." The "I" represents the individual's "impulse to engage in any new activity" (Dalton 1959, 253); the "me" is the conscience. He puts Mead's framework in historical context by pointing out that in modern society an individual has many "me's" because of his many different associations. Dalton (1959, 254) writes,

> In a sense, the individual is now able to pick and choose justifications for a great range of behaviors. Becoming more complex morally does not of course mean that he has lost his conscience! It means rather that he has become able to consider and deal with all the conflicting interests and values around him. He has in effect become a plurality under one skin.

In this formulation, the individual autonomy of the "noble entrepreneur" model is maintained, but no longer by natural individualism. Now the individual autonomously picks a justification from an inventory of justifications determined only by his/her range of experience and his/her choice of appropriateness.

This characterization of the individual seems extremely one-sided given Mead's continuous reminders that the individual "self" is first and foremost socially determined. Mead (1934, 222) wrote,

> But even in the most modern and highly-evolved forms of human civilization the individual, however original and creative he may be in his thinking or behavior, always and necessarily assumes a definite relation to, and reflects in the structure of his self or personality, the general organized pattern of experience and activity

exhibited in or characterizing the social life-process in which he is involved, and of which his self or personality is essentially a creative expression or embodiment.

Hence, Dalton's formulation of a "plurality under one skin" underestimates the fundamental dependence this "plurality" has on society. The society, according to Mead, has a "general organized pattern of experience." It is not simply a field of "conflicting interests and values." Dalton's "plurality" is clamped to an "organized pattern," and this is the American pattern that pleases itself to see individual selves as purely unique (Lasch 1979).

We are told that the dichotomy between individual and organization has a long history in the field of organization theory. Dalton (1959, 271) quotes Barnard (1938), Argyris (1957), and others on the "dehumanizing" aspects of work in large formal organizations. Indeed, Dalton (1959, 271) informs the reader that the tension is at least as old as the "fifth century B.C.." This leads him to reflect,

> However, recognizing the timeless element allows a better appraisal of the individual's part in the conflict. Today's tempo is faster, but the underlying process is the same. And it may be said that the rapid pace is less painful than the strain between appearance and being for individuals who exhaust themselves maintaining unassailable fronts (Dalton 1959, 271).

In other words, the "plurality under one skin" can escape the dehumanizing strain of formal organization by switching selves, thus taking pressure off maintaining "unassailable fronts." But this creates a social problem: How does the group regulate individual pluralism in order to maintain itself as a group?

Morality constrains individuals so they can live and work together (Rieff 1987). Dalton follows the Rousseauean tradition, however, that sees this regulation as constraining individual creativity and well-being. Mead (1934), Dalton's main source in these matters, saw the self as fundamentally social. The opposition between individual and organization, then, is false to the extent it conceals the social nature of man/woman. The human being requires social materials, most notably, for Mead (1934), a shared language, to inform self-consciousness. Dalton's concept of the individual, motivated by a belief that the individual is threatened by rational organization, loses sight of the fact that the source of both its survival and creativity is its social and moral heritage.

In Dalton's (1959, 258) view, the organization forces the individual to individualize. He writes,

> Oversimplifying, one can say that ceaseless reorganization of the system hinders the matching of roles and occupants. This arises in part from the system's inconsistent, and usually unavoidable, excess of demands over returns to occupants, who respond by initiating corrective counter claims. In *qualifiedly* accomplishing its rational ends, the system unwittingly coerces its occupants to *qualifiedly* realize the personalizing urges innate to them.

Note the reductive language of people as "occupants." For Dalton, the organization has ends that form independent of the people who pursue them. This reification of "the system" is necessary to establish the dichotomy between individual and organization. Dalton drops the individual into the organizational machinery and "the system unwittingly coerces" him to pursue his/her self-interest. Systems in Japan, however, apparently having a bit more wit, are more apt to create "wide-spread homogeneity of interests" (Levine 1955, 68). Hence, Dalton's dichotomous relation between individual and organization is unwittingly American in its asocial and amoral ascriptions.

Once the individual starts "personalizing," it swells to overfill its formal office. The central means Dalton uses to explain this process is the concept of "ambiguity." Ambiguity is the absence of clear information which, in Dalton's work, is almost a synonym for "informal organization." Because there is "ambiguity" between organization roles and organization ends, the individual has a creative space to express his "personalizing urges."

More than stimulating individual creativity, however, "ambiguity" is the context for successful organization action. Dalton (1959, 258) writes,

> The individual manager is caught in a scheme of rational, emotional, social, and ethical claims. . . . If he regards compromise as immoral concession, and fears a harmony that brings certain side commitments with uncertain complications, he withdraws to his formal shelter, and watches others find their way through ambiguity to dominate policy and take higher roles. Ambiguity thus selects those most able to absorb, or resolve and utilize, conflict for personal organizational ends.

The concept of "ambiguity" is, therefore, the center of Dalton's theory of management: by positing a chaotic environment, it underwrites both the individual's autonomy and creativity (if not the autonomous individual itself), and the whole process of compromise and deception in what Dalton calls "strong" management. The concept is rationalist in the sense that it is defined in terms of the limits of information about means-ends relationships.

It is also this theoretical relationship—organization "ambiguity" underwrites autonomous individual—which gives meaning to Dalton's conflict analysis. The very Hobbesian (1651) pronouncements, strangely updated for bureaucratic warfare—"competing with all for individual credit" (Dalton 1959, 253)—rest upon presumptions of autonomous individuals battling under conditions of "ambiguity." Hence, more than conflictual and political, Dalton's theory of management is, at bottom, rationalist, or, more precisely, neo-rationalist (Simon 1945). Dalton's (1959, 107) depreciation of "formal organization"—"irrelevant controls . . . not enough based on intimate knowledge of people and conditions and kept up-to-date"—is also a result of the assumption of pervasive "ambiguity." The lopsided informal-formal dichotomy, therefore, has the same bias that was found in the individual-organization dichotomy: it presents an exaggerated picture of the autonomy and creativity of the individual.

Thus, despite his criticism of the role of rationality in organizations, Dalton, through the concept of ambiguity, hands off rational prowess to the individual. Dalton's "individual" uses rationality to outwit both organization rationality and moral constraints. The individual's behavior "is increasingly based more on what he anticipates than on what he has been" (Dalton 1959, 254). This is clearly wrong except in the sense that the individual ignores his/her moral upbringing to increase his/her options in an increasingly competitive social environment. Dalton forgets the point that the individual's disconnection from the past is a major cause of the changing social environment (MacIntyre 1984). Indeed, the individual purposefully creates "ambiguity" as a strategic advantage over its competitors. Dalton also misses the point that the "pick and choose justifications" mode of moral management is actually a breakdown in moral commitment (Rieff 1987). "Ambiguity" is his neo-rationalist god-term to justify this absence of community.

Words such as "evade," "elude," "tacit," "resistance," "illegal," "falsify," "conceal," "manipulate," "conspire," "deceive," "covert," "subvert," "distort," "disregard," "escape," "devious," "fiction," "mask," "secret," "mislead," etc., dominate Dalton's ethnographic description. Interpersonal relations are clearly treacherous. He (1959, 164) occasionally throws in a moral statement—"compromise to preserve the uncompromisable"—but we never find out what is "uncompromisable." There is no discussion of ultimate values. Indeed, the data is dominated by self-interested behavior.

Clearly, the "maze of shifting ties" before Dalton's eyes is undeniably American (1959, 106). But Dalton did not want to see what Tocqueville (1850, 507) had seen before him: "individualism at first only dams the springs of public virtues, but in the long run it attacks and destroys all the others too and finally merges in egoism." Writing more than a century after Tocqueville, Dalton universalizes American individualism to avoid confronting its dishonest and destructive aspects. This only entrenches these aspects further. Only collectively sanctioned moral ideals can provide the controlling symbolic needed to integrate self-interested behavior into a social whole (Rieff 1987). Without individual moral commitment, there is no way to relax the "maze of shifting ties" and the self-serving "ambiguity" it generates.

The Theory of Management Ethics

Dalton is no idealist. Compromise is central to his understanding of management, morality, and even history. He (1959, 245) writes, "To sanctify either formal or informal approaches to the exclusion of the other, when concession is necessary, is immoral and overlooks the fact the very rules and principles being fought over are products of compromise." This formulation is characteristically Dalton. The first part—compromise is required between obeying rules and taking responsibility for their concrete consequences—is true in practical affairs (Weber 1946). The second part, all rules and principles are products of compromise, is not true: fierce commitment to ideals is a key part of entrepreneurial history (Schumpeter 1934). Furthermore, it implies an attitude that in principle is ready to compromise all principles. This excessive rationalism undermines all rules and principles by removing their key support: belief.

In Dalton's theory of management ethics, there are two moralities, one implied in formal organization and one implied in informal organization. This is the root of the problem. Not only does the manager have to find compromises between stated morality and an uncooperative, continuously changing social world, but he also has to find compromises between two systems of conflicting moral principles. Dalton sees the need for compromise everywhere because conflict is everywhere. Conflict is everywhere because the "cultures" he studied are centered on self-interested behavior with an insatiable desire for personal rewards (for example, one executive built his home with company materials and company personnel on company time). Dalton's management "ethics" is an attempt to justify this culture and the self-interested behavior it encourages. Ultimately, he can never resolve the moral conflict because he does not have a consistent moral position by which to evaluate it. This is why he continuously goes outside of morality to biology, economics, history, etc., to find a justification. This is also why his (1959, 245) solemn praise throughout the book for "core principles" rings hollow: he never states one. It is impossible to do so with two moral systems. Two moral systems mean no moral system.

This leads Dalton into a fundamental contradiction, when, at the end of the book, he defines morality. The definition seems oddly disassociated from the justifications running throughout the case analysis. He (1959, 243) writes,

> All decisions imply choice and can therefore be regarded as moral acts. But when decisions directly involve others, as in organizations, and are made in an atmosphere of uncertainty, they become acutely moral.

I interpret this as meaning that one has a moral responsibility not to hurt others by one's decisions; and uncertainty increases one's responsibility. Veblen (1961) has pointed out that these kinds of moral sentiments in the competitive economic system are secularized reformulations of the traditional Christian ethic of brotherly love. However, Dalton's text is filled with praise of conflict and competition and acceptance of deception and manipulation. Indeed, as was shown, his text is an effort to justify this behavior. The contradiction is particularly sharp in his use of the purely amoral biological justifications. "Protective coloration" is a survival mechanism. There is nothing moral about it.

Dalton's use of a traditional concept of morality is misleading when in fact his entire ethnographic effort is aimed at delegitimating "moral fixity." He cannot have it both ways. In the last sentence of the book, he (1959, 272) advises those who worry about excessive organization control to "refocus" their concern on the "ethic of protective coloration among thinking animals." The notion of "thinking animals" is Dalton in a nutshell. At bottom, he exaggerates the role man's/woman's biological nature plays in his/her social behavior at the expense of the cultural. This is why the "ethic of protective coloration" contradicts his basically Christian definition of morality: animals are not religious.

Dalton is not religious either. His underlying cynicism about religion is reflected in an analogy he uses to explain bureaucratic rationality. "Like the Sabbath," he (1959, 266) writes, "rationality inescapably compromises with social demands." There is, however, nothing inescapable about it. Strict observance of religious doctrine is alive and well in many parts of the world (Gellner 1992). Dalton's view that it is not is a projection of his own disbelieving attitude toward religion. That he even equates sacred rules with bureaucratic rules (something he does on several occasions, 1959, 30, 100) shows his inability to grasp the meaning of sacredness to the believer.

Dalton's concept of the "strong manager" reflects his own values. Similar to Dalton's openness to compromising Sabbath rules, the "strong manager" is open to compromising organization rules. Dalton (1959, 247) writes, "Pulled between official and unofficial claims on themselves, they are less morally disturbed than the weak because they and their followers variously influence the system and profit from it." Dalton does not notice or is not concerned with the tension, sometimes contradiction, between this extreme self-interest and his often-stated value "gain for the organization." It is important because this value is the closest Dalton comes to a concern for the whole, that is, to morality. Hence, Dalton's preference for aggressive men—the "social lion" is the prototype for the "strong manager"—dominates his theoretical constructions, the interpretations they make possible, and most certainly his sense of morality.

Dalton (1959, 231) could perhaps argue that the "strong manager" has "rare judgment" in knowing how far to compromise. However, since there is no legitimate standard of morality, it must be "rare" indeed: it is logically impossible. Furthermore, if this magical judgment is so rare, how is it possible for the type of organization Dalton studies, with its tens of thousands of employees and extensive management structure, to function? It seems obvious that this type of organization needs more moral leadership than "rare judgment" would allow. Hence, Dalton cannot avoid the excessive self-interest in the management system as a whole. He (1959, 247) admits that "the strong can of course be immoral," but, without giving a reason, says they are "usually not." He emphasizes their positive side: creativity and flexibility. This lack of analytic balance also evidences his individualistic bias and apologetic purpose.

Ultimately, Dalton's theory of management ethics is a reversal of traditional Western moral beliefs. In Dalton's judgment, managers are weak when they resist change and cling to rules. But there is no way to completely separate specific organization rules from the traditional belief in obeying rules. That "weak" managers express "moral disturbance" (Dalton 1959, 228) in the face of a systematic breakdown of respect for rules represents the last whimper of a dying culture that preached obedience to rules. Dalton's condemnation of this culture and his praise of the new culture of continuous compromise, represents further progress for Enlightenment "rationality" as it enters the nonrational domain of ultimate ethical values. Dalton does not realize that the new social system he is helping to usher into the world of management will be weak and dangerous exactly because the "strong" have so little "moral disturbance."

Conclusion

Despite decades of documentation of ethically questionable behavior in the sociology of organization literature, the question of management ethics has seldom been addressed. It is the purpose of this chapter to reopen the ethics debate within the sociology of organization literature by providing a textual analysis of Melville Dalton's discussion of morality in his classic study, *Men Who Manage*. Specifically, I contrasted the concept of moral tradition with Dalton's contingent approach to moral analysis. My purpose was to evaluate Dalton's contribution to the field of management ethics. Five points will be made.

First, Dalton utilizes several universals to make his case about the role of morality in society. Perhaps the central one is to define "human nature" in terms of a gregarious, "social lion" type individual whose deepest instinct is creativity. By universalizing this rather American fantasy, Dalton biologically justifies individualism as the central social value. This follows an Enlightenment tradition originally argued by Rousseau in the eighteenth century and advanced by others in the nineteenth century, Nietzsche being a particularly relevant forefather to Dalton. The problem with raising the individual above the group in importance is that it springs the individual loose from moral traditions. Moral traditions are important because they provide moral standards developed over multiple generations, giving social life a stable and continuous regulation of interpersonal relations.

Second, Dalton also follows modern thought in using "reason"—or in Durkheim's (1961, 20) ironic words, the "authority of reason"—as a substitute for traditional moral authority. This is most clearly seen in another universal that Dalton employs to make his case about the role of morality in organization, economic effectiveness. Dalton argues that economic effectiveness is a more appropriate standard for managerial behavior than moral tradition, which reduces managerial options, because it leads to gains for the organization as a whole. However, as MacIntyre (1984) points out, this prioritization leads to the breakdown of moral authority because the category of effectiveness is only applied in terms of satisfying desires. The question as to whether the desires are good or bad is not part of the effectiveness criteria. Hence, Dalton's reliance on effectiveness as a substitute for moral traditions, misconceives the problem of morality as one of satisfying appetite rather than of limiting behavior. The result is that management is left to operate in a moral void.

Third, Dalton argues that compromise is the central means to broker conflicts between morals and the organization goals and self-interests of executives. As we saw, "moral fixity" does not meet the criteria of effectiveness. However, just as "moral fixity" is ineffective in terms of economics, compromise is inadequate in terms of morals: it has no end. Compromise as a moral principle cannot provide a stable moral order because its deliberations beget more compromise. The proper role of compromise is to rescue moral tradition from intractable moral conflicts. However, as the central moral principle in its own right, it reduces morality to politics. As we saw in Dalton's ethnography, a culture of compromise stimulates self-positioning, manipulation, and deception, not self-constraint. Only a moral system based in tradition can have even a small chance of avoiding domination by political forces because being based in the past not only provides continuity and thus stability, it also puts morals somewhat above the "creativity" and desires of the current political scene.

Fourth, Dalton uses the concept of "ambiguity" to explain his central theoretical concern with the relation between formal and informal organization. Because organization behavior is ambiguous, individual creativity is vital for accomplishing organization ends. For the same reason, formal rules are impotent. However, in praising the creative individual's ability to profit from ambiguity, Dalton misses the deeper point that the "creative" individual is a primary cause of ambiguity. It is because of the loss of a social whole—a controlling moral demand system that integrates the individual into collective purpose—that the "creative" individual is dominant in the first place. "Ambiguity" is Dalton's rational justification for cultural disintegration. The abstraction "gain for the organization" is an economic misnomer for the loss of a moral whole.

Finally, it is a curious fact that Dalton pays so little attention to the influence leaders have on the organizational cultures he so carefully documents. Certainly he knew that some of the greatest writers—Plato, Machiavelli, Hobbes, and Freud, to name a few—considered leadership to be of central importance for the quality of interpersonal relations that develop in groups. But for Dalton, the leaders are merely competitively advanced specimens of democratic individualism. He focuses instead on the "system." This allows him, however, to absolve each individual of moral responsibility, especially the leader. Their unending appetite for material rewards and personal power undoubtedly contributes to the morally weak cultures that pervade these organizations. By creating a theoretical framework that reduces morality to an obstacle that creative managers should compromise, Dalton gives legitimacy to this state of affairs. It is in regard to this situation that moral continuity with the past can act as a constraining force against over-stimulated self-interest. Without it, the social lions will lower the standard of morality to the extremely unstable level that maximizes their own desires.

Part 3

Ethical Rationalism

4

Management Ethics Without the Past: Rationalism and Individualism in Critical Organization Theory

Since the Enlightenment our attachment to the past has been greatly weakened, in some areas of social life it has almost ceased to exist. This characteristic of the modern mind is seen as an overreaction. The modern mind has lost the capacity to appreciate the positive contribution the maintenance of the past in the present achieves in social life, especially in the sphere of moral conduct.

In the field of organization theory, nowhere is the past as explicitly distrusted as in critical organization theory. The maintenance of the past in the present is seen as a potential carrier of oppressive and unjust social relationships. Perpetual critique is advocated as a means to uncover these oppressive and unjust relations and prevent any new undemocratic relations from becoming established.

I present a historical and cultural analysis of the modern attitude toward the past and develop a concept of moral tradition to analyze critical organization theory's ethical assumptions and implications. In so doing, an effort is made to rectify the exaggerated confidence critical organization theory places in rationalism and individualism and to recognize the ineluctable role traditions play not only in organizational life, but also in the way we theorize about organizations.

It is worth remembering Karl Marx's (1844) dictum that all criticism begins in the criticism of repetition. It shows not only the dependence of criticism on what it criticizes, but also the dependence of criticism on the past. The part of organization theory that most centrally relies on criticism—critical organization theory (for example, Alvesson and Willmott 1992a)—has developed without the benefit of this part of Marx's teaching. In critical organization theory, the dependence of criticism on the past has been forgotten. This is important because maintaining part of the past in the present is required to provide continuity and stability in moral conduct (Arendt 1968; MacIntyre 1988; Rieff 1985; Shils 1981).

In this chapter, I will develop a conceptual framework to analyze the role of the past in the establishment and maintenance of moral conduct, with special attention to the relationship between moral commitment and criticism. This involves developing a concept of *moral tradition* that is used to analyze the moral linkages between the past and the present. I apply this framework to the analysis of moral assumptions and moral positions in critical organization theory. I intend to make two contributions to the field of organization theory: one, to propose a conceptual framework that can be used to analyze the role of the past in the ethical aspects of organization theory; two, to analyze the attitude toward the past specifically in critical organization theory in order to determine what effect the past has on its moral assumptions and implications.

The moral intention of critical organization theory can be seen in how it defines the condition of current management practice. It assumes that the "central problem of management resides in the social relations of production which *systematically* foster and sustain very limited and often distorted forms of communication" (Alvesson and Willmott 1992b, 7). In this formulation several key moral assumptions of critical organization theory are apparent. First, organizations are assumed to be brought into existence by "social relations of production" in which power exercised by managerial elites is used to reproduce certain social arrangements and stop others from coming into existence (Benson 1977; compare, Clegg 1977; Jermier 1985). Second, it is assumed that these social arrangements are "arbitrary" in that they result from historical and political processes that have no special legitimacy (Benson 1977; Deetz 1992; Alvesson and Deetz 1996). Third, the primary means by which these social arrangements are maintained are "distorted forms of communications" which keep employees from exercising their own rational powers and self-interests (Clegg 1977; Alvesson and Willmott 1992b; Alvesson and Deetz 1996). Hence, critical organization theory assumes much of management practice is unfair and oppressive. It seeks to change these unfair and oppressive practices and to institute its own moral preferences.

The central influence on critical organization theory is the work of Jürgen Habermas (Alvesson and Willmott 1992b). For Habermas (1979; 1984), the problems of modern social organization can only be solved by more democracy. Hence, critical organization theorists seek to re-establish the ideals of the Enlightenment. In Alvesson and Willmott's (1992b, 9) words, they wish to create a "more autonomous individual who ... can master his or her own destiny in joint operation with peers." Thus, their moral intention is to criticize established social relations to advance the goals of individual autonomy and democratic decision-making in organizations.

I take issue with critical organization theory's political and ethical goals, because by focusing completely on the autonomy of the individual and the capacities of individuals to participate in democratic decision-making, they neglect the role of the past in contributing to the moral integrity and stability of social relations. By one-sidedly pursuing individual autonomy and rationality, they take for granted the moral character of the individual and greatly de-emphasize the accomplishments of previous generations. This is, in my opinion, surely to result in a lowering of moral standards and a vulnerability toward extreme individualism and/or extreme collectivism.

Before analyzing critical organization theory in detail, the following section will review the historical and cultural context of modern organizations and develop a concept of moral tradition. This concept will then be used to analyze critical organization theory.

The Authority of the Past and Management Ethics

1. *Historical Background.* By the middle of the eighteenth century, after several centuries of decline, Christianity was no longer the dominant moral orientation in Western civilization (Arendt 1968). It was replaced in about a half century with faith in secular rationalism and its anti-communal and ahistorical individualism (Gellner 1992). Politically, the values of individual equality and liberty became commonly accepted (Lukes 1973).

However, Christianity did not disappear. Its moral fervor was incorporated into the secular dynamism driving Western culture. The result was a massive intensification of man/woman's moral demands on society (Polanyi 1966). A new, more powerful moral perfectionism developed. Polanyi (1969, 13) formulated the new perspective thus:

> Its argument is simple and yet to be answered. If society is not a divine institution, it is made by man, and man is free to do with society what he likes. There is no excuse for having a bad society, and we must make a good one without delay.

Secular rationalism led to great benefits and humanitarian improvements. It also, however, led to personal nihilism and political immoralism, escalating in the Holocaust and the total wars and revolutions that scarred the twentieth century. Polanyi (1969) explains this process as one of *moral inversion:* Once Christian authority was fatally weakened by science, men/women became conscious of themselves as sovereign individuals. Rousseau (1755), for example, praised uncivilized man/woman as the "noble savage" who was uncorrupted by the knowledge of good and evil. Morality, losing its home in Christian social ethics, found its new expression in the idea of the *natural* individual. The result was the inversion of morality: the idealism inherent in Christian morality, which had been held superior to the individual, was secularized and incorporated into the idea of the individual itself.

Once morality became inverted through the growth of modern individualism, it became immanent in brute force. Great humanitarian efforts were initiated, but almost immediately excesses became apparent, that is, the Reign of Terror (Burke 1795). Implicit moral motives no longer speak in their own voice and are no longer accessible to moral arguments (Polanyi, 1969). This is the road from modern individualism to modern immoralism. Thus, modernity is not only an age of impersonal control (Alvesson and Willmott 1992b; Deetz 1992; Burrell 1994), but also an age of moral excess (that is, fanatical demands for social perfection). Modern individualism, formed through the developments of rational skepticism and immanent perfectionism, led to nihilism as a form of moral protest against the imagined futility and dishonesty of all human moral ideals. A demand for total change is implied, though, as we will see in critical organization theory, explicitly only criticism of the past and present is advocated.

Before modernity, all societies made use of moral traditions. Indeed, the anthropologist Louis Dumont (1986) argues that moral traditions are a necessary requirement for social organization. Dumont (1986) refers to moral traditions as "outworldly" because of their ideal structure. In modernity, however, outworldly values collapsed into inworldly values; that is, moral values are seen as inherent in things and processes of the social world. The modern individual, instead of being socialized into an outworldly moral belief system in order to cultivate knowledge of good and evil, becomes an autonomous player in a fully self-legitimated world (Dumont 1986). As early as in Hobbes's

Leviathan (1651), however, it was realized that an aggregate of autonomous individuals only governed by their own wills, would lead to governments which tend towards absolute power and be indifferent to morals. This is another aspect of modern individualism and the loss of outworldly moral traditions: the modern state emerged bearing absolute values—that is, the government as the final arbitrator between itself and its citizens (Hobbes 1651). Thus, in a sense, the modern state emerged with the absolutism of the Church, but without its moral heritage.

These developments influenced the character of modern management and organization. Modern managers, lacking any training in moral traditions, are only limited in their actions by organizational authority. However, organizational authority, as MacIntyre (1984) points out, is void of moral traditions and is little more than successful power. Modern organizations, like modern states, tend to only consider the costs and benefits of any particular action (Jackall 1988). Exxon's attempt to avoid responsibility before, during, and after the Valdez disaster is a dramatic example (McCoy and Fritsch 1996). Managers, infected by the moral void in the organization, become manipulative arenas themselves as they try to present the costs and benefits of any course of action to their own advantage (Rieff 1987).

2. *The Past as a Moral Model.* Without the transmission of traditions, societies and organizations lose the capacity to stabilize and appreciate moral standards. The implications for modern culture are considerable. First, Max Weber (1946) argued that the tragic nature of action has been forgotten; that is, without memory of the past, we tend to forget that the results of any action can have a dual nature, and be both good and evil. This suggests a cautious attitude towards change alien to secular rationalism. Second, there is no permanent solution to any important problem in human life (Shils 1981). The optimism of secular rationalism has given rise to one change after another, but each solution creates new problems—for example, economic development created wealth but simultaneously damaged the environment. Clearly, mere change does not guarantee the existing will be replaced with something better. Third, in the Laws, Plato argues that a life without piety to the past courts grief. It prevents continuity of character that makes psychological stability impossible and thus undermines the development of trust between individuals. Finally, piety toward the past secures the existence of personal role models by which individuals can

cultivate and direct their moral development. When we give up the ability to admire what is best in the past, in the hope of freeing our creativity, we usually end up being dominated by the clever among us (Mill 1831). We lose Abraham Lincoln and gain Lee Iaccoca.

Much of the criticism of tradition (usually discussed in terms of "culture" in critical organization theory), has been based on misunderstanding it as a hegemonic (Deetz 1992), monolithic (Willmott 1993), or "unthought consensus" (Clegg 1977). But traditions in organizations, as in societies, are nearly always vague. As Linda Trevino and Katherine Nelson (1995) point out about the famous Johnson & Johnson company credo: Its application in the Tylenol crisis was hotly debated and the final actions had much to do with the marketing background of the CEO who knew the importance of timing in the release of information. There is seldom complete agreement on the meaning of organization traditions except for a few formally promulgated beliefs, and even these have multiple interpretations (Kunda 1992).

Such "monolithic" control as traditions muster, is from an overlay of overlapping combinations of beliefs (Shils 1981). For example, a marketing manager who exaggerates the quality of fast food chicken can be said to be under the same tradition as a finance manager who is trying to cut the marketing manager's advertising budget, in that they are both following the tradition of profit maximization. Thus, within the "same" tradition there are not only different levels of differentiation and specificity, but also different interpretations and emphases. Clearly, every tradition offers the possibility of a variety of responses and actions. Indeed, other companies with creeds similar to Johnson & Johnson's reacted differently in similar crises (Trevino and Nelson 1995). Even though traditions are approximate, intermittent, partial, and shifting, they do give a background of consensus to organizations which provides organization members with some degree of common beliefs and common perceptions. Without them, organizations could not have continuity over time.

The importance of the past in providing continuity points to the indebtedness of those working in the present to those who came before them. Beliefs are not just shared with contemporaries, but also with predecessors. The Johnson & Johnson creed, for example, is over fifty years old. Traditions are accumulations of experience that have been rationally reflected upon, added to and corrected by each generation (Shils 1981). To imply, as critical organization theory does, that we can rationally choose our beliefs is very misleading. No generation creates most of what it uses, believes, and practices (Shils 1981). For example, in the management of an organization, the tradition of management and the traditionality of interpersonal relationships, work habits, organizational routines, etc., are implicit in the focus on particular goals that are being formulated and/or implemented. Hence, all knowledge requires a vast tacit (and inherited) context in which it makes sense (Polanyi 1966).

Rationality cannot be used to obliterate tradition as long as there is a need for order (Shils 1981). Organizations need traditions to reproduce their shape and identity over time. Furthermore, as long as individuals wish for meaning beyond their functional roles, they will use traditions to maintain and reproduce what they find meaningful. As long as organizations need rules and categories and as long as individuals cannot create these for themselves when the occasion arises and for that occasion only, traditions will be needed (Shils 1981). Indeed, as long as the separate actions of individuals are inadequate to meet their desires, organizations will be necessary. Where there are organizations, there will be authority and authority will become enmeshed in traditions to stabilize and reproduce it. Finally, traditions will be desired to maintain the sense of collectivity, which not only transcends the individual but transcends his/her contemporaries too. This sense of belonging to something that has depth in time is an important aspect of providing depth in meaning. Without it, as Hannah Arendt (1950) has argued in her study of totalitarianism, we become open to action without limit.

3. Memory is a Moral Decision. The past carried in a tradition is the perceived past, not the past that historians attempt to discover. The perceived past is recorded in memory and writing and is capable of being retrospectively reformed by those working in the present. Hence, tradition is a process of selection (Arendt 1968). Tradition implies a process of valuation whereby choices are made about what is valuable and what should be continued.

This process of valuation cannot be taken for granted. Human actions are the most evanescent of things, quickly disappearing if effort and energy are not expended to represent them. To be represented, it must be remembered. The past does not need to be remembered by all who enact it, because memories leave an objective deposit in tradition and traditions are carried forward by a continuing chain of transmissions and receptions (Shils 1981). However, to become a tradition and remain a tradition, a pattern of thought or action must be remembered.

It is this chain of memory that makes it possible for organizations to go on reproducing themselves over time while also changing (Shils 1981). The process of reproduction is guided by what organization members remember about what they themselves said and did, what they perceive and remember of what other persons expect and require of them, and also those claims to which they remember being entitled by virtue of particular qualifications such as skill, title, appointment, and ownership (Shils 1981). These expectations and entitlements are reproduced and carried forward by the memories of individuals, written records, and the interconnected memories and records of others. In this way, by keeping some of its past in the present to sustain a set of interconnected identities through time, an organization is preserved.

It is in this context that I assert memory is a moral decision. It is a moral decision because by choosing what to remember, we influence the responsibilities we acknowledge, the actions we take, and thus the effects we have on others. In MacIntyre's (1988) terms, we can only make moral decisions inside moral traditions because these traditions make it possible to challenge, debate, and finally make moral decisions. Clearly, these decisions are influenced to some extent by what we remember. Memory is a moral decision because we can forget what we learned from the past and, in forgetting, lose or weaken the framework in which moral reasoning takes place.

On the organizational level, moral traditions—exhibited in decisions and actions—provide the internal spine of the culture that maintains managerial integrity. These traditions need to be criticized to correct abuses in decision-making and actions, but if the criticism is too constant or carried to the point where the moral tradition is no longer capable of transmitting moral guidance, the organization runs the danger of deteriorating into a collection of self-interested manipulators, or worse.

This is the cost of being sprung lose from the past. Historical memory is the basis of moral decision. This is a dimension that is grossly under-appreciated in critical organization theory with its call for "perpetual critique" (Deetz 1992). Management ethics requires moral constraints rooted in historical memory. We need an acute memory of the suffering that has been caused by organizations in the past and continues to be caused in the present. By remembering the past, we have the basis to inhibit ourselves from that relentless optimism that pushes for endless change. We need to learn a cautious attitude toward change so to uncover its use for self-justification and power-seeking.

Critical Organization Theory: Description and Analysis

1. *Basic Assumptions in Critical Organization Theory.* Equality, reflexive questioning, and democratic process are central concerns in the writings of critical organization theorists. It can be seen in their focus on the relation between discourse and power. In the words of Alvesson and Willmott (1992b, 12),

> According to CT, the practices and discourses that comprise organizations are never politically neutral. Sedimented with asymmetrical relations of power, they reproduce structures in which there is differential access to valued material and symbolic goods. Top management is routinely privileged in decision-making and agency-setting and in defining and shaping human needs and social reality. An objective of CT is to challenge the centrality and necessity of the dominant role of elites in defining reality and impeding emancipatory change.

Asymmetrical relations of power lead to distorted speech and false consensus (Morgan 1992). Following Habermas (1971, 1979), critical organization theorists seek "ideal speech" which enables free and rational communications with the goal of approximating a genuine consensus (Steffy and Grimes 1992; Alvesson and Deetz 1996).[1] They recommend using Habermas's (1984) universal validity criteria—comprehensibility, sincerity, truthfulness, and legitimacy—to evaluate different statements (Forester 1992; Nord and Jermier 1992; Alvesson and Deetz 1996). It is assumed that by unmasking the discourses used to maintain relations of power, change and equality can be brought about (Steffy and Grimes 1992).[2]

The fact that power relations are maintained in discourse implies that they can be difficult to recognize due to their "taken-for-grantedness." Critical organization theorists thus seek to expose these hidden relations. Deetz (1992, 43) writes, "Reproblemitizing the obvious requires identifying conflicts which do not happen, pulling out latent experiences which are overlooked, and identifying discursive practices which block value discussion and close the exploration of differences." Critical organization theorists literally seek to establish a "culture of critical discourse" (Nord and Jermier 1992, 216), based on "perpetual critique" (Deetz 1992, 36), in order to freely and collectively criticize organizational forms and search out alternatives (Benson 1977). The goal is to create an "opening to the future" (Deetz 1992, 35) that undermines established imperatives based on financial, political, or traditional control (Alvesson and Deetz 1996). This will require "continuous reconstruction" so that a new regime does not simply replace the old one (Benson 1977, 18; compare, Deetz and Mumby 1990; Alvesson and Willmott 1992c).

At the center of this emancipating project is the transformation of the self. Alvesson and Willmott (1992c, 441) write,

> To justify their critique of contemporary illusions and social unhappiness, CT researchers have appealed to the idea that, at the core of individuals, is a (potentially) unified, rational autonomous subject—a subject that is currently alienated and degraded by the socially unnecessary demands of capitalist work organizations.

This potentially rational and autonomous subject can be developed through the inculcation of the value of critical self-reflection. Values must be "consciously chosen," otherwise, as we will see in critical studies of organizational culture, individuals become indifferent or nihilistic toward established systems of meaning (Willmott 1993, 533). An even deeper problem, however, is that the emancipatory project causes anxiety and insecurity because it takes away answers and replaces them with questions. However, critical organization theorists believe it is only through informed choice, made possible by autonomous individuals carrying out critical analyses, that democratic practices can be maintained and the inherent moral quality of social reality can be experienced (Willmott 1993).

Three points will be made on critical organization theory. First, the formulation of morality implied in critical organization theory is highly individualistic. The achievements of autonomous individuals consciously participating in democratic decision-making are seen as both inherently moral and will result in moral outcomes. This is the assumption of immanent perfectionism that, as we have seen, leads to moral inversion—the loss of moral limits (Polanyi 1969). In organizations, dominant majorities have routinely mistreated race, class, and gender minorities (Kanter 1977). Critical organization theory's goal of ensuring voice for these minorities does not change the fact that democratic process cannot guarantee ethical results. What is needed in addition to democratic process is a specific tradition of pursuing justice.

Second, along with an exaggerated faith in democratic process, critical organization theorists offer faith in the rational capacities of individuals. It is assumed that if individuals are freed of the controlling power of discourses by critical self-reflection, they will make "rational" (that is, fair and good) decisions. But individuals stripped of the authority of the past have not always been fair or good. Indeed, it is known that capitalism is a great freer and rationalizer of individual energies (Schumpeter 1942), yet this freedom and rationality has at times led to greed and destructive disregard for others. Here too, critical organization theorists seem to arrive at a one-sided position. Historically, rationality outside the controls of nonrational authoritative values has been as destructive, if not more destructive, than oppressive and unfair social traditions.

Third, establishing a "culture of critical discourse" (Nord and Jermier 1992, 216), that seeks to problematize established beliefs and continually support differences, is certain to weaken collective moral structures. The ability to critically evaluate beliefs and actions is no doubt a required capacity for any individual or group, but to build consensus or solidarity on this capacity alone is both one-sided and unwise. Along with criticism, commitment needs to be cultivated. The tobacco industry, for example, has for decades criticized information on the harmful effects of smoking, without ever demonstrating a commitment to the well-being of their consumers (Trevino and Nelson 1995). Clearly, individuals, to work and live together, must have a shared sense of justice and limits to individual action (Arendt 1968). This sense cannot arise from a culture of criticism because criticism only begets more criticism; it can only come from the transmission of ethical values from one generation to the next because this is the only practical way to maintain a common base (Chapman 1967). In modernity, this process has been disrupted by the culture of criticism. To continue to think that traditions can be replaced by criticism greatly exaggerates the capacity and nobility of rationality as well as misunderstands that traditions are an irremovable part of human social existence. We have been privileged with great moral traditions, our highest responsibility is to master and improve them from our own experience.

2. *The Attitude Toward the Past.* Critical organization theorists are distrustful and suspicious of the past. In contrast, their attitude toward the future is one of hope for freedom and progress. The key assump-

tion they make is that "the world is socially constructed and can be remade" (Jermier 1985, 75). For critical organization theorists, "socially constructed" means illegitimate. It is a rationalist rejection of the tacit nature of culture. It is common to find the words "arbitrary character" (Benson 1977, 6), or "arbitrary nature" (Alvesson and Deetz 1996, 200) associated with the process of social construction, that is with culture. Since beliefs are considered arbitrary, critical organization theorists claim independence from and superiority over their cultural inheritance. The result is a rejection of the past. Alvesson and Willmott (1992c), for example, recommend protecting the ambiguities of the empirical situation in order to be able to challenge any particular account of it. Alvesson and Deetz (1996) assume words like "women" and "worker" are power-laden distinctions and not legitimate representations of reality. Deetz (1992, 30) is optimistic that a better life can be made in the "next moment." The established present is seen as illegitimate by definition.

Critical organization theorists look particularly closely at appeals to the truth in any social setting. In Forester's (1992, 62) words,

> By refining Habermas's attention to a 'double structure of speech', we come to examine specifically the micropolitics of speech and interaction (Habermas, 1979). Quite contrary to prevailing misinterpretations of Habermas, we come not to expect any idealized truth-telling; instead we look closely at the ways in which appeals to truth (and quite differently, truthfulness) serve varied and significantly contingent, variable ends (Forester, 1985, 1991). . . . Similarly, too, for the contingencies of consent, claims to legitimacy and cultural conventions, and the contingencies of trust and forms of attention.

Hence, truth too is seen as constructed from "arbitrary representational practices" (Alvesson and Willmott 1992b, 13), that are merely historical and political in nature (Alvesson and Deetz 1996). The past is seen as little more than the record of winners and losers in the interminable political struggle that explains the relations of domination in the present. Critical organization theory is thus intensely present-oriented in that the only legitimate beliefs are ones that are consciously, rationally, and collectively developed in a current dialogue. All other forms of belief are seen as distortion carried over time through language (Alvesson and Willmott 1992b). Language must be continuously examined for these implicit power-laden beliefs.

The centrality of individual consciousness in critical organization theory is also a factor in its attitude toward the past. Since critical organization theorists assume that the only form of legitimate belief is achieved through rational discussions between individuals, they seek to increase participation in these discussions. Willmott (1993, 521) writes,

> Even though definitive authoritative judgments about the morality of a discourse (e.g., the corporate culture literature) are unobtainable, their absence does not exclude the possibility of engaging forms of discourse that strive to enrich our appreciation of the moral dimensions and significance of lay and scientific practice . . . the challenge is to revive and reconstruct the life of science in ways that incorporate the deployment of critical reason to re-member the normative, moral-political quality of all forms of human activity.

By reformulating the word "remember" as "re-member," Willmott is changing the significance of memory from a diachronic to a synchronic mode; that is, memory is no longer an instrument to recall a specific past, but becomes an instrument to implement critical organization theory's timeless ideal: individual, conscious participation in all human activity. Participation (politics) replaces tradition (culture).

Two comments will be made on critical organization theory's attitude toward the past. First, in claiming that social constructions are arbitrary, critical organization theorists imply that evil is only a product of the past and once individuals are freed to rationally choose their beliefs, a better life can be created. This one-sided argument transfers the evil potential of human beings to the abstract past or cultural system. This shift in responsibility for action from the individual to the cultural system or "social constructions" is misleading because only the individual can have a choice and the responsibility to exercise the choice morally. This transfer of moral responsibility encourages self-justifications and power-seeking because it discredits the cultural constraints against them.[3]

Second, Willmott (1993) argues that the role of memory in organizations should be to "re-member the normative, moral-political quality" of human activity; that is, to increase individual participation in all forms of human activity. In this way, the individual can participate in creating the moral rules and political goals that effects him or her. This argument collapses the distinction between morals and politics. Moral and political are hyphenated because Willmott assumes they are both subcategories in critical organization theory's father category of social control. With the individual as the fundamental value, "memory" is transformed into a timeless defense against social control. Hence, memory is removed as the spine of moral consistency and instead becomes a stimulus to critical participation. In this context, moral decision would become difficult at best because commitments, through which moral standards are maintained, would be greatly weakened (MacIntyre 1988). By turning their back on the moral value of the past, critical organization theorists greatly lighten the moral weight of the present.

3. *The Assumption of Naturalism.* The overarching ideal in the desire to question all assumptions, traditions, and beliefs is the belief in rationality. People and organizations are seen as not rational enough. People do not understand their "specific interests" (Alvesson and Deetz 1996, 198), or their "genuine needs and wants" (Alvesson and Willmott 1992c, 435), because their rational capacities are constrained by "systemic processes that produce active consent" (Alvesson and Deetz 1996, 199). Once the distortions to rational thinking by power and class interests are uncovered, the individual will be free to make unbiased choices (Nord and Jermier 1992) and pursue "suppressed values such as autonomy, creativity, and pleasure" (Alvesson and Deetz 1996, 200).

This commitment to uncover the "suppressed values" of autonomy, creativity, and pleasure points to the foundational assumption inherent in critical organization theory. I refer here to the assumption of *naturalism.* Naturalism is a philosophy that originates in the eighteenth century, which claims the immanent freedom and rights of man/woman in opposition to spiritual and cultural demands. Ironically, critical organization theory's central commitment to reflexively question all beliefs is not applied to its foundational assumption. For example, in his critique of Herbert Simon's theory of bounded rationality, Forester distinguishes between bounds that are alterable and ones that are just plain "human." He (1992, 61) writes, "But Simon's account was concerned neither with the role social structures may play in a given case to bound rationality, nor with those bonds which might be otherwise, bounds that are 'unnecessary', alterable and contingent, not arguably part of being human." Or Alvesson and Deetz (1996), in discussing the "naturalization" of the social order, distinguish between false naturalization and "life processes." They (1996, 199) write,

> In naturalization a social formation is abstracted from the historical conflictual site of its origin and treated as a concrete, relatively fixed, entity. As such the reification becomes the reality rather than life processes.

Hence, even behind their analysis of the illusion of "naturalization" is the society-nature dichotomy.

The writer who has most developed the assumption of naturalism is Hugh Willmott. Willmott (1993, 531) writes,

> Earlier it was argued that, lacking instinctual closure, the openness or indeterminacy of human existence is accompanied by an imperative to accomplish (normative) closure 'for all practical purposes' (Garfinkel, 1967). The sense of order bestowed by this 'second nature' provides a way of coming to terms with, a fundamental 'lack' in human nature (Bauman, 1976). Perversely, the very possibility of realizing the freedom of this 'lack' also depends upon the cultural world of 'second nature'. For it is 'second nature' that conditions and constrains how human freedom is interpreted and realized.

Hence, Willmott's theory of culture rests on the assumption that human existence is fundamentally pre-cultural. He sets up a nature-culture dichotomy that assumes culture is a "'second nature'." This assumption delegitimates culture, because it turns culture into an instrumental solution to the foundational problem of existential indeterminacy. This leads Willmott (1993, 533) to conclude that since human life is fundamentally indeterminate, the "central *moral* issue" is to create social institutions that increase contemplation of competing value-standpoints and appreciate the importance of making informed choices. Willmott desires an "age of responsibility" (1993, 540), where the awareness of indeterminacy leads to an awareness of the "normativity of knowledge" (1993, 542), and thus to an openness toward diversity and pluralism.

Four points will be made on the assumption of naturalism. First, the assumption of naturalism is an anti-tradition tradition. Its Enlightenment forerunners were romanticists, like Rousseau (1755), who argued against the corrupting influences of society and custom. The basic romantic idea is still the same. A society-humanity dichotomy is set up as an uncriticized foundational assumption that is both the source of their anti-tradition and anti-culture animus, and of their ahistorical rationalism and individualism. This is another example of critical organization theory being as much under the yoke of tradition as the traditions they are criticizing. Critical organization theory is replacing commitment to with suspicion of the cultural history of Western civilization, based on their foundational assumption of a natural humanity.

Second, the goal of increasing individual creativity is a traditional aim of modern individualism. The important aspect of this aim is that the individual is expected to be creative independent of any criteria of what creativity means. In his study of the creativity of writers, however, T. S. Eliot (1932) found that creativity originates in tradition and is dependent on tradition for not only its resources, but also its motivation. Creativity is impossible without commitment. In modernity, the interest in creativity has led to a great increase in cultural activities, but with the result of the general lowering of their quality. In management education, for example, this can be seen in the increasing number of programs designed to stimulate individual creativity (Boyatzis 1995), while many students are unable to adequately read and write. When change (or creativity) becomes dominant over tradition, the result is a general breakdown in cultural standards and the quality of cultural creations.

Third, critical organization theory's interest in increasing the pursuit of pleasure (Alvesson and Deetz 1996) is another offshoot of modern individualism. Culture, instead of being an edifice of moral discipline, becomes a vehicle for endless experience. Endless experience without any criteria for establishing its meaning or value results in experience becoming infinitely dispersed and uninteresting. Boredom and impatience become central characteristics of this attitude toward life (Rieff 1990). All too often, this leads the search for new experience beyond moral limits. Tom Wolfe (1987) provides a detailed sketch of just such a "Master of the Universe" in his character Sherman McCoy, whose defining trait is an incapacity to feel guilty for greed, marital infidelity, and even manslaughter.

Fourth, it is worth examining in what sense critical organization theorists see themselves as pursuing ethical ends. Willmott (1993), for example, claims that human existence is fundamentally indeterminate. Since no moral values can be privileged in an indeterminate universe, he arrives at moral relativism. This argument, however, ignores the whole history of our civilization (Taylor 1989). This shows the true purpose of the assumption of naturalism: it is to justify a rejection of inherited belief. Hence, ethics for critical organization theorists rests on the assumption of ahistorical individualism. This disregard for the accomplishments of past generations is characteristic of the modern mind (Mill 1831).

4. *Application to Organizations and Management.* From its beginnings in the 1970s, critical organization theory defined "organization"

in terms of "established social relations" (Heydebrand 1977, 87), that were maintained through a process of social construction mediated by the "present structure of advantages and disadvantages" (Benson 1977, 7). Hence, critical organization theory originates as a "critical-Marxist theoretical orientation" (Heydebrand 1977, 98; compare, Benson 1977; Clegg 1977), with its classic concern for domination of one group by another.[4] It is important to note that critical organization theory, from its beginnings, grasps domination in both its material (Marx 1844) and ideal or symbolic dimensions (Weber 1904–05). This orientation gives rise to the central concerns of critical organization theory: resistance to organizational control (Clegg 1977; Willmott 1993), against processes of reification and ideology that constrain rationality (Benson 1977; Jermier 1985; Alvesson and Willmott 1992c), and support for individual emancipation and democratic process in organizations (Benson 1977; Alvesson and Willmott 1992b; Alvesson and Deetz 1996).

Critical organization theory seeks to humanize work in organizations. Alvesson and Willmott (1992b, 4) write that "research is self-consciously motivated by an effort to discredit, and ideally eliminate, forms of management and organization that have institutionalized the opposition between the purposefulness of individuals and the seeming givenness and narrow instrumentality of work-process relationships." Some of the specific goals that critical organization theorists pursue are that work should be designed to conform to bodily, cognitive, and emotional needs, not vice versa (Steffy and Grimes 1992); they argue for equal opportunity to contribute to production systems, so as to meet human needs and lead to individual development (Alvesson and Deetz 1996); finally, they support workplace democracy, quality of work, gender equality, environmental protection, and informed and independent consumption (Alvesson and Willmott 1992b). An example of critical organization theory applied to management education is Nord and Jermier's (1992) effort to have managers in Human Resource Management (HRM) study the history of HRM to undermine the objectivist bias in this field.

Inside the disciplines of management and organization, critical organization theory has also encouraged the examination of the role of theory and methods. Early on it was recognized that organization theory has a "control function" and is unreflexive and ahistorical (Clegg and Dunkerley 1977). This enabled organization theory to support oppressive social relations. A similar critique has been applied to marketing. Glenn Morgan (1992, 143) writes,

> Drucker and Kotler present marketing as a neutral tool. What they neglect to consider is that the discourse of marketing itself constitutes social relations as it becomes applied; it does not stand aloof from them. It actively participates in the self-constitution of subjects through commodities . . . .It produces a consumer of goods and services wrapped up in them as part of self-image. The self is voided of moral character, and appearance becomes everything.

Morgan, using critical organization theory, shows that the claim of neutrality by the marketing profession is an illusion. By showing the broader social and psychological effects of marketing, he argues for the acceptance of social responsibility by the profession.

On the methodological level, Steffy and Grimes (1992) have argued that validation criteria must include input from the organizations and individuals studied. Only in this way, can organizational research lead to empowerment and democratic action. The key aim should be strategies to attain/sustain consensus.[5] The researcher is responsible to go beyond narrow problem-solving to report the historical and cultural context in which the "problem" is set. Otherwise, the researcher becomes a part of the power system and the research supports the system of domination. The researcher and the research must necessarily seek to be an agent of change towards enlightenment and emancipation.

Two points will be made on critical organization theory's application to organizations and management. First, the strong influence of Marxist theory on critical organization theory can be seen in its core concerns with resistance, ideology, and emancipation. This points out an important paradox: critical organization theory depends upon the dominance of what it criticizes. If critical organization theory ever succeeds in destroying the object of its criticism, it will itself necessarily change from a challenging creed to an organizational discipline to protect the victories it has won. Critical organization theorists, wary of this problem, attempt to defend against it by calls for perpetual critique.[6] However, this does not remove the paradox of critical success: either it becomes an organizational discipline or practices perpetual critique and exists in a state of excessive autonomy.[7] Indeed, excessive autonomy is a condition for the growth of totalitarian organization (Dumont 1986). Hence, critical organization theory leads to three possible outcomes: it remains dependent on what it criticizes, institutes an organizational discipline, or institutionalizes perpetual critique and becomes vulnerable to totalitarian organization. The first shows the limits of its ethics, the second contradicts its moral and political commitments, and the third shows the potential terror of the combination of its individualism with utopian openness.

Second, critical organization theory has an important contribution to make, it seems to me, in its capacity to analyze structures of power. Its inheritance of a theory of history and a political sociology from Marxism focuses its attention on power and control. Clegg's (1977) exegesis of the political implications of organizational theory, Heydebrands's (1977) analysis of the process of rationalization in professional organizations, and Morgan's (1992) criticism of the moral tunnel vision of marketing managers are all helpful and laudable. But critical organization theory's insistence on replacing greed and manipulation with individualism and rationalism, shows its inability to learn the lesson of the Enlightenment: man/woman cannot command him/herself, it is a contradiction. Following Polanyi (1969), we can call this the tragedy of moral inversion.

5. *The Critique of Corporate Culturism.* Critical organization theorists are very sensitive to the management of culture in organizations. Willmott (1993, 534) writes,

> In effect, corporate culture programmes are designed to deny or frustrate the development of conditions in which critical reflection is fostered. They commend the homogenization of norms and values within organizations. Employees are selected and promoted on the basis of their (perceived) acceptance of, or receptivity to, the core values. More generally, employees are repeatedly urged and rewarded for suspending attachments to ideas and mores that do not confirm and reinforce the authority of the core values. Cultural diversity is dissolved in the acid bath of the core corporate values. Those who kick against the monoculture are 'moved sideways' or they are expelled.

Willmott (1993) refers to this process as one of "imprinting" core values. He considers it a form of "nascent totalitarianism," because it is "systemic and totalizing" and attempts to "control all self direction" (Willmott 1993, 523-4). It begins in recruitment and is continued through training programs. This is different from scientific management, which attempts to eliminate the nonrational aspects of work and different from the human relations school which patronizes employee feelings and sentiments. The corporate culture movement attempts to "colonize" human emotions (Willmott 1993).

Willmott (1993) argues corporate culturism is successful because it provides employees with a solution to the indeterminancy of human existence: it provides existential security through the creation of stable meanings. The problem is that employees no longer have to think about and make moral choices between competing values. In other words, corporate culturism is unethical because it encourages freedom from moral responsibility. Employees learn to trade their responsibility for security from existential anxiety and are rewarded with financial and career success in the process (Alvesson and Deetz 1996). From the point of view of critical organization theory, their "marginal gains" are far outweighed by the support they give to an oppressive system that stifles their autonomy, development, and wider interests (Willmott 1993).

The argument connecting corporate culturism with totalitarianism assumes that corporate culturism leads to a form of mind control. Jermier (1985, 79) writes,

> The anesthetized . . . worker is so skilled at programmed rationalization and diversionary consumption that he or she barely notices the recurring surgery that separates and subjugates true self (cf. Laing, 1965). There is no counterforce or retaliation since this worker mistakes even capricious and surplus repression as natural and inevitable; there is no noticeable injury, hence no reprisal.

Workers live as if in an eternal dream. Alvesson and Willmott (1992b, 9) note the use of "ego administration" to make employees fit with the demands of mass production and consumption. A process of "remembering and forgetting" induces employees to pride themselves on being autonomous individuals, while simultaneously collectively following the uniform definitions of the corporate culture (Willmott 1993, 545). Willmott refers to this process as "doublethink" and considers it the hallmark of totalitarianism (Willmott 1993).

On a more general level, however, the totalitarian nature of corporate culturism is seen as an "extension of instrumental rationality" (Willmott 1993, 518). This is a common theme in critical organization theory. Steffy and Grimes (1992, 183) find similar forces at work in human resource management in the form of "behavioral technologies, measurement systems, and governing policies." Indeed, some forms of behavioral technologies operate on a subversive level. Alvesson and Deetz (1996, 204) write,

In work organizations, conflicts between practical reason (emphasizing the removal of repression) and instrumental reason (focused on the maximization of output) are portrayed as avoidable through the use of optimal management methods such as jobs enrichments, QWL, TQM, corporate culture and so forth, which simultaneously produce human well-being and development as well as high quality and productivity. Basic political issues are then transformed into technical problem-solving.

To counter this process, Willmott (1993), using a Weberian framework, argues for the re-emergence of *value-rational action* which allows individuals to assess the meaning and worth of a range of competing value standpoints and then choose between them.

Even though some employees do resist the instrumental rationality of corporate culturism, the situation does not enable the development of value-rational action. Willmott (1993) uses Gideon Kunda's (1992) Tech Corporation as a case example. Employees at Tech were not inclined to internalize corporate cultural values, but since Tech culture promoted "openness," even independent behavior was seen as fitting in with the corporate culture. The result of this manipulation of meaning was universal cynicism. What is important here is that once universal cynicism became the pervasive social condition, it resulted in corporate dominance. The reason for this is that cynicism led to "role playing" and one can only play a role so long before the role turns into the real self (Willmott 1993). Thus, as cynicism increased and a nihilistic atmosphere was established, employees became less able to evaluate competing values, because they lacked a "critical standpoint" (Willmott 1993, 538). Hence, they had no reason to reject any role offered to them. To avoid the inner confusion, many employees clung to the corporate culture to secure stable meanings.

Two points will be made on corporate culturism. First, several critical organization theorists see corporate culturism as totalitarian, because they imagine it as a form of mind control based on the centralized rationalization of values. It is worth comparing this definition of totalitarianism with the one developed by Hannah Arendt (1950). For Arendt, totalitarianism is based on the systematic breakdown of moral and legal relationships, so that the individual is not told what to think, but cannot think morally at all. Control is based on the complete uncertainty of the social environment. By contrasting Arendt's view with the instrumental rationality view of critical organization theorists, it can be seen that the instrumental rationality view exaggerates the level of mind control, because individuals are still able to think in an organizational environment that markets a streamlined set of values.[8] The effect from propaganda on the internal life of the individual is limited, as opposed to the complete breakdown of reliable social relations which leaves the individual utterly helpless and malleable. My analysis leads away from the mind control theory and suggests that "corporate culturism" is at least partly generated by collective demand and that employees have a responsibility for its creation.[9]

Second, more importantly, in his analysis of Gideon Kunda's (1992) study of Tech Corporation, Willmott (1993) does recognize the phenomenon of universal cynicism. In this corporate culture, the distinction between control and resistance was destroyed and an environment of meaninglessness was created. This is similar to Arendt's (1950) definition of totalitarianism and has little to do with instrumental rationality but with the destruction of meaning. As Willmott (1993) points out, these individuals lost a "critical standpoint" and were unable to tell right from wrong. They happily joined the corporate culture to secure a stable social environment, thus accepting corporate self-definitions. I find this part of Willmott's analysis of corporate totalitarianism compelling because it concentrates on the element of meaninglessness in the exercise of control.[10]

Conclusion

In this chapter, a concept of moral tradition has been developed to analyze the attitude toward the past in theories of organization. I argued that moral traditions are essential for providing stability, continuity, and coherence for ethical beliefs. It was also argued that a concept of moral tradition is needed to counter the excessive reliance on the modern belief in rationality in the field of organization theory. Moral traditions are needed to maintain memory of what was learned in the past and what ethical treasures were created out of this experience.

The main problem I see with critical organization theory is its inattention to the positive aspects of attachment and commitment. In seeking to establish a culture of critical discourse, it greatly emphasizes criticism over commitment. Indeed, its deepest impulse is one of distrust for attachment and a need to examine its implications for control. This impulse originates in eighteenth century romanticism and is inseparable from an unrealistic reliance on the rational capacities of man/woman. Part of the problem is that it desires to completely spring loose the individual from the past. This complete focus on the life-span of the individual seems to be related to the hedonism of modern culture. It presents a loss of our connections to those who came before us; a disinclination to learn from, carry forward, and build on the best accomplishments of the past.

Tradition is protean. Critical organization theorists mistakenly see it only as constraining, but tradition is also creative. Critical organization theory is itself a tradition extending back 150 years to Marx, or 70 years to the Frankfurt School. In any case, tradition can be stimulating. Its tradition of ideology critique, for example, can stimulate our freedom by enabling us to understand the jargon and misrepresentations of much of modern communications. Ideology critique misunderstands itself, however, when it rejects its own traditionality and strives for perpetual critique. This is an example of the exaggerated confidence in rationality which is characteristic of critical organization theory. It is based on the Enlightenment's fresh hatred of tradition. In order to fully develop into a social and moral theory of organization, critical organization theory must acknowledge the ineluctable role of the past in the present and recognize its positive contribution to moral conduct.

Only in this way can critical organization theory establish an understanding of morality that is not a subcategory of politics. By collapsing morality into politics, critical organization theory is left with an unrestricted reliance on the thin base of the present. Critical organization theorists hope to substitute democratic process as the ethical form of politics, but a democracy of untutored individuals does not necessarily guarantee ethical decision-making. Critical organization theorists' one-sided belief that evil only comes from systemic distortions, denies the dark side of man/woman. Indeed, the result of its effort to criticize all tradition will be the inevitable concentration of power in top management. Moral traditions are essential as alternatives to political control in organizations.

Notes

1. Benhabib (1992), however, argues that Habermas's discourse ethics is not about reaching a consensus, but about stimulating agency and efficacy, dialogue, conversation, and mutual understanding; and about practicing the reversibility of perspectives and mutual respect which are the bases of the bonds that hold society together. On a more political level, she argues that "ideal speech" should be used

as a "yardstick" to uncover underrepresented interests. It involves the "right dose of fantasy" to collectively promote conflict resolution strategies (Benhabib, 1992, 49).

2. Mingers (1992) is critical of Habermas for assuming change can be brought about merely by rational enlightenment. Alvesson and Deetz (1996) mention that Habermas has been criticized for exaggerating the potential of rationality and consensus, and for assuming a too benign and benevolent view of human kind. Willmott (1993) is also skeptical that individuals can always be persuaded by a better argument. This is what leads these writers to an interest in Michel Foucault's (1980) writings on power/knowledge. Nonetheless, these writers remain committed to the critique of systems as opposed to developing a balanced view of individual/group limitations.

3. Paul Moser, the head trader at Salomon Brothers government bond trading desk, is a case in point. Moser, having the opportunity to greatly increase profits if he found a way around federal law, fraudulently put customer names on Salomon bids. His justification for his actions was simply that he disagreed with the law (Hertzberg and Cohen 1992).

4. Jermier (1985) has argued that privileged classes are behind a concerted effort by the "cultural industry" to grossly over-stimulate demand so as to divert and control the attention of workers. Or more generally, Alvesson and Willmott (1992b) argue that the central problem of management is that managers are unaccountable to their subordinates.

5. Steffy and Grimes (1992) state that in organizational psychology, the bulk of the research focuses on control and regulative issues, not dynamic ones such as power, conflict, politics, and ideology where research is needed to stimulate emancipation.

6. Critical organization theorists admit, however, that critical theory has "perverse effects" and "oppressive potential" when it lands in the hands of elites (Nord and Jermier 1992, 218; compare, Deetz and Mumby 1990). However, if critical theory has "perverse effects" when used by elites, what is to stop "perpetual critique" from being misused? Indeed, for Hannah Arendt (1950), totalitarianism is based on continuous criticism of anything that stands in the way of power.

7. Thomas McCarthy (1993) argues that without ceasing to criticize organizations, we cease to be participants.

8. Furthermore, corporations exist in pluralistic societies that make the possibility of corporate totalitarianism most unlikely. The problem is societal: extreme pluralism and individualism leaves employees with little sense of their own values. Arendt's (1950) theory of totalitarianism is more useful for capturing the central role of meaninglessness, as opposed to the imprinting of core values, in totalitarian organizations.

9. Indeed, in a democracy, leaders usually follow the desires of their constituents (Tocqueville 1850). Critical organization theorists miss this possibility, because their idealization of democracy prevents them from seeing some of the negative aspects of a plebian and callow democratic culture. Willmott (1993) does recognize the collective demand for corporate culture, but he attributes this to the inability of employees to accept the fundamental indeterminacy of social life. Psychological security, for Willmott, is a bad thing. Apparently, he arrives at this conclusion because of his belief in the nobility of a purely rational existence. Psychological security, however, is a fundamental and legitimate need of human beings (Sullivan 1950). An empty acceptance of indeterminacy will only create

more insecurity. We need to remember that rationalism not only helped create the meaninglessness of modern life, it also was not able to control the terrors that resulted from it.

10. Nonetheless, I reject Willmott's (1993) concept of a "critical standpoint," because it assumes the rationalist/individualist myth of being able to criticize standing nowhere.

5

Micro Matters: The Aesthetics of Power in NASA's Flight Readiness Review

The primitive stuff of institutions is the individuals who staff them. This is seen in the plasticity of relations between leaders and followers. In this chapter, I argue that excessive managerial control was a critical factor in determining the Challenger launch decision-making process. Specifically, I show that NASA's Flight Readiness Review was ritualized through the aesthetic techniques of visualization, expectation, and repetition that intensified dependency relations. Aesthetic instruments as tools of power are a common but mostly unrecognized problem for organizational cooperation and communications. At NASA, a culture of conformity developed, characterized by the exaggerated centrality of the leader. Conflicts existed both between groups and within individuals, but were suppressed. This interpretation is contrasted with Vaughan's (1996) use of institutional theory to analyze the disaster. Vaughan concludes that the decision process was primarily the result of macro (institutional) forces that determined the work group culture and thinking. What is at stake in this debate is our understanding of the role of individual responsibility in large bureaucratic organizations. In contrast to Vaughan this chapter holds that moral choices were a central and problematic aspect of the decision-making process.

In his book *Moby-Dick*, Herman Melville (1851) demonstrates how, shortly after the *Pequod* sailed, Captain Ahab was able to transform an extremely diverse collection of individuals into a single vehicle in pursuit of his insane aim. Melville's account exemplifies that leadership and the reaction to it are a fundamental part of collective action.

The purpose of this chapter is twofold: first, to introduce a theory of aesthetic functions in organizational politics for the study of leader-follower behavior (Rieff 1990); second, to use this theory to reanalyze the data on NASA's Flight Readiness Review (FRR), a decision-making process designed to ensure that all requirements, including safety, were met before launch approval. I will focus on the FRRs leading up to the *Challenger* disaster. I will show how the aesthetic theory of politics can contribute to our understanding of the social psychology of large group dynamics, specifically how *spectacle* can be used to solidify the leader's control over the group. I will discuss how this process was at work in NASA's FRR, undermining its intended design to stimulate investigation and debate, and how this process contributed to the *Challenger* disaster.

The "aesthetic" can be defined as that activity which people use, by means of symbolic forms, to communicate feelings to others who are thereby influenced by them (Rieff 1990). In this definition, aesthetic activity is political. In other words, aesthetic activities join individuals together in the same feelings to carry out organizational purpose.

So far, the research on disasters has not considered the role of aesthetic functions in decision-making. Gephart (1984), Hynes and Prasad (1997), and Turner (1976) consider the political aspects of disasters, but focus primarily on *inter*organizational conflict. Weick (1993) analyzes issues of unity, but does so in terms of the fragility of sensemaking processes, not political issues. Vaughan (1996) analyzes cultural influences on decision-making, but does so in terms of institutional forces influencing unconscious cognitive structures, giving little attention to semi-autonomous micro-level developments such as leader-follower dynamics.

The study of aesthetic functions in politics is closely aligned with psychodynamic approaches to the study of disaster as these approaches tend to focus on the emotional aspects of interpersonal relations (Kets de Vries 1991). There also is a long tradition focusing on leader-follower relations (Freud 1921). In the study of an oil refinery disaster, Hirschhorn and Young (1993), for example, discuss social defenses developed to control anxiety, leading to a disregard for danger. Schwartz (1990), in his study of the *Challenger* disaster, finds organizational ideals invested with narcissism to such an extent as to lead to feelings of organizational omnipotence. Elmes and Barry (1999), also employing the concept of narcissism in their study of mountain climbing disasters, argued that accomplished team leaders ignored safety regulations in trying to satisfy self-inflated clients. The theory of aesthetic functions in politics builds on this literature by developing knowledge about how the symbolic structure of group unity can be manipulated to inhibit open discussion and debate.

Research in the social psychology of conformity and obedience is also an important basis for explaining how aesthetic instruments can be used for organizational domination. Asch (1951; 1955), Milgram (1963), and Janis (1972) have found powerful tendencies toward conformity in the individual's relationship to various kinds of authority. This body of literature will be used to explain conscious and unconscious group pressures that lead to individual self-censorship and force consensus. Whereas this literature focuses on small groups, the theory of aesthetic functions in politics will demonstrate some of the ways obedience and conformity are enacted in large groups. Turquet's (1974) work on leadership and the tendency of small groups to focus too much on their own emotional needs will also be used to show how leaders can take on magical powers in the eyes of followers. In large groups, magical powers can be transferred to organizational processes and structures (Diamond 1991). In this regard, my work builds on Schwartz's (1990) analysis of organizational narcissism in the NASA decision-making process.

This chapter analyzes aesthetic influences on decision-making in the *Challenger* disaster in terms of micro-level dynamics. I argue that these micro-level dynamics are partially autonomous from macro-level forces. This is a counter-point to Vaughan's (1996) important work that exaggerates the role of macro–forces in determining work group decision-making, missing the importance of individual moral responsibility. The following section reviews relevant literature and offers a conceptual framework. This will be followed by a brief overview of the *Challenger* case. Then I will analyze the FRR in terms of the way aesthetic images are used for political purposes. In the conclusion, I will make recommendations to resolve destructive levels of aesthetic domination.

Literature Review and Conceptual Framework

Studies of disaster have a natural interest in the notion of forewarning. In Turner's (1976) study of three disasters in the United Kingdom, he concludes that some forewarning is usually available. Large-scale disasters develop over a long time period and involve considerable resources. Turner (1976) uses a concept of cultural knowledge to explain why developing disasters are not noticed. For various reasons—epistemological or political, for example—cultural knowledge does not accurately represent reality. It originates in historical and institutional processes that have a life of their own, separate from changes in industrial and technological organization. Thus, dangerous events, carrying the potential for disaster, remain unnoticed.

Turner (1976) finds that cultural knowledge was used as a defense by inside groups to reject the perceptions of outside groups. Differing perceptions were not seen as disagreements over reality, but as attempts to wrest power away from insiders. Hynes and Prasad (1997), in their study of a Canadian coal mine disaster, note the role of power relations in the development of disaster. The miners were not unionized and so were forced to go along with management's disregard for safety. Concerning the *Challenger* disaster, Vaughan (1996) develops a notion of the "culture of production" to show how production pressures had become part of the organizational culture from sources both inside and outside the organization. In her research, the concept of culture suppresses the notion of organizational power, replacing the study of conflict with a notion of totalizing and unconscious institutional forces.

The notion that events leading to disaster are difficult to discern or are invisible also is found in Perrow's (1984) theory of "normal accidents." He argues that disasters involve a complex interaction of design errors, equipment failure, and operational mistakes. An unforeseeable dynamic evolves making complex systems disasters only understandable in retrospect. These disasters are "normal" in the sense that they naturally arise from complex and tightly coupled systems. The complexity and amount of information is so great that crucial warnings are overlooked, or communications between subgroups are misunderstood (Turner 1976).

Weick (1993), in his study of disaster among firefighters who parachuted into a wilderness area to fight a forest fire, focuses on the structure of social interaction. He finds that when there is a sudden loss of rational, orderly relations among group members, both the sense of what is happening and the capacity to rebuild this sense are lost. More precisely, there is an interactive disintegration between the system of individual roles and the process of sensemaking. In Weick's case study, firefighters were overwhelmed by the surprising strength of the fire and lost their capacity to work together as a team. Key in Weick's (1993) explanation of the group breakdown is the group's minimal shared past. In the sudden crisis, they lacked the interpersonal resources to reestablish roles and relationships. When established and shared interpretive schemes and role relations break down, Weick (1993) recommends that group members redouble the effort to reaffirm role relations, or that the single individual tries to create new understandings which can be used to build new role relations.

Weick's explanation is built around the notion of structure, both cognitive and social. This tends to lead him to emphasize shared knowledge at the expense of personal knowledge (Polanyi 1958). This can be seen in his review of Vaughan's (1996) study of the *Challenger* disaster (Weick 1997). He (1997, 395) writes about the fateful decision to launch the *Challenger*:

> The teleconference participants were the medium by which the invisible hand of NASA's rules, beliefs, and procedures converted [risk] uncertainty into certainty. The system knew that the *Challenger* should not be launched under conditions that were this far outside the experience base. But this dispersed knowledge could not be assembled credibly, because the people who ran the teleconference were far removed from the murky technology, shims, improvisation, and tacit understanding that engineers used to make the shuttle fly.

Weick's concepts of structure and structuring lead him to give the "invisible hand of NASA's rules, beliefs, and procedures" the central role in explaining the disaster. Personal decision-making and responsibility recede into the background. As I show in the case overview, the *Challenger* data does not support this picture of an invisible culture controlling decision-making while individuals lacked enough knowledge to recognize the threat to flight safety.

Vaughan's (1996) study of the *Challenger* disaster takes a similar approach. Her central concern is with a process she calls the "normalizing of deviance" (Vaughan 1996). She seeks to explain why NASA overlooked or somehow missed a stream of information that pointed to dangerous problems with the o-rings. Her extensive research shows that all the danger signals were "normalized" or interpreted as acceptable risks, that is, within the risk parameters established by NASA. In trying to explain what in retrospect were clearly erroneous decisions made by dozens of highly qualified engineers and engineering managers, Vaughan utilizes a vast array of concepts, but the central one, I believe, and the one primarily used to explain the irrational process of normalization, is "institutional theory" (DiMaggio and Powell 1991). Vaughan (1996, 198) writes about how the institutional context gave rise to a "culture of production" which led to and insulated a defective decision-making process:

We see how the premises of decision making about the [o-rings] existed before any specific managerial actions. The salient structural condition was NASA's institutional history: politics, competition, and scarcity. The culture of production contributed to the persistence of the work group's definition of the situation because their actions were normative and acceptable within this larger cultural context. The culture of production comprised the institutionalized belief systems of the aerospace industry, the engineering profession, the NASA organization, and Marshall Space Flight Center. Each cultural layer was in many ways distinctive; nonetheless, aspects of one carried over and interpenetrated the next. The greater the degree of institutionalization, the greater the resistance of cultural understanding to change. Deeply embedded in this framework of institutions, the work group's cultural construction of risk was less vulnerable to challenges and intervention.

By arguing that institutional history leads to the development of a "culture of production" which determines decision-making on the work group level, a great deal of work group experience is being ignored. Vaughan's (1996) use of the "new institutionalism" leads her to frame her analysis in terms of collective cognitive structures rather than the complexity of individual and interpersonal experience. Her interview data, for example, has little information about feelings or interpersonal conflict. In effect, by positing universal (and unconscious) forces that "permeated the organization, operating forcefully but insidiously in a prerational manner, influencing decision making by managers and engineers without requiring any conscious calculus," she drops individual moral responsibility from her explanatory framework (Vaughan 1996, 68). (See Collins [1981] for a critique of the tendency of institutional theory to reduce micro behavior to macro forces.).

Gephart (1984) comments on the tendency in the disaster research to rely on rationalist assumptions that limit explanations of disasters to collective errors in perception and judgement. Vaughan is arguing that the "culture of production" determined work group decision-making by steering it away from objective reality. Gephart (1984) argues that this approach implies that accurate collective agreement on the nature of reality is possible. Vaughan (1996), for her part, is pessimistic about any such accuracy, but only because of the prerational processes of institutionalization. Hence, the notion of objectivity is assumed in her analysis and she sees her task as explaining how decision-making falls short of it.

Gephart (1984) offers an alternative explanatory framework, that is, sensemaking as a political process. Instead of the institutionalization of layers of homogenizing culture, Gephart seeks out the practices that produce and maintain different perceptions of reality. He assumes that since there is a social distribution of interests, motives, and knowledge, it is likely that different people will see reality differently. Sensemaking involves issues of power because different views of reality imply a struggle between views for dominance of organizational action. Hence, the occurrence of a disaster is a political accomplishment on the micro level, not just a cultural and cognitive one. Applied to the *Challenger* disaster, the model of political sensemaking would see processes of institutionalization as affecting different individuals and groups differently. The conflicts and acts of domination that funnel diverse opinions into a decision outcome become the focus of analysis.

There is a stream of literature since the 1950s that addresses the question of how conflicts over perceptions are resolved on the work group level. Experiments carried out by Asch (1951; 1955) show that no matter how sure individuals were of their perceptions, when they stood alone against a majority, 75 percent of the time they changed their opinions—to some extent—and their views into agreement with the majority. Even when the majority was instructed to make extreme mistakes, subjects tended to conform to the majority position. It is important to note that when the experiment was altered to give the minority subject a supporter, the subject invariably resisted majority pressure. Thus, it was the condition of being alone that was decisive for predicting conformity.

Milgram (1963) carried out experiments on the phenomenon of destructive obedience. His research demonstrates that the majority of randomly chosen subjects willingly follow orders to apply what they believe to be dangerous levels of electrical shocks to other participants in the experiment. Many of the subjects applying the electrical shocks were visibly distressed by their actions, but nonetheless continued to follow orders. Clearly, there are micro-level dimensions to the study of obedience.

Janis (1972), studying major government decision-making fiascoes, develops a group dynamics theory of decision-making he calls "groupthink." The central assumption is that powerful pressures are brought against dissidents in cohesive groups. Group consensus is cherished and protected by group members because consensus allows group members to contain anxiety and maintain comfortable levels of self-esteem. When dissidents raise questions about error or risk, conflict is generated and disturbing moral issues surface, both of which require effort to address and are unsettling. By developing illusions of invulnerability or assumptions of inherent morality, all this can be avoided. The result is a decline in reality testing capabilities and moral judgement. The groupthink concept applies to the FRR in that 90 percent of the participants did not speak in what was supposed to be an open, adversarial decision process.

Another theory of work group pathology that focuses on primitive forms of bonding is developed by Turquet (1974). He argues that all groups have rational or purposeful elements and what he calls "basic-assumptions" (Turquet 1974). Basic-assumptions have to do with the emotional needs of the group. Problems arise when basis-assumption needs overwhelm goal-seeking behavior. Group members become de-skilled, suffer a loss of memory, and their sense of time is impaired. These last points about memory and the impairment of the sense of time are of particular interest because, as Weick (1997) notes in reference to the *Challenger* disaster, during the ongoing attempt to understand o-ring damage, engineers continually forgot their previous explanations as they created new ones to account for the latest evidence.

Work groups are not always reasonable and balanced. Regressive emotional behavior can become tangled up with organizational tasks and structures. In their study of Mount Everest climbing disasters, for example, Elmes and Barry (1999) find team leaders with years of safe and successful climbing experience making fatal decisions while trying to meet the inflated demands of high-paying clients. Diamond (1991) finds the excessive use of organizational control systems such as bureaucratic rules or hierarchical authority to contain anxiety. Decision processes became ritualized, losing their focus on organizational goals. In the study of the FRR, it will be shown how the decision process became ritualized through the use of aesthetic instruments of control.

Hirschhorn and Young (1990), in their study of disaster at an American oil refinery, find another form of organizational regression. Workers used a defense mechanism called *splitting* to manage their anxiety in a high-risk work environment. Members of one work group felt safe and in control by splitting their "good" feelings from their "bad" feelings (that is, feelings of danger and inadequacy) and projecting the latter onto another group. The organizational situation that had caused their anxiety thus remained unchanged. Hirschhorn and Young (1993) note that by splitting the "good" from the "bad," decision-making processes tend to become ritualized and seen as infallible or magical. In the *Challenger* case, confidence in scientific method and the FRR process replaced confidence in the particular decisions that were being made.

A key element in understanding regressive work groups is leadership. Turquet (1974) argues that in basic-assumption groups the leader is the only one who matters. This centrality is based on the leader's role in satisfying the emotional needs of basic-assumption groups. Hence, though it appears from the outside that the leader is dominating, the "domination" is based on a collusive interdependence with followers. The fantasy is that all responsibility is left to the leader, he/she will magically take care of everything. This complete absence of leadership sharing is a defining characteristic of the basic-assumption group.

Turquet (1974) finds that in large groups (groups too large for members to know each other personally), basic-assumption needs can be met through the individual's identification with the organization as an encompassing whole. In regressed groups this experience takes on an oceanic feeling of oneness which can easily be projected onto the leader. Followers can become an audience for the leader, vicariously participating in the leader's greatness, lost in the ongoing activity, blindly hopeful. As was mentioned, 90 percent of the personnel coming to the FRR did not speak. They formed a silent audience, identifying with the leader's domination of the proceedings.

This mythic dynamic between leader and followers, where the leader assumes near total control, has been insightfully analyzed through its aesthetic structure (Rieff 1990). The image of the whole that becomes so mesmerizing to followers and leaders alike functions as a symbol of prestige that is used to create union among the disparate followers. Without this symbolic structure pointing the way, group members could not develop the same feelings and perceptions, which in basic-assumption groups is the ultimate goal. When unity becomes an end in itself and serves no higher purpose, it serves merely the exercise of power.

The loss of any values beyond a desire for unifying control is one of the chief signs of organizational pathology. Domination through aesthetic forms requires the ritualization of communication and interpersonal relationships. Rieff (1990) argues there are three essential elements in this process: *visualization, expectation,* and *repetition.* Visualization as a ritual of power functions by largely replacing discussion with spectacle. Speech is not used so much for argument, but to communicate demands through states of feeling. This form of influence is familiar in televised political advertisements where the image presented is more powerful than the accompanying text.

The second element in the use of aesthetic forms for domination is the ritualization of expectation. By concentrating expectations on the activity of the leader, the leader's importance is dramatized. The attention of subordinates is focused and their emotions heightened. Jackall (1988), in his study of managers, finds one CEO who routinely humiliated his president in public. The expectation of this behavior was a company ritual that sent the message to all the company's managers that it could happen to any one of them. This increased their awareness of the CEO's overwhelming power and the increased awareness, in return, further increased the CEO's power.

The final element of domination through the use of aesthetic forms is repetition. Repetition functions to create and encourage expectation through the restatement of the aesthetic theme in differing contexts, and by the cumulative weight of new details. At "Tech Corporation," for example, Kunda (1992) finds the same corporate images were relentlessly repeated on the company home page, posted in public places, distributed in the mail, encountered in workshops, and used as decoration. As a result, these images became part of the conventional knowledge of everyday life that participants used to understand the present and imagine the future.

Case Overview

On January 28, 1986, shortly after takeoff, the space shuttle *Challenger* exploded killing five astronauts, an aerospace engineer, and a schoolteacher. The cause of the disaster was leakage of hot motor gasses through defective o-rings that ignited the external fuel tank. The shuttle technology was unprecedented and contained hundreds of parts that were considered unproven and had to be continuously evaluated. Questions about the o-rings dated back to the beginning of the space shuttle development in 1977. In the course of the 28 flights that took place between 1977 and 1986, the o-rings, along with many other parts, did not function flawlessly. In fact, over the course of these flights, the o-rings showed increasing, though inconsistent, deterioration. Engineers and engineering managers attended to the o-ring problems throughout this period, continuously evaluating, analyzing, and attempting to remedy them, always concluding that the o-rings posed acceptable risks.

On Flight 51B, April 29, 1985, however, they discovered the primary o-ring had burned all the way through and the secondary or redundant o-ring, the integrity of which was a key part of their acceptable risk justification, had sustained severe damage. At this point, at Morton Thiokol (the manufacturer of the solid rocket motors of which the o-rings were parts) conflicts arose over whether the latest o-ring deterioration represented a threat to flight safety (van Gigch et al. 1988; Winsor 1988). Warnings of potential disaster and complaints about severe time pressures interfering with testing and research show up in internal memos; disagreements develop between engineers and engineering managers as to the level of flight risk. Disagreements about flight risk between engineers and managers continued right up to the *Challenger* launch decision when, under pressure from Marshall Space Flight Center managers, Morton Thiokol managers reversed the decision of their engineers and recommended flight for the *Challenger* the following morning.

There were four main NASA organizations involved in the space shuttle program: NASA headquarters with overall responsibility in Washington, D.C.; Johnson Space Center with mission control responsibility and oversight of the entire shuttle program in Texas; Kennedy Space Center with launch responsibility in Florida; and the shuttle program headquarters at Marshall Space Flight Center in Alabama. Morton Thiokol headquarters is in Utah. The NASA culture, originating in the late 1950s, was built around technical exactitudes and military-like discipline (Vaughan 1996). In the mid–1970s, however, because of a change in governmental priorities, NASA's budget was cut and never restored (Marx et al. 1987). Top NASA administrators became preoccupied with raising money (Brody 1986). In the process they made promises, particularly in regard to making the shuttle program profitable, that they did not have the resources to keep. It was in this context that Ronald Reagan announced on July 4, 1982 that the shuttle was "operational" when, in fact, this was far from true (Vaughan 1996). By being defined as "operational," the flight schedule was greatly increased, safety reviews were cut, and civilians were put on flights. Money and time were not available, however, to redesign poorly performing parts such as the o-rings.

The budget cuts lead to jealous competition among the Marshall, Johnson, and Kennedy space centers (Brody 1986). My focus is on Marshall Space Center because Marshall had primary responsibility for the o-rings. Marshall had developed a culture that sought to contain problems internally (Minkes 1988). The top administrator at Marshall was William Lucas. He had been trained in the original NASA culture of the 1960s and was known for demanding high standards of engineering precision (Brody 1986). He was also known as a "master bureaucrat [who] created an atmosphere of rigid, often fearful, conformity" (Vaughan 1996, 218). He set up competition between managers to meet deadlines, conform to technical details, solve technical problems, follow rules, and be efficient, safe, and successful.

The decision-making process at the Marshall Space Center had become dysfunctional because of a context of excessive fear and anxiety. I will show how aesthetic functions in the key decision-making mechanism, the Flight Readiness Review (FRR), helped create this context. The FRRs took place at four levels throughout NASA's hierarchical system. Their purpose was to decide whether the shuttle was ready to fly and fly safely. The process worked from the bottom up. It started at level IV where contractor engineers gave presentations on flight readiness to contractor management; on level III, contractor management presented to the relevant project manager at Marshall; on level II, Marshall project managers presented to the project manager at Johnson; and on level I, the same project managers who present at level II presented to top NASA administrators. All FRR levels were designed to be adversarial to ensure rigorous debate. Most of the work was done on levels IV and III, only a relatively small number of items were passed up and reviewed on levels II and I (Vaughan 1996).

Because Marshall had three important shuttle components—the main engine, external tank, and solid rocket booster—Marshall had an extra review called "level 2 1/2," formally designated the "Marshall Center Board FRR" (Vaughan 1996). The Marshall Center director, William Lucas, ran this review. This step allowed him to review all information before it left Marshall. My analysis will focus on the Marshall Center Board FRR because this review brought together Lucas, the Marshall project managers, and a large number of other Marshall and Morton Thiokol personnel, thus providing the fullest picture of Marshall leadership, organizational dynamics, and organizational culture. The primary data I will analyze is from an interview Vaughan (1996) conducted with Larry Wear, Marshall Solid Rocket Motor Project Manager, who headed up the Marshall level IV FRR and participated in the Marshall Center Board FRR as both presenter and observer.

The Flight Readiness Review and the Aesthetics of Power

> *"Of course the Commandant is the kind of man to have turned these conferences into public spectacles."*
>
> —Franz Kafka
> "In the Penal Colony"
> (1919, 158)

The technical culture at NASA was based on scientific principles and positivistic methods; most of all, truth had to be quantitatively demonstrated. Analytic models, bench tests, field tests, and comparisons of predictions with performance, all formulated quantitatively, were the legitimate currency of analysis and decision. Even when engineers expressed "concern" about observed booster joint damage, the unquantified information was not enough to stop the next flight (Vaughan 1996, 257). Since carrying out quantitative research takes time, there was a "predisposition to continue launching" in the short and even medium-term (Vaughan 1996: 263).

However, I would argue that in scientific research "concern" is the origin of discovery (Weber 1918b; Roberts 1997). By accepting only quantitative data as legitimate, management undermined a key source of scientific discovery, tacit knowledge (Weick 1997). Tacit knowledge is a central component of discovery, because it enables intuitive creativity to order and reorder complex data sets without demonstration as a means to create new potential solutions which can then be investigated (Polanyi 1966). Hence, by making time-consuming quantitative research necessary before arguments could be presented, management stifled the discovery process and, in effect, turned time into a tool of power.

The "technical culture" was nowhere better enforced than in the Marshall Center Board FRR. This FRR met formally and frequently to evaluate and decide flight readiness. It had a 12-member board chaired by William Lucas. Larry Wear, Marshall Solid Rocket Motor Program Manager, describes:

The [FRR] would be held in a humongous conference room that looks like an auditorium. It's an open meeting. There might be one hundred–one hundred and fifty people there. Be a whole raft of people, ninety percent of whom weren't going to ask you any questions . . . .it's a great drama. Sometimes people give very informative, very interesting presentations. That's drama in a way. And it's an adversarial process. I think there are some people who have, what's the word, there is a word for when you enjoy somebody else's punishment . . . masochistic, they are masochistic. You know, come in and watch Larry Wear or Larry Mulloy or Thiokol take a whipping from the Board. There are people who I think actually come to watch that element.

It's serious work. There are reputations at stake, not just individuals, but the Center itself. . . . You don't leave the Center to give a significant briefing unless the Center senior management is aware of what you're doing, and that Board was a means of doing it. He [Lucas] was looking after the institution's image and his own. One reason is because he becomes a member of this thing, as it gets on up higher. He doesn't want to go to the high-level board and sit there and then be embarrassed by what his people are saying.

There are standards to be upheld. He challenges the technical information. Lucas and the Board ask very hard questions, going into details much deeper than what's presented to them in the charts. You've got to be able to answer any question. And he challenges the style of the presentation. He [Lucas] requires you to present the things up to the standards of Marshall Space Center, and I heard him say several times, he'd stop something and he'd turn to the man's boss, and he'd say, "Jim, I just don't believe this represents the standards of this Center, do you?" Of course, Jim would say, "No, sir, I certainly don't." (Vaughan 1996, 219-20).

This FRR produced considerable anxiety. Presenting there was likened to being in a "fishbowl" (Vaughan 1996). It also produced intense competition between groups to look good in this ultimate of public displays.

Vaughan (1996: 275) reports that the FRR structure was "deliberately created to seek unfavorable information that challenged the decision to accept risk and fly." We know from research in organizations, however, that formal structure can be substantially altered by informal relations (Dalton 1959; Hynes and Prasad 1997). It is important to remember that only a handful of the 100 or more people attending the Marshall Center Board FRR actively participated. Hence, though the FRR was designed to be "adversarial," it was most of all intimidating. The objective for presenters was not to debate, but "to answer any question." It was not so much a "review" as a grilling. It is significant that a flight was rarely delayed because of FRR deliberations (Vaughan 1996). Indeed, as I will show, the central effects of the FRR were to inculcate fear, demonstrate power, and punish the wayward. It was, above all, a ritual of management control.

To understand the FRR ritual it is important, I think, to draw attention to the fear that the FRR created. If an engineer would question the decision process without quantitative evidence, he/she was taking "an occupational risk, jeopardizing the engineers' professional integrity, causing them to lose face" (Vaughan 1996, 249). In this sense, the scientific paradigm was used at the FRR as a weapon of intimidation. However, it was used to intimidate for other reasons than to demand quantitative data. Leon Ray, Marshall engineer, stated, "If a guy is too conservative, he's "shootin' down launches"; if he's too conservative, you will find someone else in that position" (Vaughan 1996, 230). Hence, "scientific" methods were used for other reasons than interpreting fact; they were used to enforce the flight schedule.

The FRR ritual was the primary mechanism for creating the social and emotional transformations that resulted in the unified "scientific" culture. This can be seen in Larry Wear's imagination of the FRR. To begin with, he stated that the conference room where the FRR was held was "like an auditorium." This characterization highlights the public nature of the FRR, that it was a collective enactment. It also gives us the first clue to the centrality of seeing in the experience of the FRR. Auditoriums are places where large groups can watch presentations by individuals or smaller groups. The FRR was not a place for scientific debate; it was a place to observe a message. The audience did not hear debate; they saw criticism (that is, power). In this context, seeing is believing; thinking was not much required. This is the first transformation that the FRR ritual performed: It transformed participants into spectators.

It's important to note that the 100 or more people who attended the meeting were not required to come. They chose to come. The FRR was an open meeting. It was an interesting and/or significant event to them. That "ninety percent" of them did not speak shows the passive nature of their participation. They did not affect the meeting through activity, but merely by bearing witness. They observed what happened. Having 100 or more people silently observing the meeting lent legitimacy to the meeting. Weick (1997, 396) refers to this process as the "silence of consent." However, this "silence" grows loud as participants later inform others of what happened. Furthermore, the silence of consent implies that each of the participants knew that if they did speak up, they would most likely be alone. Aloneness, as was shown in the experiments of Asch (1951) on the effect of group pres-

sure on individual decision-making, strongly correlates with conformity. The FRR atmosphere was not conducive to open communications.

The FRR was a "great drama." It was packed with emotion, interest, plot, stimulation, conflict, and story. It focused the mind on its
message, at once entertaining and informing. The presentations were
informative, and that is a drama "in a way." But the deeper drama for
the audience was in getting to see individuals severely criticized and
careers destroyed. Wear felt the audience enjoyed seeing "somebody
else's punishment."[1] This was the essence of the FRR: a large audience was focused on the severe criticism of an individual. They were
all sharing the same feelings: the pleasure of seeing someone else
punished and/or the fear of knowing it could happen to them. Which-
ever identification particular individuals made, they were identifying
with an authoritarian management structure. Identification implies
obedience (Freud 1921). This is the second transformative dynamic of
the FRR ritual: By creating passive identification, the FRR at once
established and legitimated an authoritarian management culture.

There are two basic ways the FRR ritual successfully created passive identifications. First, it did so by creating *expectation*. Individuals
were attracted to the FRR because they expected to see peers severely
criticized. The drama was created by the expectation of this excite-
ment (Aristotle 1968). Expectation focused their attention, channeled
their interest. Indeed, the drama functioned to rivet their attention; it
generated a strong emotional and mental attachment to the event. This
is what gave the event its transformative power. By employing a standard aesthetic device—the progression of expectation—the FRR ritual
transformed participation into spectatorship, thus creating a unity (Rieff
1990). The result was a culture of passivity, the flipside of "science"
as power.

The second way the FRR ritual created passive identification was
repetition. By continuous repetition of severe criticism, passive observation became habitualized. Visualization as an aesthetic device is
very powerful when repeated. This also fueled the ritual's transformative power; it became, as can be seen in Wear's description, a central
institution in the Marshall organizational culture. It continually repeated the culture's key themes: the centrality of Mr. Lucas, everyone's
dependence on Mr. Lucas, "scientific" standards, Mr. Lucas's power
to make and destroy careers, and the competition between individuals

and groups to win Mr. Lucas's favor. These themes suggest that Marshall personnel were acting as a basic-assumption group, that is, overly focused on their own emotional needs (Turquet 1974). This can be seen in the obsessive importance of the leader; a great deal of attention simply went into observing his exercise of power. The result was a heightened feeling of dependency and thus a concern for security. Just how intense the concerns for security were can be measured by the extent of the passive participation.

Thus, out of a collection of engineers and managers from diverse backgrounds and multiple projects, a unity was created. The aesthetic functions of the FRR ritual were indeed powerful. They created the "technical culture." However, it can be seen that the scientific standards of the "technical culture" were only the first layer of this culture. The deeper layer was the centrality of Mr. Lucas and his use of power to create the drama of the FRR. Indeed, in this context the "scientific standards" should be seen as an organizational control device. They were used not only to criticize, but also to limit possible action. The FRR did not challenge flight recommendations so much as the opposite: It made it difficult to stop the flight schedule. By turning participants into spectators, the FRR ritual solidified a regime of power.

Mr. Lucas appears distinctly as an individual in Wear's description of the FRR ritual. Indeed, he is the only one. The ritual allows only for three roles: the one (usually Mr. Lucas, but occasionally the Board) who criticizes; the person who is criticized; and the many who passively observe. Except for Lucas and the Board, there is a loss of individuality in the other two roles. The vast majority of participants become spectators of the ritual itself, watching it unfold as if by an inexorable power. The audience is dissolved into the process. By becoming spectators of themselves, they become instruments of organizational power. The loss of individuality in the FRR is a key mechanism in the transfer of power (Schwartz 1990). The loss of individual autonomy is replaced by the all-powerful autonomy of "science." "Science," not the individual, becomes responsible for decision-making. This exaggerated investment in method suggests that "science" and the FRR process have taken on magical properties in the minds of some participants (Diamond 1991; Hirschhorn and Young 1990; Turquet 1974). This is implied when the individual puts his/her faith in a method or process but then takes no personal responsibility for it. It is as if the process works by itself, magically.

The context of intimidation in the FRR ritual is central to achieving this loss of individual responsibility. It was not the technical culture per se that caused irrationally narrow thinking, but its use as an instrument of power. The managers and engineers attending FRRs were keen on avoiding responsibility for "holding up a launch" (Vaughan 1996, 242). As we saw, it was not just the production schedule that was at stake, but the individual's career progress. It is in this social environment that the *Challenger* disaster must be understood. Individuals made choices in response to the intimidating environment. These choices must be seen as moral choices because they impact others. Hence, these choices had to run the gauntlet of the individual's sense of guilt (Freud 1936).

The FRR ritual, however, offered a means to avoid this morally disturbing and potentially career–damaging personal decision. By transferring individual responsibility to the FRR process, the individual could flee the difficult decision. Vaughan (1996) argues that the scientific paradigm was a legitimate macro–institution that justified the rules for evidence at the FRR. This belief leads her to conclude that legitimate institutions and the rules derived from them were responsible for the tragic outcome (Allinson 1998). However, I argue that the individual is reduced to an automaton in this explanation. The fact is that there were "concerns" about safety that were not reported because of a lack of quantitative evidence. Larry Mulloy, Marshall Solid Rocket Booster Project Manager, for example, did not include his "temperature concerns" in his FRR presentation because he could not answer all questions that would be asked (Vaughan 1996, 222). In so doing, he made a decision to protect himself or trust the decision process. If it was the former, then a moral choice was made; if it was the latter, then a transfer of responsibility took place between the individual and the process. Given that the lives of astronauts and civilians were at stake, one would think that the transfer of responsibility would generate at least some discomfort.

In the Marshall culture, however, there is evidence that the significance of death was repressed. Death was referred to by the engineers as having "a long day ... [or] ... a bad day" (Vaughan 1996, 253). Hynes and Prasad (1997) find jokes about death at a coalmine operating in an unsafe work environment before an explosion at the mine killed 26 people. Indeed, Janis (1972) finds that laughing about danger was a typical characteristic of groupthink. In the high-pressure environment at NASA where a culture of fear had been established, it seems likely that the engineers repressed their feelings about death as a means to avoid the anxiety they felt about the risks they were taking with other people's lives. The repression of death, in this context, can be seen as a means to avoid individual responsibility. It dovetails, on the organizational level, with the FRR ritual, that turns participants into spectators. The FRR ritual, then, can be seen as the organizational mechanism that translates the outside pressures that Vaughan identifies—for example, Reagan's premature announcement that the shuttle was operational—into individual behavior.

Nonetheless, there are several reasons why turning the FRR screw into the hearts and minds of participants cannot be completely accounted for by Vaughan's theory of unconscious macro forces. First, as was shown in the case overview, several engineers at Morton Thiokol wrote memos disagreeing with the conclusion that it was safe to fly. If universal macro forces were dominant, these disagreements would not have arisen. Second, we saw that engineers and managers feared giving presentations at the Marshall Center Board FRR run by Director Lucas. The harshness of this FRR and the fear it generated were not part of the institutional context. Clearly, they can be better accounted for by the management style of Mr. Lucas. Third, the research on conformity and obedience concludes that individuals tend to conform to majorities and/or figures of authority. In the FRR both a silent majority and dominating leader were present, supporting the view that semi-autonomous organizational dynamics were a key factor. Fourth, the death jokes suggest that the engineers were suffering discomfort with the decision-making process (Freud 1938). If they were truly under the sway of institutional criteria that justified the flight risks, they would have little need to release anxiety through jokes about death. Finally, if the institutional context controlled the minds of participants to the extent Vaughan argues, the fear, anxiety, and tension of the FRR process would never have arisen. There would have been no need to punish the wayward and demonstrate power. Consensus would have been a less conflicted outcome.

Conclusion

This analysis of the Marshall Center Board FRR suggests that conformity enforced by fear was a key factor in rendering the decision process dysfunctional. Participants in the FRR feared severe criticism or career setbacks from "poor" performance at the FRR. The result was exaggerated basic-assumption needs, especially for security. This is why a culture of passivity was established at the Marshall Space Center. By not participating, engineers sought to avoid attack.

It appears that the original design of the FRR was intended to avoid just such an outcome. By establishing a bottom-up process, different responsibilities given to different groups, and multiple levels of review, the decision process was structured to maximize debate, argumentation, and confrontation. What went wrong? First, the culture established at Marshall undermined the FRR structure. Second, the contractor system made it difficult for Morton Thiokol to confront its client, Marshall, for fear of losing its contract (Winsor 1988). What is needed in this situation is extra vigilance to maintain a culture that balances suspicion of ideas with trust that criticism will not bring retaliation. A balance must be found between destructive levels of competition and stifling conformity. Marshall found its home in the latter. While a balance is always hard to achieve and maintain, in a high-pressure environment including a contractor relationship, it might well have been impossible.

The key to achieving the balance is leadership. The leader must be a first among equals, willing to accept criticism of his/her own ideas and accept the same treatment generally given to everyone else (Janis 1972; Turquet 1974). Lucas, on the contrary, dished out criticism but did not establish an atmosphere where his own opinions could receive the same treatment. This exaggerated the centrality of his role in the organization and encouraged the fantasy that he was responsible for everything and had everything under control. What Lucas needed to do was use his centrality to establish himself as a role model who was willing to listen to criticism and not retaliate. He needed to establish norms that it was safe to convey bad news and important to communicate doubts. This would increase the chances that someone would speak out and, as Asch (1955) notes, dissent by one increases the independence of others. In Asch's research, the presence of dissent resulted in fewer errors. Dissent is also a key source for the formation of subgroups which Weick (1993) considers to be important for training the leader and increasing organizational adaptation.

For leaders to create a culture of debate and discussion, they need the support of the broader organizational context. Clearly, as Vaughan's

(1996) detailed analysis of NASA's institutional history demonstrates, Lucas did not have this support. He operated in a pressure-cooker environment with top level administrators more focused on fund-raising and public relations than on organizational management (Brody 1986). In this environment, the culture of conformity at Marshall became isolated. The multiple levels of review at the FRRs were designed to catch errors in scientific logic, not pathologies in organizational culture. The culture of conformity, repeatedly dramatized in the FRR process, permeated the behaviors of Marshall managers. On the night of the unprecedented *Challenger* launch decision, after Marshall managers pressured Morton Thiokol managers to reverse their launch decision, Vaughan (1996, 328) reports that the Marshall managers did not report the conflict to Director Lucas because they did not want to "—wake the old man—." Or were they trying to avoid his wrath?

With organizational leadership operating in a basic-assumption mode, it is difficult to avoid the development of a dysfunctional organizational culture. One possible counterforce to the break down of leadership is the professional culture of the engineers. In this case, the engineers were, along with the managers, swamped by the organizational culture. If the engineers had been clearer about and more committed to their own professional standards, they might have had the emotional and ideal resources to resist top management's confusion.

Note

1. Of course, Larry Wear meant "sadistic" when he said "masochistic" as the "word for when you enjoy somebody else's punishment." This unconscious slip by Mr. Wear suggests the repression of sadistic or aggressive urges. Hence, just as Wear felt the audience enjoyed watching peers get crucified, Wear too had a strong attraction to it. So strong, in fact, he had to repress it. A key meaning of the "scientific" culture, then, was its significance as power. In other words, the severe criticism in the name of "scientific" standards was a vehicle for the expression and pleasure of power.

Part 4

Ethical Relativism

6

The Revolt Against Cultural Authority: Power/Knowledge as an Assumption in Organization Theory

Foucault-inspired organization theory has interpreted the Enlightenment effort to make reason the foundation for human freedom as a failure. Reason is seen as developing into "disciplinary knowledge," which dominates modern organizations and the individuals who live and work in them. In fact, the individual's very identity is the means by which the individual is enslaved. Knowledge is thus seen as nowhere separate from power.

In this chapter, I will use a concept of traditional authority to examine Foucault-inspired organization theory and its power/knowledge conceptual framework in terms of their ethical and cultural implications.[1] My approach will highlight the Foucault-inspired misinterpretation of the effect of the Enlightenment on modern organizations, its rejection of the authority of the past as a basis for moral order, and its impossible attempt to find "freedom" through the destruction of cultural authority.

Developments in the modern period, roughly the last two hundred years, have had both good and evil effects on human life. On the positive side, great strides have been made in such areas as the rule of law, democratic government, equality of opportunity, and the rights of minorities (Selznick 1992). On the negative side, the present age has experienced organizations designed for totalitarian killing run similar to modern manufacturing plants (Bauman 1989). Involved in both of these phenomena is the modern idea of *reason*: reason has played a central part in the democratic revolutions of the eighteenth century and the mass murder campaigns of the twentieth century.

Modern history clearly has implications for organization theory and practice (Burrell 1994). Reason, or what is usually discussed in terms of rationality (Schluchter 1981), plays a central role in modern organi-

zational life. The literature on evaluating this role has been characterized as a heated debate (Power 1990). On one hand, modern management theory has been concerned primarily with rationalizing business
organization in terms of top management control (Scott 1992). On the
other hand, postmodernists argue that this combination of rationalizing
processes and control has led to totalitarian domination in organizations (Burrell 1988; Cooper and Burrell 1988). The postmodernists
recommend a process of "deconstruction" to dismantle the oppressive
nature· of these rationalizing processes (Cooper, 1989; Linstead and
Grafton-Small 1992).

A third position, closely allied with that of the postmodernists, is
critical organization theory (Alvesson and Willmott 1992a). Critical
organization theory, like postmodern organization theory, is against
the "narrow instrumentality" of rationalizing work-process relationships (Alvesson and Willmott 1992b, 4).[2] However, following Habermas
(1971), and splitting from the postmodernists, critical theorists seek to
save reason from its enslavement in the "distortions and inequalities
that have developed historically" (Mingers 1992, 98). Critical organization theory seeks to create "ideal speech" through which individuals
can "communicate freely and reach consensus" (Morgan 1992, 147).
The key to securing ideal speech is to dismantle "asymmetrical relations of power" (Alvesson and Willmott 1992b, 12). In Habermas,
however, there is an "almost total lack of sustained discussion of
power" (Mingers 1992, 106). Habermas's "ideal speech" is just that—
an ideal. Critical organization theorists thus call for the development
of a theory of power (Mingers 1992; Morgan 1992). This has resulted
in a shared interest with the postmodernists in the *power/knowledge*
framework of Michel Foucault.

For Foucault, reason is inseparable from power because it exists,
socially, as "disciplinary knowledge" (Townley 1993). Disciplinary
knowledge turns knowledge into a system of domination by creating
universal definitions of reality and of the individual's place in it that
limit and constrain the possibilities for thought and action. Knowledge
is seen as a subcategory of power, since it is used for social and
psychological control (Taylor 1984). Critical organization theorists have
learned, using Foucault's framework, that accounting (Power and
Laughlin 1992), marketing (Morgan 1992), and human resource management (Steffy and Grimes 1992) are just some of the disciplines that
"adversely delimit the self at work" (Steffy and Grimes 1992, 188).

The disciplines of management theory have thus become invisible prisons within which workers are controlled and oppressed (Deetz 1992).

In this chapter, I examine this view of modern culture and management and the power/knowledge framework as they are used in the writings of critical and postmodern organization theorists in terms of their ethical and cultural implications. I use a nonmodern concept of traditional authority to carry out the analysis (Arendt 1968; MacIntyre 1984; Rieff 1985). The concept of traditional authority has three main components. First, it posits the authority of the past; that is, the authority of the past is seen as essential for the maintenance of a stable social (thus moral) life by ensuring continuity between the past, present, and future. Second, for a life to be meaningful, the individual must belong to a social whole that maintains a hierarchy of beliefs. Third, beliefs require boundaries that define what is included and what is excluded. Hence, in the analysis of Foucault-inspired organization theory, I will be concerned with how the past is viewed, how moral boundaries are treated, and what relationship the individual has to the group.

As we apply a concept of traditional authority to modern culture, it will be seen that the key characteristic of modern culture is not reason, but cultural fragmentation. In fact, the Foucault-inspired position criticizing reason as a totalitarian unity will be shown to be a particular variant of rationalism itself, in the form of Nietzschean skepticism. Instead of assuming that the Enlightenment has led to universal systems of domination, I will show that the original impulse of Enlightenment thinking—an attack on patriarchal authority—has been broadened out to an attack on authority in any possible form. The Foucault-inspired criticism of "power/knowledge relations," with its search for individual "freedom," represents exactly this intolerance of authority. It is the last possible stop on the Enlightenment road to a world of nihilism, where even individual identity is rejected.

In essence, critical organization theory and postmodern organization theory have interpreted Foucault as collapsing the distinction between authority and power. For them, all discipline has become power/knowledge. This reduction raises individual autonomy to the supreme value while simultaneously devaluing collective existence. Indeed, in critical organization theory, cultural authority is seen as totalitarian oppression, suffocating its central goals of individual empowerment and democratic process in organizations. However, as will be shown, the extreme individualism underlying the critical and postmodern position can only increase the role of power in organizations, because the rejection of cultural authority leaves nothing remaining except power. Democracy is, after all, a political process attempting to regulate power interests.

The Decline of Culture in Modernity

The distinctive characteristic of modern culture is fragmentation. A key force in modern cultural fragmentation is capitalistic economic organization because it generates a continuous need for new products and new markets (Jameson 1984). This need has led to the implosion of all cultural boundaries due to the continuous transformation of time and space (Marsden and Townley 1995). In this setting, words and symbols lose their traditional relationship to referents, transforming social and cultural organization. Class cultures that had once controlled cultural habits and meanings have mostly disappeared. Consumption-oriented behavior has become the key modality of modern culture, especially in the decades since the great economic expansion and technological development that followed World War II (Heller 1993). Moreover, since consumption is based on a constantly changing pluralization of tastes, cultural identification has become shallow and unstable.

The loss of class organization has also had a negative effect on politics because classes have been part of the foundation of representative government. Corporations now dominate the social landscape, but they are not "life wholes" (Heller 1993). At bottom, they are functionally motivated. This has further increased what Tocqueville (1850) considered a natural tendency in modern democracies, toward "mass society." In mass society, individuals make little or no identifications with the range of social groups between themselves and the intimidating image of the society as a whole. Stauth and Turner (1988, 519) have referred to this condition as "cultural egalitarianism" because equality acts as a social leveling mechanism, thus undermining the social distinctions needed to define classes or groups. Importantly, the effect of this leveling on culture is destructive because, as the individual gets lost in the crowd, public opinion becomes "a sort of religion, with the majority as its prophet" (Tocqueville 1850, 436). In addition, this particular "prophet," having a very short memory, does not provide consistent moral leadership (Riesman, 1950; Stivers, 1994).

Democratic cultural tendencies toward extreme individualism and toward domination by a fickle majority have been criticized by intellectuals as a loss of moral standards over the past two hundred years. Some intellectuals have called for a return to stable structures of cultural authority (Burke 1791; Bell 1976). Other writers, however, have pointed out that intellectuals have not fared well in terms of social status in the culture of egalitarianism (O'Neill 1988). Their role as protectors of a dominant culture has been lost, and it has been argued that their claims of extreme individualism and moral decay have been exaggerated (O'Neill 1988). I doubt, however, that these claims have been exaggerated, given the wide-ranging acceptance totalitarian regimes have received from their citizens in this century (Bauman 1989).

Intellectuals have responded to the fragmentation of modern culture in numerous other ways (Stauth and Turner 1988). One way that affects our view of moral truth is Friedrich Nietzsche's (1886) announcement of the "death of God," which recognized the release of the individual from Christian structures of moral authority. Nietzsche encourages the individual to develop a robust skepticism: "What is falling, that one should also push!" (Nietzsche in Kaufmann 1974: 109). With Nietzsche, Enlightenment individualism takes a fantastic step beyond political autonomy toward psychological autonomy from all cultural authority.

Foucault-Inspired Organization Theory and the Loss of Historical Memory[3]

Culture is the war before the shooting starts. This has never been so apparent as it is in modern culture, with its central value of individualism and the endless creation of cultural "innovation" that has resulted from it. Importantly, in organization theory, the original Enlightenment notion of reason has remained a robust competitor in the cultural wars that it originated. In critical organization theory, reason can be seen in its central goal of *emancipation*. Alvesson and Willmott (1992c, 435) write, "Central to CT is the emancipatory potential of reason to *reflect* critically on how the reality of the social world, including the construction of the self, is socially produced and, therefore, is open to transformation." In this view, organization conflict can be resolved through "better discussions" because moral shortcomings are "constrained by better negotiations rather than by community principles" (Deetz 1995, 223). Hence, confidence in reason ("better negotiations") and distrust of collective moral structures ("community principles") are integral to critical organization theory.

In this view, however, reason is not free to do its transformative work. In modern life, reason has become imprisoned in culture and the result is totalitarian systems of rational domination (Cooper and Burrell 1988; Willmott 1994). This is the conclusion of both critical organization theory *and* postmodern organization theory. Although there are numerable influences, an unambiguous relation to Nietzsche can be discerned. This can be seen clearly in Foucault-inspired organization theorists, who reject modernism's assumption of a rational and autonomous person, because the rational person is seen as manipulated. Deetz (1992, 37) writes,

> Disciplinary power resides in every perception, every judgment, every act. In its positive sense it enables, and negatively it excludes and marginalizes . . . .Rather than analyzing power in the organization as if it were a sovereign state, the conception of power has to be reformed to account for this more massive and invisible structure of control. Administration has to be seen in relation to order and discipline if its power is to be understood. . . . It is not just the rule and routine which become internalized, but a complex set of practices which provide common sense, self-evident experience and personal identity.

Identity itself is seen as the lever of manipulation and control. Thus, there is a call to "de-center" the subject (Burrell 1988). This is to be accomplished through "disciplines of 'de-subjection' which accept and promote a lived acceptance of the contingency and discontinuity of 'nothingness' of self-identity" (Willmott 1994, 90). In other words, the individual must avoid any commitment to a stable identity. Self-identity must remain mobile. This is to be carried out through a process of "perpetual critique" (Deetz 1992, 36).

The idea of de-subjection raises a few problems. First, by critiquing all structures of cultural authority, the individual will be forced into a state of pure contemporaneity. But living in a state of the pure present, if it were possible, would make life meaningless because meaning requires stable symbolic and linguistic structures connecting the present with the past (Dilthey, 1883). Second, living in a condition of "contingency and discontinuity" would destroy the boundary between internal perception and external reality (Winnicott 1971). Without a stable self, how would the individual know what is not-self?

Despite the impossibility of de-subjection, this view has had a wide influence. Gergen (1992, 217), for example, writes of a critical suspension of one's own beliefs and recommends instead the view that there be "no language of understanding placed beyond the boundaries of potential." In other words, all beliefs must remain relaxed to avoid stifling potential ideas. This position appears to come more than dangerously close to nihilism, though Gergen believes that the real danger is in taking ideas too seriously and thus closing off pragmatic options. However, pragmatism, in continuously reevaluating ends, tends to reduce ends to means (Dumont 1986). As a result, managers find themselves incapable of taking moral positions (MacIntyre 1984). It would seem that Gergen, Willmott, Deetz and others believe they can somehow destroy their identity and have it too.

Another example is Clegg (1995, 163), who states, "What one takes to be sacred and what one takes to be profane depend utterly on relations of meaning." The anguished question of conscience drops out of his understanding of the sacred. His reference to the sacred as a "language game" destroys the idea of what the sacred signifies: a deeply personal commitment to faith in revealed truth. Indeed, Knights and Willmott, in a telling loss of historical memory, speak of the "religious worldview of the Dark Ages" (1989, 536). They appear to collapse all of religious history into the "Dark Ages." But it was precisely the crumbling of ancient religion that was an important cause of the Dark Ages (Masaryk 1994; Arendt 1968).

The entire discussion of modernism in the field of organization theory has taken place in a historical vacuum (Reed 1993). Burrell (1993, 79), for example, writes, "Rationality, regularity, science and technology, calculability, and prediction are almost always predicated upon a modernist project." This statement completely ignores the historical connection between processes of rationalization and nonmodern religion: "At all times and in all places, the need for salvation . . . has resulted from the endeavor of a systematic and practical rationalization of life's realities" (Weber 1915, 353). In fact, "modern" rationality originates in Christian "outworldly" individualism[4] and can never completely separate from Christian holism, because modern individualism is not understandable without a hidden residue of this outworldliness, that is, without a hidden faith that truth is possible

(Dumont 1986). Hence, with the loss of religious belief, modern rationality becomes a blind nostalgia, unconsciously assuming the existence of a whole it consciously rejects. This can be seen even in a modern mainstay such as accounting, where the audit, developed in the twelfth century at the height of Christian civilization, was used for the purpose of controlling goods, money, and people (Hoskin and Macve 1986). Thus, the distinctive feature of modernity is not its rationality or regulation, but the loss of any system of belief in which they make sense (Rieff 1987).

The discussion of rationality in Foucault-inspired organization theory has been stunted by the assumption that all relevant history begins in the eighteenth century. We read that modernity is totalizing and controlling (Cooper and Burrell 1988), and that the modern hope of emancipation has not shown much progress (Burrell 1994). Such discussions ignore the fact that eighteenth-century political individualism arose out of sixteenth-century religious individualism (Weber 1904–05; Tawney 1962). Indeed, the Enlightenment consumes all attention; the Reformation is completely forgotten. If the Reformation were remembered, however, the tendency to categorize universal beliefs as "totalitarian" would be recognized as historically false, because the label "totalitarian" would have to be applied to all Western religious history. In other words, Foucault-inspired organization theory cannot theoretically distinguish, for example, between the modern phenomenon of Stalinism and nonmodern Christian social ethics. Deetz (1992, 43), for example, states,

> To understand modern domination, we must take the routine, the commonsensical and the self-evident and subject them to reconsideration. The more distant dominations by the Church and kings were not simply forced on subjects but were routine and ritualized, reproduced in innumerable practices; they were consented to but not chosen.

This equating of modern organizational domination with Christian social ethics is misleading because Christian social ethics is a historical precursor to the rule of law, democratic government, and equality of opportunity (Troeltsch 1992), while Stalinism, for example, has no such connections. Foucault-inspired organization theorists grossly misread and simplify Western cultural history.

Postmodern and critical organization theorists have abandoned history as a motivation for human action (O'Neill 1988). This enables them to set up the strawman "modernism" as a foil to justify their attack on all cultural authority. In spite of their rejection of the authority of the past and their attack on modern reason, however, they still need a foundational assumption on which to base their position. They find this assumption in "nature." Knights and Willmott (1989, 542), for example, write, "The very openness of human subjectivity, which arises from the condition of being at once a part of, and apart from, nature (Bauman 1976; Giddens 1979) leads us to seek security in those social identities that are both available and valued in society." Alternatively, Cooper and Burrell (1988, 100) write of the "immanence of the body" as the fundamental element in social life. This return to nature as a foundational assumption is a return to one of the central themes in nineteenth century social science enamored, as it was, with the revolution in biology (Rieff 1979). Historically, it also represents a revolt against the Christian duality of flesh and spirit. A form of naturalism, then, replaces Western cultural history as a foundational assumption in critical and postmodern organization theory. Not only does this foundational assumption symbolize the timeless present; ironically, it goes uncriticized.

Upon this despiritualization of Western culture, critical and postmodern organization theorists build their case against Reason. They see reason as "disciplinary knowledge" in modern organizations because it constrains the natural autonomy of the individual (Townley 1993). In this view, all of the social sciences are seen as knowledge structures used in domination (McCarthy 1993). Sociology, social work, law, psychology, and most certainly management and organization theory are implicated. Just as psychology is used to persuade the individual to adjust to (thus accept) the external world (Willmott 1994), theories of leadership and organization are used to develop discourses and classification schemes that reproduce systems of power (Knights and Collinson 1987; Burrell 1988; Steffy and Grimes 1992). By rejecting Western cultural history, positing the "naturalness" of the individual, and assuming all discipline is oppressive power/knowledge, critical organization theory and postmodern organization theory elevate individualism, although only implicitly, to the role of their supreme value.

The Power/Knowledge System and the Individual

The power/knowledge framework assumes that before something can be governed or managed, it must first be known (Townley 1993). Knowledge delineates an analytic space and in so doing is implicated in relations of power, because that "space" becomes both a structure of perception and a means of intervention that controls the behavior of individuals (Townley 1993). Indeed, Foucault (1980) argues that it is impossible for knowledge not to engender power.

The power/knowledge concept is based on the idea of organized activity as a "unitary flow" (Cooper and Burrell 1988). There is a wish to see the whole of human activity as part of a single control system. Cooper and Burrell (1988, 105) write:

> A genealogy of system and organization begins with the recognition that representations and structures derive from a more fundamental process of materiality and energy. Ideas, images, discourse itself are now to be viewed as a material force that dissolves the conception of the human world as a series of divisions. This view is elaborated in a key postmodern text by Deleuze and Guattari in which social 'bodies' are defined as productive 'machines' which are continually engaged in the processing of matter (Deleuze and Guattari, 1983). The unitary point of view taken by Deleuze and Guattari rejects the representations of separate social terms, which means the concept of the productive machine applies to everything in the human (and natural) world: machines are individuals, groups, organizations and whole societies. This approach also means that we have to reject the usual conception of machines as extensions of human power; in fact, Deleuze and Guattari argue that man is actually an appendix of machines.

Clearly, the emphasis is on system, and the system is conceived as total. The individual is seen as highly dependent. Burrell (1988, 228) writes, "As the reader peruses this page, the gestures, the posture, the attitude, 'the dressage' adopted in this literary task are part of the political anatomy of society."

It comes as no surprise, then, that "prison" is chosen as the metaphor for organization (Burrell 1988; Linstead and Grafton-Small 1992; Parker 1992). Burrell (1988, 232) writes,

> The real point is not that most of us do not live in carceral institutions and can therefore escape from their discipline but that, as individuals, we are incarcerated within an organizational world. Thus, whilst we may not live in total institutions, the institutional organization of our lives is total. It is in this sense that Foucault's comment 'prisons resemble factories, schools, barracks, hospitals which all resemble prisons' has to be understood.

Hence, all organizations are essentially alike because their fundamental characteristic is that they are part of, according to Burrell (1988), a pervasive bureaucratic administrative apparatus. Power/knowledge is an omnipresent system of total control.

Truth plays the key role in this totalizing system. Truth becomes a tool of power. Power "produces reality . . . [through] . . . rituals of truth" (Foucault in Townley 1993, 522). These rituals control the individual internally by manufacturing belief. Foucault (1980, 131) repeatedly reminds us that "truth is not the reward of free spirits [but] . . . a thing of this world . . . [that is] . . . produced only by virtue of multiple forms of constraints." Each society creates its own "regime of truth" to control its population (Foucault, 1980, 131).

Foucault's view has attracted a considerable amount of criticism. McCarthy (1993, 54), who would agree that there is a "political economy of truth," sees the assumption of totalizing systematic control as diverting attention from questions of who possesses power, by what right, and who profits and suffers from it. He sees the framework as one-sided, replacing the abstract individualism of utilitarian theory with an equally abstract holism. We gain a greater sensitivity to the constraints of macro-structures like bureaucracy, but by seeing *only* these macro-structures, we falsely reduce the individual to insignificance.

Taylor (1984) argues that Foucault never explains how this totalizing system actually works, how power is able to achieve such totalizing systematicity. Taylor (1984) claims that Foucault reifies language, giving it absolute dominion over action, but in reality language never achieves such a level of control. Action always has partial independence. Like McCarthy, Taylor (1984) finds Foucault's totalizing system one-sided. The individual can always move to another organization and even within the same organization, the level and kind of power are different in different contexts (Dalton 1959).

Knights and Vurdubakis, however, argue that these views of Foucault are themselves one-sided. They claim that in a correct interpretation of Foucault, power relations can be seen as developing for "socio-historical reasons" and thus cannot be a "seamless web" (Knights and Vurdubakis 1994, 177-8). Power relations compete with and contradict each other and are seldom stable. Indeed, quoting Foucault, they observe, " 'power is only exercised over free subjects' ," thus " 'at the very heart of the power relationships. . .are the recalcitrance of the will and the intransigence of freedom' " (Foucault in Knights and Vurdubakis 1994, 179).

Despite Knights and Vurdubakis's (1994, 191) "paradoxical" reading of Foucault and despite claims to the contrary, however, they conclude:

> Foucault is not just saying that we need to support human rights as well as problematize their foundations and transformation – but that this support and problematization should proceed simultaneously; that is to say, we need to remain skeptical at one and the same time precisely of those rights that we support (and perhaps campaign for), if only to avoid the kind of self-subjugation or project identification which stifles critical judgment.

This is "skeptical" indeed. The ambivalence about "identification" takes us right back to the systematicity of oppressive power: identification itself is oppressive and the individual must guard against it by not identifying. Not much "recalcitrance of the will" here. Knights and Vurdubakis (1994) do recognize their problem and the problem with Foucault's concept of power/knowledge (they call it a "negative tool"), but they do so only in passing after spending their whole effort trying to justify the possibility of "resistance" in the Foucauldian world of systematic power.

It is an irony of Foucault-influenced organization theory that it has led to such great sensitivity to the use of "unexamined totalizing assumptions" (Knights and Vurdubakis 1994, 186), while its own use of power/knowledge "is totalizing itself" (Reed 1993, 168). The reader is repeatedly warned that "'structures' and 'contingencies' are abstractions that do not *do* anything" (Willmott 1994, 88), but then we find that power is so systematically "embedded in social practices . . . [that it] . . . transforms individuals into subjects . . . [making] . . . interpretive procedures" impossible (Knights and Willmott 1989, 540). In other words, power is so deeply embedded in organizations that the individual's opinion is always false. This position is extreme. Its theoretical formulation makes it impervious to contradictions from ethnographic fieldwork. In this sense, it resembles religion or myth more than science. It completely dismisses the complexities of history, psychology, and ethics. This reduction of everything, including our cultural heritage, to power/knowledge seeks a world of complete contemporaneity: an impossible world of the democratic now, where godlike individuals completely create themselves without any type of internalized social constraint.

The Popularity of the Power/Knowledge Framework

In attempting to understand the popularity of the power/knowledge framework among critical and postmodern organization theorists, a few general observations can be made. First, in an age dominated by bureaucratic control and overwhelming complexity, the idea of an impersonal power system in which power is everywhere and no one is in control, may have some intuitive appeal—and certainly speaks to the frustration generated by modern bureaucracies and the "personalities" that go with them. This helps to explain the popularity of the power/knowledge framework, but not its usefulness. Its usefulness in organization theory, however, has mostly been limited to an abstract polemic against the oppression of modern organizations (Thompson 1993).

Second, much of the interest in the power/knowledge framework in the discipline of organization theory can be found in writers influenced by "radical organization theory." Radical organization theory originates in the Marxist critique of capitalism (Marsden and Townley 1995). The power/knowledge framework fits well with the Marxist framework because both stress system-wide issues with only a secondary focus on the individual. Indeed, Marx considered psychology a derivative category of economic structure. It would appear, then, that the power/knowledge framework is liable to some of the same criticisms as the Marxian framework itself. Particularly relevant in this context is Marx's attempt to erase historical memory. For example, there is his conceptual metamorphosis that transforms the "sabbath Jew . . . [into the] . . . real Jew . . . [whose] . . . worldly god" is money (Marx 1844, 34). The power/knowledge framework also implies a destruction of historical memory in its reduction of all ideal existences to their implications for control.

Third, the power/knowledge framework democratizes power. Unlike many theories of power—Pfeffer (1981) and Mintzberg (1983), for example, show how power is exercised by one person or group over another—the power/knowledge notion of power includes everyone. Symbolically, power becomes the great equalizer because of its systemic character. One might say that the power/knowledge notion of power is "politically correct." The attraction of this notion is, I think, the fact that in a democratic "culture" where the "death of God" has turned all values into commodities which can be exchanged, discarded, or destroyed, the notion of cultural authority is questioned everywhere and its authoritative nature is perceived as mere power. The power/knowledge framework of systemic power relations thus appears to capture the pervasiveness of power, but without acknowledging the historical loss of cultural authority that created this situation. This is the misleading understanding of power that is promulgated by critical organization theory and postmodern organization theory.

Fourth, the conceptualization of power/knowledge is scientific in the sense that, unlike religious myths, it attacks transcendence. The power/knowledge framework clearly follows in the Enlightenment tradition that seeks freedom for the individual from oppressive systems of belief. Whether one recalls Descartes, who distrusted custom, or Marx, who saw religion as an "opiate," the warnings of Foucault-inspired organization theorists against systemic rationalities carry on a tradition of rebellion against communal authority. It is this rebellion and this desire for an impossible autonomy that continue to make the power/knowledge framework attractive today and lead many distrustful minds along the absurd road of endless criticism.

Power/Knowledge and the Loss of Moral Boundaries

The ethic of endless criticism can be seen clearly in Cooper and Burrell's (1988, 101) Foucault-inspired advice that one should try to avoid the "haste of wanting to know." Belief also is to be avoided. Postmodern "rationality is based not on finding answers to problems but of 'problemizing' answers" (Cooper and Burrell 1988, 101). The goal is to know how thoughts are put together to "force" an answer. As was seen, truth is a subcategory of power in the power/knowledge framework. It follows that truth is oppressive. It further follows that the road to freedom requires not only perpetual critique, but also a will to "'possible transgression'" (Foucault in McCarthy 1993, 62). Clearly, Foucault is heir to Enlightenment skepticism or what Nietzsche (1887, 307) called "intellectual cleanliness at any price." It is this faith in the kind of criticism that criticizes everything but itself that postmodern and critical management theorists have found in Foucault. But when criticism itself is what is most readily accepted, how do we cultivate the difference between right and wrong?

The Foucault-inspired perspective reduces all belief, all ethics, and all religion to the game of politics. The individual must become skilled at transgression in order to win. It is hard to imagine how the commit-ment and sacrifice required for organization will be forthcoming if all belief is rejected or at least questioned and all discipline is seen as oppressive. Indeed, as Reed (1993) has commented, postmodernism becomes absurd when pushed to its logical limits. Without stable, unquestioned internal (that is, moral) controls, all social order would become dependent on external controls. This, in fact, is what is hap-pening (Elshtain 1995). The continuing increase in police forces and prisons in the United States today follows from the breakdown of internal discipline. "Prison" is truly becoming more important, but not as a metaphor.

But since critical and postmodern organization theorists see stable moral boundaries as tools of power, they agitate for complete open-ness. Deetz (1992, 35-6) writes,

> The modern corporate power is not a monolithic extension of class politics, but more like a web of arbitrary asymmetrical relations with specific means of deci-sion and control . . . .The force of these arrangements is primarily in producing order, forgetfulness and dependency . . . .Our opening to the future is better seen in the perpetual critique of each consensus and claim to rationality, but not for the sake of better reasoning and new consensus. The recovery of lost conflict and the retention of on-going decision-making against presumption and closure can be developed as the central critical goal.

Yet the absence of inner controls and the consensus on which they are based would open up potential action in all directions, including re-verse directions. Historically, an attitude of openness to action has been the defining trait of the totalitarian character (Rieff 1985). Hitler's motto was "Everything is possible" (Arendt 1950, 138). Hence, with-out internal controls, the totalitarian character is open to *any* action required to accomplish its goals. *Totalitarian* means total openness. In organizations, a population of "open" individuals can be easily con-trolled and easily organized for criminal purposes (Bauman 1989). This is the lesson of the Holocaust. The Holocaust grew out of an atomization of society that resulted from a historical breakdown of cultural authority (Arendt 1950). The postmodernists are wrong to assume that totalitarian killing is reducible to instrumental reason gone wild (Burrell 1988; Stauth and Turner 1988)—another explanation through abstraction that is characteristic of the postmodern perspec-tive. We must stop blaming ideas for immoral behavior. Only the individual can take responsibility for her/his actions.

Truth/Knowledge and Organizational Morality

It is this misidentification of instrumental reason as the essence of modern culture that leads Foucault-inspired organization theorists to argue for individual autonomy as their ultimate goal. However, without a stable organizational culture in which common sense and common standards act as a safeguard against the openness or "freedom" that these theorists call for, we become vulnerable to totalitarianism. Shared belief is required to stabilize self-respect. History demonstrates that self-respect will be sought in one way or another. Better that it should be found in the *truth/knowledge* of time-honored organizational traditions than in charismatic or democratic totalitarianism (the latter a predictable problem for critical and postmodern organizational theory, because their celebration of individualism and contemporaneity leaves them vulnerable to pressures for conformity).

Freedom must be limited in order to be meaningful. This truth has been forgotten, but it has been taught by many, from Socrates (MacIntyre 1984) to Durkheim (1925) and Freud (1930). The notion of power/knowledge is supposed to demystify oppressive systems, but its extremism will result in the general weakening of cultural constraint. Cultural constraint makes social life possible by putting limits on all of us; it is the only way to make life meaningful and thus livable. Those who would make psychological openness the key value in a social philosophy and perpetual criticism the key means of achieving it, will find that the destruction of cultural constraints is inevitable. This will lead to a loss of freedom—because freedom is meaningful and organizationally practical only within specified limits.

Truth/knowledge is the essence of culture. By making truth a subcategory of power, Foucault relativizes culture, making truth impossible (Taylor 1984). Taylor argues that this relativization of culture is invalid because our culture has a history. We have a truth that is independent of power. Our truth exists in the present, while based on the past and pressing into the future (Arendt 1968). The range of meaning is limited.

Critical and postmodern organization theorists forget these limits because they forget history. Instead, they seek a world without limits (postmodernism) or a completely contemporary world populated by fully rational decision makers (critical theory). But these worlds are impossible. They both assume that only the System can be evil, and that once it is destroyed, man/woman will again become innocent. But evil has been pervasive in human history in all kinds of social systems. Evil is a part of human life because it arises from the loss of the good (Augustine). This is why all societies before the modern period instituted systems of moral demand to cultivate the good. These systems were separate from, but related to, political control. Critical and postmodern organization theorists have reduced these two systems to one, the political. Critical organization theorists claim that only democratic process is needed to regulate social life in organizations. Their blaming of evil on abstractions, misunderstanding of the role of moral truth in history, and wish for a completely contemporary social life demonstrate a naive conception of the inner life of the individual and the relationship of the inner life to the social world.

Organizations require established moral systems in order to maintain moral behavior; a democracy of criminals will not produce good results. Moral standards must be deeply internalized in the individual to be strong enough to resist the questionable opportunities and rewards common to organizational life. The pragmatism of Deetz (1992), for example, is problematic because it depends completely on the rational capacities of individuals. However, democratic moral standards tend to be reduced to the aggregate self-interest of the individuals involved (Tocqueville 1850). Moral standards must be autonomous from political process to some extent in order to avoid being drowned in power politics. Organizations require truth/knowledge as the basis of their moral demand system. Truth/knowledge must be maintained in organizational traditions, which should change, but with a concern for continuity and maintenance. Only in this way will the individuals' powerful tendency to rationalize selfish and destructive behavior be confronted with a moral standard that is independent of that rationalizing capacity.

Conclusion

All organizations have a past, and the way they relate to their past is key in determining how they act in the present and how they plan for the future. From the past we get the moral weight to counterbalance the lightness of our present acts. It is the past, and the past only, that can provide moral depth through tradition. Tradition provides a road map through our past to point out the moral treasures and show us what their worth is. The destruction of tradition in modernity is a great loss because we have lost contact with the moral lessons of those who have come before us and can no longer learn from their experience. Perpetual criticism condemns us to perpetual ignorance.

Why is tradition an important concept in the study of organizations? Tradition makes possible the investigation of moral stability or the lack of it over time in the experience of organization members. Moreover, tradition is essential to establishing and maintaining an ethical frame within which the organization can operate. It is a form of constraint that provides approval for some actions and disapproval for others. The power/knowledge framework, designed to throw off the burden of the past, leaves individuals unconstrained in the face of the immediacy of their desires. This remarkable belief in the goodness of the unconstrained individual, freed from the evil of the oppressive System, expresses an act of faith that is humbled not at all in comparison with the world's great religions.

What it does not do, however, is demonstrate any basis for organization morality. The concept of tradition, on the other hand, directs organizations to come to terms with their indebtedness to people who have come before them. This enables organizations to benefit from past accomplishments, especially those of a moral nature, that can be idealized to provide moral guidance in cases of conflict or in the face of ethically ambiguous opportunities to produce a profit. This will help resolve some of the cultural ambiguity that organization theorists have been pointing out for decades. Ambiguity has an internal relationship to individualism. Shared moral traditions in organizations can at least temper the unpredictability of organizational politics, a root cause of "ambiguity."

Why is the concept of tradition essential in analyzing and evaluating the contributions of critical organization theory and postmodern organization theory? These frameworks, with their great sensitivity to cultural structures of oppression are one-sided. They greatly underestimate and misconstrue the importance of moral and cultural authority. Indeed, they reduce ethics to individual freedom; and critical organization theory goes so far as to posit an unhampered democratic process as the ultimate goal for organization ethics. But unethical people cannot be saved by democratic process. They simply reduce it to democratic power politics—an empirically familiar version of power more so than the abstract "power/knowledge" system. Hence, the concept of tradition points up the naive idea of organization ethics inherent in both critical organization theory and postmodern organization theory.

More importantly, the concept of tradition, with its sensitivity to historical context, was able to demonstrate these theories' misunderstanding of both the historical context of the Enlightenment and the effect it had on modern organizations. The concept of tradition is of importance for the very reason that the Enlightenment attacked all traditional authority. The attempt of critical organization theory and postmodern organization theory to begin history with modernity implies all nonmodern (especially traditional) forms of social organization are oppressive. Not only does this deny the irremovable fact of tradition in human social life, but the central role of religion in Western civilization for several millennia is dropped as if it were an irrelevance from the "Dark Ages." This shows up in the extremely limited grasp of ethics and extreme reduction of belief to oppression. Hence, critical (that is, modern) organization theory and postmodern organization theory grow out of the same root: the Enlightenment attack on traditional authority. Their own unique contribution, which is systematized through their reading of Foucault, is to extend the attack to *all* forms of authority.

The concept of tradition is essential, then, in evaluating what a completely contemporary world would be like, for that is what these two theories, with their reduction of ethics to individualism and religion and tradition to oppression, have to offer. Tradition represents an opposite, ideal type to the endless contemporaneity of endless criticism. Tradition assumes that there are positive values to be found in our history (Christian humility, for example) and that these values are not only worth preserving, but also worth following. Tradition stands against complete openness to possibility, because action can produce evil as well as good. Tradition implies cautiousness toward our freedom, because the evil potential of man/woman cannot be reduced to a System—capitalist, power/knowledge, or other. Thus, destroying culture in the process of eluding power/knowledge amounts to a dangerous and doomed project.

How can the concept of tradition be used to analyze organizations? First, historical analysis is a necessary part of studying the cultural aspects of organizations. Historical analysis should be combined with the analysis of symbolic structures. A necessary part of grasping symbolic structures is understanding their origin and change over time. In this way, traditional elements in the culture of an organization can be identified. All organizations have these elements. Once the traditional elements have been discovered, the concept of tradition can be of use in analyzing the role they play in the life of the organization; that is, how are individual-group relations regulated, what is the range in which moral behavior is sanctioned and how are transgressions dealt with, and how is the past maintained in the present and passed on over time? In this way, it is possible to evaluate the stability of the organization culture and to determine the public or shared nature of organization life. Of course, I refer here to the "culture" that can be discovered only through an extended period of ethnographic fieldwork, and not to any crafted ideology coming out of top management.

Second, the concept of tradition is essential for analyzing the ethical character of an organization. I agree with Durkheim that an ethics that is easily open to change or that easily changes lacks a definitive part of moral culture: discipline. For a group to be ethical, it must internalize ethical principles. Thus, change in ethical beliefs must include a character change which, to be meaningful, is slow and difficult to achieve. A rapid change in ethics is a bad thing, since it implies shallowness. This is a major problem with pragmatism; it is too closely aligned with modern rationality and its naive view of man/woman. The concept of tradition focuses on enduring moral patterns over time, thereby concentrating on the less conscious aspects of morality. Here the hierarchical nature of moral values can be investigated through their dominance in actual decision-making situations. The concept of tradition helps us to analyze the hairline difference between legitimate authority and power, a difference completely lost in Foucault-inspired organization theory.

Notes

1. This will include Foucault's influence on *both* the literature in critical organization theory and postmodern organization theory.
2. I am using the word "theory" in the original Platonic sense as an instrument for vision. Critical management studies and postmodern studies of organization, since they enable us to see organization in particular ways, are thus seen as theories of organization.
3. I am very much aware that some of Foucault's work is notable for its historical analysis. This chapter is not intended as a critique of Foucault's work. Nor is it a critique of the ways in which organization theorists have interpreted Foucault's

work. It is intended as a critique of the ways in which some of Foucault's ideas have been used by organization theorists.
4. Christian outworldly individualism posits that man/woman is an individual-in-relation-to-God. Thus, the outworldly individual subordinates worldly relationships by rationalizing his/her conduct in terms of the teaching of Christ.

7

Playing with the Pieces: Deconstruction and the Loss of Moral Culture

This chapter investigates the assumptions and implications of the notion of deconstruction as they are found in writers concerned with organization theory and organization ethnography. Deconstruction, and postmodernism generally, is shown to be a continuation of modernity's attack on cultural authority and its celebration of the ideology of individualism with its concomitant of endless criticism. Deconstruction posits the oppositional nature of language and symbolism as a "violent hierarchy" and seeks to overturn this hierarchy to achieve human freedom. This reading of the repressive aspects of culture is shown to undermine the essential dynamic of culture, which is a recurrent splitting of what is from what is not in the process of forming meaning.

By opening up structures of meaning to expose their repressed contents, deconstruction aspires to question all authority. This is particularly threatening to the ethical aspects of organizational culture, because it suggests a continuous attempt to question the boundary between right and wrong. Indeed, orders of right and wrong are seen by deconstruction as mere political attempts at controlling an organization. Ethics is reduced to politics; authority is confused with power.

I argue here, instead, that stable structures of meaning are needed over time to found a traditional and thus legitimate base for business ethics. Contrary to deconstruction's goal of opening meaning to its repressed opposite, I assert that memory should be seen as a moral decision. Business ethics requires stable moral standards and, no less, the capacity to believe in them.

In his story "In the Penal Colony," Franz Kafka (1919) portrays the repressive nature of culture as a prison. This is the modern imagination, a post–religious imagination that can experience authority and discipline only in terms of oppression and pain. Since the middle of the eighteenth century, this perception of all types of authority has been a growing trend (Arendt 1968). By the late twentieth century, in the project of postmodernism, it has reached its most advanced, one is tempted to say terminal, stage: all cultural boundaries are considered oppressive and are to be deconstructed. Kafka's fictional image of culture as penal colony is now an accepted, in some places popular, approach to the study of social organization.

In postmodern organization theory, the prison metaphor (and the attack against the principle of authority that it represents) is used as the central image of organization (Burrell 1988). Linstead and Grafton-Small (1992), for example, begin their discussion of the literature on organizational culture by quoting Alexander Solzhenitsyn on life in a Siberian labor camp. The reader is informed that the prisoner in the story "could be any of us" (Linstead and Grafton-Small 1992, 331). But could it be? Are the similarities between employees and prisoners in democratic societies more important than the differences? I think not. One must forget the prisoner's guilt to think it so. It is this position, beyond good and evil, that underlies the postmodern attack on all authority seen in the organizational culture literature. The position is theoretically unbalanced, socially and morally destructive, and all the more popular for it, having found a ready home in the confused individualism of the present age.

In this chapter, I will review the general attack on cultural authority as it is found in postmodernism, and then analyze the assumptions and processes of deconstruction as they have been presented in the discipline of organization theory. Postmodernism is notoriously hard to define, as it is found across the social sciences and humanities and has evolved differently in different disciplines. For purposes of this chapter, I will define postmodernism as a theoretical framework focusing on the role of language and symbolism in the phenomenon of social and psychological control.[1] Deconstruction is seen as a particular method and philosophy in use within the postmodernism movement for dismantling linguistic and symbolic structures.

Deconstruction poses serious problems for the discipline of organization theory in that its calls for an "opening" of cultural and linguistic forms will destabilize already unstable ethical structures. The fact that organization theory generally ignores ethics makes the threat posed by deconstruction hardly noticeable. Ironically, we owe thanks to postmodernism in that its greatly exaggerated quest for liberation from cultural forms draws attention to the neglected role of ethics in the cultural aspects of organizations and organization theory. In any case, ethics requires distinctions between right and wrong (Aristotle 1982), and the deconstructive goal of "ceaseless moving between terms" (Linstead 1993b, 112) breaks the spine of ethical judgment. I will develop a theory of culture that posits moral and traditional authority as essential to maintaining standards of ethical conduct in organizations. I agree with deconstructionism on the points that language is oppositional in nature and that cultural forms repress their opposites. However, instead of concluding from this that cultural repression[2] acts as an unethical, oppressive system of power, I will show that repression is the essential dynamic of culture and is required for creating meaning, particularly for creating meaningful distinctions between right and wrong in any particular culture (Rieff 1979, 1985). Traditional authority maintains an element of repression through its repetition of past cultural forms. Through tradition, then, repression protects ethical standards from being dissolved in the endless critique that is the birth sign of the modern/postmodern mind. In a world of massive change, only the continuity of tradition can stabilize and legitimize a business ethics.

Memory Is a Moral Decision

In a recent issue of the management journal *Organization Studies* (1995, 16:4, 553-7), a debate of sorts takes place concerning the meaning of knowledge and truth as basic assumptions inside the field of organization theory. All four participants—Parker, Clegg, Jackson, and Carter—assume that the two endpoints in the debate about cultural assumptions are realism or objectivity on one hand, and relativism or subjectivism on the other (Parker 1995b; Clegg 1995a; Jackson 1995; Carter 1995). Parker attempts to stake out a third position, a "middleground," that the other three writers criticize severely.

This debate—and it is similar to the vast majority of management literature on the subject—defines the two key values of modernity as rationality and individualism. It is assumed that knowledge is posited as either objective (rationalism) or subjective (individualism). In the case of the four debaters, who all favor the subjectivism/relativism position, they have learned from Foucault, Derrida, and others that rationality is neither objective nor true, but is enmeshed in a sociolinguistic field benefiting some social actors, to the detriment of some others. Thus, all four debaters (Parker is ambivalent and that is why he is ridiculed) assume that relativism in one form or another is the only acceptable social basis for organization theory. Where all religions have broken down to sects of one, how else can we protect freedom of belief?

The whole debate rejects the possibility of an enduring management ethics, because any consensus is seen as just another attempt by some individual or group to exercise power over some other individual or group. This is the modern/postmodern mentality: it begins with the assumption that the individual is the autonomous unit of social organization (Hobbes), and proceeds to the assumption that cultural wholes are stifling obstacles at best, or terrorizing tools of oppression at worst (Foucault). Management ethics is basically ignored by organizational theorists, despite its general acceptance, if superficial use, by management practitioners, because of the former's suspicion of cultural wholes, or what they call "meta-narratives."

By granting real existence only to individuals, however, relativism subordinates relations between individuals. This is the modern reversal of the traditional assumption that relations are primary (Dumont 1986). Indeed, this unquestionable assumption of the autonomous individual, in the face of the primacy of cultural wholes in *all* previous civilizations, indicates the depth of repression modernity applies to collective beliefs. Morality is now seen as located in the conscience of the autonomous individual, while being simultaneously severed from collective belief. This creates a "theoretically unbridgeable chasm between *is* and *ought to be*" (Dumont 1986, 244). Denied the possibility of a moral culture, the individual must establish his/her own relation between representation and action (see Jackson 1995). Thus, relativism creates a subhuman world of objects and things to which the individual may choose to superadd values, but then again may not. With the denial of the whole, modern and postmodern intellectuals have made the instrumental point of view decisive.

Despite their repression in modern culture, cultural wholes cannot be destroyed. We still make sense of reality by formulating our experience into hierarchical levels, where the higher level explains the lower. For example, it is widely held in American business culture that the value of profit is of higher importance and subordinates the value of social responsibility (Friedman 1970). The subordination is clearly seen in the common tendency to view corporate philanthropy in terms of "payback" (Carr 1968). Hierarchical relations between values forming cultural wholes are an indestructible part of social existence, because collective order is impossible without them.

The problem with the repression of cultural wholes in the ideology of modern individualism is that in its one-sidedness, it has created unstable social situations in which people become vulnerable to totalitarian forms of organization. The behavior characteristic of the modern individualistic person is a single-minded devotion to private goals of family and career (Tocqueville 1850). In Germany, this atomized creature became the mass man whom Hitler organized to run his bureaucracies and carry out his crimes (Arendt 1950). A disturbing similarity between the mass man of mid-century and the postmodern theorist of today is that neither can find truth beyond mere personal opinion or practical usefulness (see the debaters for examples: Parker 1995b; Jackson 1995; Carter 1995). In Nazi Germany, nothing proved easier than destroying the private moralities of the former and redirecting the rootless moralities of individuals concerned with no more than practical usefulness (Bauman 1989). Totalitarianism is a disease of modern society in that it is the flip side of modern individualism. It stands as a revelation of the limits of relativism; that is, of the dangers of individualism that has been ideologically severed from the society that produced it. On the organizational level, as Schwartz (1990) has pointed out in the space shuttle example and others, this can easily slip into corporate goals dominating both ethical values and common sense.

The one-sidedness of individualism/relativism is nowhere seen so clearly as in the creation of the self.

> Language, according to Mead, enables the individual to "take the role of the other" because in addressing the other, the individual arouses in himself the same tendency to respond that he is attempting to elicit from the other. In adumbrating the response of the other, he is able both to "get inside" the other's mental processes and to look back on himself, the stimulus to the other's response, as he appears to the other. . . . This process . . . is "interiorized" by individuals in the form of an inner dialogue between their "I" and their "me." (Wrong, 1994, 63).

For George Herbert Mead, then, taking the attitude of the other, through language, is the essential characteristic of both selfhood and consciousness of kind. What does this tell us about postmodern relativism and its assumption that discord is equivalent to harmony in social life (Clegg 1995a)? First, social communication is the very stuff out of which the self is made. Hence, harmony is primary, discord secondary, in social life because the self must first be part of a unity before discord is possible. Second, Clegg's (1995b, 160) rejection of "empathetic insight ... [in favor of] ... discursive possibility" overstructuralizes cultural context and in the process loses touch with the feeling-self component of the individual, what Cooley (1922) calls the "my feeling." Postmodern relativism, by reifying cultural context, loses touch with how we imagine the mind of the other and, in so doing, share the judgment of the other. Ironically, as we will see, this overstructuralized view of culture and language will commit the postmodernists to seeking the freedom of the oppressed (thus autonomous) individual—a freedom that they plead cannot exist.

Through reciprocal imagining, both self and society achieve their unity (Rieff 1990). It is a moral unity because as we imagine the minds of others, we realize that sacrifice is essential to maintaining both our own self-image and to getting along with the other. Hence, without a shared sense of obligation, both self and society disintegrate internally, becoming cold and shallow. Indeed, for the child as well as for the stranger, the specific obligations of a culture are learned from the approval and disapproval of the members of that culture (Sullivan 1950). Individualism/relativism is a false ideology because it is based on an impossible autonomy.

Social acceptances and rejections, approvals and disapprovals, compose the myth that every society produces and in which it lives. The individual departs and yet maintains its membership in the collective myth in order to balance his/her self-esteem gained from social approval with the sense of guilt acquired from disapproval. Approval and disapproval are internalized. The so-called personal "truth" (Parker 1995a) or personal "opinion" (Carter 1995) of our management theorists is derived from the internalization of previous acceptances and rejections. Indeed, these "personal" sentiments evidence the sense of guilt because they assume a judgment of right and wrong. The sense of guilt poses an insurmountable problem for postmodernism because in its universality, guilt is inexplicable except as a prolepsis of faith (Rieff 1981). Each individual explains itself to itself by measuring the manner and distance of its drift through the authoritative cultural context of its social existence. This context can be accepted, rejected, or manipulated. In any case, the context is decisive. Postmodernism is the celebration of rejection. And rejection, as Tawney (1926) points out in the fantasy of the "self-made" entrepreneur, does not remove the condition of dependency. What it does do is encourage managerial manipulation of others as a norm of organizational behavior (MacIntyre 1984).

Culture is authoritative. Clegg (1995a) is right to argue that truth requires a process of institutionalization to exist, but he is wrong to assume that this can be done only through the exercise of power. This is an example of the modern confusion between power and legitimate authority. It originates in the fiction, discussed above, that the individual is the primary unit of social organization. If the group is given equal status with the individual, however, then hierarchy and authority are seen as essential to social life (Dumont 1986). The pervasive presence of the Foucauldian idea of power in Clegg's (1995b) framework appears as the modern equivalent to the traditional ideas of order and hierarchy. In Clegg, the social (moral) is reduced to the political. Note the transformation of value. However, all groups still make exclusive claims upon their members. Thus, religion is still the first and purest form of politics (Freud 1921). This is parallel to Aristotle's point that questions of justice can arise only in an already constituted community (1971). Indeed, without agreed-upon standards, the idea of justice is meaningless (Rieff 1985). Authority is original to power, because human groups are original to the individual. Clegg (1995a, b) repeats the tragic forgetfulness of modern "liberation."

Cultural authority imposes upon its members the awesome dichotomy between a meaningful and a meaningless life (Rieff 1987). Postmodernists, in scorning cultural authority, are opposing the dynamics of culture. Culture opposes the primacy of possibility, that is, the ability of man/woman to express everything and therefore nothing. Culture acts through authority to narrow possible meanings. Narrowing meaning is the dynamic of culture. Without this dynamic, culture cannot exist. This is not totalitarian oppression. Totalitarianism operates to destroy meaning in order to annihilate even the possibility of principled resistance. This is what is *totalizing* about totalitarianism (Arendt 1950).

Authority, on the contrary, is always *given*, or it is fraudulent (Rieff 1985). Authority is given not because people are dupes, tricked into controlling themselves for some systemic conspiracy, but because through the hierarchical ordering of culture they find their way to purposeful behavior (Durkheim 1925) and a feeling of self-respect that makes life meaningful and worthwhile (Cooley 1922; Rieff 1985; Sullivan 1950).

Authority, then, is essential to culture. It protects social life from the primacy of possibility that surrounds every culture. Possibility is the opposite of cultural authority. Cultural diversity cannot be an unlimited goal; its limitation is the central problem of culture (Plato 1968). No culture can tolerate unlimited diversity without being destroyed. Diversity can only exist inside a culture as a limited range of possibility. Without this "imaginary wall," individual and social purpose is impossible (Durkheim 1925). Deprivation must be the first and final function of culture. Likewise, a culture composed of continuous criticism cannot possibly carry out its meaning-defining function. To exist, culture must in some respects remain beyond criticism. The notion of being beyond criticism is unthinkable to the modern mind, with its depthless distrust of authority. This is why faith is not even conceived of as a possibility in the modern-postmodern debate between realism and relativism. The repression of faith evidences not only the endless transitional condition of modern social life, but precisely the fallacy of postmodern "openness." Complete openness, like complete individuality, is impossible.

Postmodernism is, ironically, an example of cultural repression. To be meaningful, culture must repress what it is not. Postmodernism must repress the idea of faith, because the mere idea of being beyond doubt is contradictory to the postmodern vision of cultural "openness." This is why the postmodern discussion stops at belief: belief can be doubted, faith cannot. Herein lies the problem of management ethics. Without a collective capacity for enduring commitment, management ethics becomes vulnerable to the endless rationalizations of the critical intellect. Parker's (1995b) ambivalent search for truth (faith) was intolerable to the critical intellects of his colleagues. Where Parker sought truth, they could only feel/see power: "[W]here, oh where, is some recognition of the role of power?" (Carter 1995, 574). Power is to criticism what truth is to faith. Only truth can stabilize a management ethics.

Every order of actual existence derives from the recurrent splitting motion by which the human capacity to express everything is narrowed into an acceptable range before standards of good and evil. It is true that some "voices" are repressed. Repression is truth experienced negationally (Rieff 1979). It is best that some voices are never heard.

We would all be better off, I believe, if our business culture of social responsibility was strong enough to subordinate economic self-interest. It is true, as the deconstructionists might say, that social responsibility is intimately indebted to its opposite, self-interest. But some debts must remain unpaid. To work in a culture of social responsibility, one must partially repress self-interest. Repression is the source of cultural truth. Collective representations make it operable. This created truth keeps us at a safe distance from ourselves and from each other. Cultural authority, then, protects subjectivity by surrounding it and enforcing its truth internally and externally. Moral character is predicated on cultural authority.

Of course, as in the case of America, self-interest can be idealized and social responsibility repressed. This is not typical of Western history, however, and this is exactly the point. Up to the present age, our history is influenced by great moral traditions, originating in Jerusalem and Athens. But we have lost touch with these traditions as a primary form of moral truth. The loss has resulted in our inability to conserve the past. The modern individual is obsessed with the future, because it is there that the road to prosperity begins. A tradition restricting future behavior is easily seen as an obstacle to opportunity. This "obstacle," however, carries "the knowledge of tragedy with which all action . . . is truly interwoven" (Weber 1918a, 117). To ignore tradition is to repeat unguided the paradoxical relation between intended action and outcome.

This is a dangerous type of ignorance, because it opens social action to unchecked ambition and stupidity. The great moral accomplishments in our history are worth conserving just for this reason: they carry the moral lessons of past decisions and actions. Tradition has a repressive purpose.

> On the conscious surface of a culture, the repressed content of the past is something "vanished and overcome in the life of a people." But this is just what defines the impact of memory: one's reaction to it, against it. (Rieff, 1979, 200-1).

Tradition is double-sided: it carries forward the moral vision of right conduct and the repressed guilt that originally created the moral reaction. Hence, *memory is a moral decision because it represents a choice to learn or to forget a moral lesson from the past.* Cultivating a tradition is remembering the moral lesson and updating it for the present.

Tradition selects and names, hands down and preserves, what continuous generations find valuable in human history. We need this authority in our lives because without the permanence and durability that it provides, each generation begins ignorant and inexperienced in exactly the most important questions of human existence: What will I deny myself, and what not? The present age is no exception. This is, I think, the correct context in which to read Weber's (1904-5, 182) ambivalent prognosis:

> For of the last stage of this cultural development, it might well be truly said: "Specialists without spirit, sensualists without heart; this nullity imagines that it has attained a level of civilization never before achieved."
> But this brings us to the world of judgments of value and faith. . . .

Specialists without spirit—postmodernism's reified demon, instrumental rationality—has been recognized all too well (Knights and Vurdubakis 1994; Knights and Willmott 1989; Alvesson and Willmott 1992; Parker 1995b). Perhaps this recognition acts to block a more important truth, the connection between relativism and sensualists without heart. For what kind of heart can find truth only in a "test" of its "usefulness" (Jackson 1995; Carter 1995)? This institutionalized dismemberment of the past assumes that there is no reason to get beyond the disconnectedness of our goals and the fragmented selves that arise from them. There is, however, a reason: it is the capacity to learn from the past which goods in human life are higher and which are lower. This is a teaching that business ethics has forgotten, and if left to postmodern theory, will be unable to remember.

Postmodernism and Culture: A Critical Summary

The literature on postmodernism is characterized by its disconnectedness from historical context. This disconnectedness has been referred to as "forgetfulness" (Reed 1993). Few writers have developed empirical analyses to support their theoretical speculations (Featherstone 1988). What is at stake in this forgetfulness is the connection to reality. This is of special importance because postmodernism claims that the very idea of social reality is false (Gergen 1992). The general argument about the impossibility of social reality is based on the two claims that "[a]11 is representational" (Burrell 1993, 81), and representation is irrevocably indeterminate (Cooper and Burrell 1988). Given this metaphysics, postmodern writers tend to accept uncritically the claim that we live in a "postmodern" world without corroborating empirical evidence (Kellner 1988). Indeed, Ernest Gellner (1992) argues that because of their idealization of meaning, postmodern writers ignore the non–semantic aspects of economic and political reality.

Postmodern writers tend to frame their discussions rather abstractly in terms of the transformation from "modernism" to "postmodernism." The present is postmodern and is assumed to be a "different epoch" (Parker 1992). Several writers have seen this as an exaggeration. Douglas Kellner (1988) claims that postmodern writers exclude historical continuities from their discussions. He also argues, using Baudrillard as an example, that they take "tendencies" for "finalities" (Kellner 1988). Paul Thompson (1993), speaking of Lyotard and others, argues that these writers misleadingly reduce the complex relations between cultural, economic, social, and political aspects of reality to particular socioeconomic developments. Lyotard (1984), for example, does not, according to Thompson (1993), clearly explain the relations between technology, capital, and social development to demonstrate his claim of a postmodern condition.

This lack of empirical support for their conclusions mirrors a deeper contradiction that runs through the postmodern literature. Postmodern writers problematize reference, which they take to be "reality," but they presuppose access to the real in order to make their claims about the postmodern world (Kellner 1988). If reference (reality) is so indeterminable, how is it possible for postmodern writers to analyze it? This explains the tendency noted above for postmodern writers to present their ideas in mostly abstract, one-sided polemics with little historical analysis.

There is another, related contradiction in the postmodern literature. Postmodernism claims to be speaking of a "different epoch," but it is dependent on the dominant and coherent culture of modernism to communicate its beliefs about the impossibility of belief (Rieff 1991). Hence, postmodernism is necessarily a subcultural movement and its peculiar goal of decentering culture can only exist as a goal on a subcultural level. Like the Christian Church after the fall of Rome, postmodernism would quickly transform itself into a hierarchical system if it wanted to survive in a world without order.

The political nature of postmodernism has been commented on by several writers. Interestingly, it seems to be a specific tactic of postmodern writers that their call for openness is not itself open in principle to what they call "meta-narratives" (Linstead 1993a). Kellner (1988) has pointed out, citing Lyotard as an example, the contradiction in this lack of consistent openness. Kellner (1988) goes on to note that the disallowing of meta-narratives is every bit as much a totalizing perspective as the meta-narratives themselves. In any case, as Jameson (1984) states, meta-narratives are unavoidable. It is his belief that they have not become discredited and disappeared, but have become unconscious. Indeed, it is hard to imagine that the will to order, that has been the main influence on all civilizations in human history (Weber 1922), has disappeared from the scene.

There is another contradiction to be pointed out in this context. Gellner (1992) argues that the postmodern call for openness to other cultures is impossible because postmodern theory presumes that cultural boundaries cannot exist, thus making it impossible for other cultures to exist. Hence, it is inherently contradictory for postmodernists to be committed to a "search for instabilities" (Cooper and Burrell 1988, 98), while simultaneously attempting to create, for example, "alternative gender identities" (Mumby and Putnam 1992, 467). They cannot have it both ways.

This underlying confusion in postmodern thought is related to its radical contemporaneity. For postmodernism, the past has become "an open museum, a junk store, a replay" (O'Neill 1988, 501). Doubt, a growing phenomenon in modernity from Descartes to Nietzsche, has reached an extreme form in postmodernism. Baudrillard, for example, wants to bring back all past cultures that modern writers such as Marx and Freud destroyed with their "hermeneutics of suspicion . . . [but only to] . . . play with the pieces . . . [in a] . . . kind of post-history which is without meaning" (Baudrillard quoted in Kellner 1988, 246-8). This fantasy of having the "pieces" of culture without the meaning is, of course, nonsense. Baudrillard's radical contemporaneity, however, is a theme running through the postmodern literature. The literature portrays a nihilistic universe which impossibly makes a home in nothingness.

Nothingness, or the "search for instabilities" advocated by postmodern writers, leads to a dangerous loss of limits on human behavior. Without some type of cultural constraint, the infinite potential of human behavior is unleashed. This is exactly what postmodern writers want (Burrell 1993). They appear to have already forgotten that the atrocities that have been committed in this century are also a sample of human potential (Arendt 1950). Indeed, in postmodernism, the idea of individual moral responsibility is theoretically precluded from consideration because self-consciousness is considered a myth (Linstead 1993a). On the contrary, as has been noted, they are sensitive to the controlling nature of systems of meaning. Thus, in postmodernism, control is equated with oppression. It is exactly this destruction of the ancient dichotomy between the individual and the group and of the attempt from Plato to Machiavelli to Durkheim and Freud to balance individual needs with collective requirements that I find most dangerous in the postmodern literature.

Deconstruction and Organization Theory

Postmodern writers in organization theory have not only introduced postmodernism by contrasting it with modernism, they have also forgotten all non-modern forms of cultural organization. Robert Cooper and Gibson Burrell (1988), for example, limit their comparison to two major modern positions: instrumental reason and critical theory. They quickly discount instrumental reason because of its universalizing (read totalizing, as in totalitarianism) nature and turn their attention to critical theory, which, following Habermas, seeks a universal consensus. They argue that consensus can never be truly reached. Burrell and Cooper (1988, 99) write,

> The triumph of consensus is thus similar to the destruction of opposition, for it negates the very thing, dissensus, on which it rests. In an afterward to Lyotard, Samuel Weber interprets the dissensus of the games as a '*tension* between unity and disunity' (Lyotard and Thébaud 1986: 113) and thus gives to difference and self-reference the function of an originary and irreducible *force* which pervades all social encounters as raw 'feelings of envy, jealousy, and rancour' (Lyotard and Thébaud 1986: 106). Difference is thus more than a theoretical concept since it takes on the force of elemental passion, a kind of prime energizer. Human action is thus seen to step from drives beyond direct human control; behavior, individual or institutional, is essentially a reaction to an originary force.

Hence, consensus too starts to look like a totalizing and oppressive goal. Cooper and Burrell (1988) conclude that "agonistics," or contest, is vital to maintaining a state of continuous provocation, which will defend organizations from the totalizing tendencies inherent in modern reason and consensus.

Cooper and Burrell (1988) present the contrast between a totalizing modernism and a liberating postmodernism outside any historical context. The fact that *all* previous civilizations instituted some kind of controls or limits to enable people to live and work together is forgotten (Dumont 1986). Along with the loss of memory, postmodern theorists have presented an overly simplistic view of modern organizations by ignoring important cultural developments such as the great increase in entrepreneurship and the extensive development of nonprofit organizations, neither of which is dominated by universal reason (bureaucracy) or universal consensus (ideal democracy). Postmodernism seems to need to be obsessed with a universalizing oppression in order to justify its extreme rejection of any kind of limits. Ironically, given its all–is–representational ethos, postmodernism seems to have typical modern aspirations of self-realization and self-perfection which, managerially, are formulated as a sort of "'entrepreneur of the self'" (du Gay 1994, 132). In this sense, "postmodernism" is part of the continuing pluralization of modernity (Heller 1993); that is, part of the historical era that makes the private well-being of the individual the highest end in life.

Pluralization, or self-centeredness, can be a problem too, however. In organizational terms, as an end in itself, it can lead to miscommunication and conflict (Barnard 1938; Schein 1992). The postmodern preference for agonistics seems to suggest some sort of radical pluralism with no past, no truth. Kenneth Gergen (1992), for example, is optimistic that an open attitude toward language will enhance an organization's survival. On the contrary, however, contest must be carefully limited or it can encourage irrational behavior and become destructive to an organization (Baum 1993). And even if contest calls forth the noblest motivations, the process itself can be easily manipulated by a clever top management (McSwite 1995). Thus, agonistics is a one-sided attempt at decentralization that will break down civility or be reversed through corporate manipulation.

Perhaps more than anyone else, it has been Jacques Derrida who has sensitized organizational theorists to the oppressive potential of language (Cooper 1989). His general argument is that language is oppositional in nature (for example, "group" requires the repression of "individual" for its meaning), and thus, to the extent that any semantic structure is clear, it implies the suppression of some potential voices. Derrida proposes a process of "deconstruction" to release the repressed meanings (Cooper 1989). Deconstruction has been used by organizational researchers to analyze the repression of feminine issues in organizations (Martin 1990; Mumby and Putnam 1992), and the repression of nonscientific assumptions in scientific management texts (Kilduff 1993).

Philosophically, however, the idea of deconstruction goes deeper. Cooper (1989, 480-1) writes,

> For [Pondy and Mitroff] language appears as a mere carrier of information and meaning. For Derrida, in contrast, language is a structure of material marks or sounds which are in themselves 'undecidable' and *upon which meaning has to be imposed* . . . .Applied to organizational analysis, this means that organization always harbours within itself that which transgresses it, namely, disorganization . . . .Derrida starts from the position that human experience is pervaded by an existential 'ambivalence' which in turn serves as the drive to organize.

Hence, organization not only contains its opposite; this double reality is the origin of the will to organize. Thus, organizing is necessarily a political act, but not for the classic reason of the separation into rulers and ruled (Plato 1968). The deeper reason is that human attempts at defining the meaning of language go farther than they are needed as a heuristic device and become fixed and repressive (Linstead 1993a). Hence, organizational culture, whatever the content, is repressive (Linstead and Grafton-Small 1992).

Deconstruction, then, represents a new way of thinking. All previous thinking, according to Derrida, has ignored the role of language in the transmission of thoughts (Cooper 1989). Derrida uses the notion of "logocentrism" to capture the central importance of *logos* (word, reason) in Western culture. Logocentrism acts like "the law" to control human affairs. Indeed, Cooper, quoting Norbert Elias, goes on to equate "logocentrism" with the "civilizing process," which was "'concerned far more with the problems of the object of knowledge than the subject of knowledge'" (Elias in Cooper 1989, 482). Hence, the problem is the cultural process itself. It is a repressive system of knowledge, carried through and hidden in language. This is the radical new insight that deconstruction brings: language and culture are bound together in a process of universal repression.

Language thus becomes the key villain in an implicit, undemocratic plot hidden deep within organizational culture. Potential voices have been repressed, and the repression is not even recognized. Cooper (1989, 482-3) writes,

> The civilizing process is thus guarded against further, and possibly destructive, analysis by securing it in a metaphysical foundation which serves to 'hide' it from critical view. It is precisely this work of mystification that deconstruction aims to reveal . . . .In overturning it is recognized that texts are structured around binary oppositions (e.g., good-bad, male-female) in which one of the terms dominates the

other. As Derrida writes: '. . . we are not dealing with the peaceful co-existence of a *vis-à-vis*, but rather with a violent hierarchy. One of the two terms governs the other (axiologically, logically, etc.), or has the upper hand. To deconstruct the opposition, first of all, is to overturn the hierarchy at a given moment' (Derrida 1981a, 41).

The "violent hierarchy" has little to do with top management; it is the repressiveness of language that silences potential voices in organizations. Cooper (1989) follows Derrida in a wish to "overturn" this hierarchy.

I will make four points concerning the process of deconstruction. First, Cooper's belief that organization always harbors its opposite, disorganization, within itself is misleading. The idea of antithetical meanings being active in words is Freud's (1910). The crucial concept here is repression. Derrida's removal of the process of repression from social reality and positing it solely in language is indeed questionable. Language takes on a life of its own independent of the people who use it. This reification of language loses the driving force of repression in the Freudian sense, that is, the socialization process by which the individual is narrowed into a member of a culture. As John O'Neill (1988) points out, in this view language never has a local value. But this is exactly what language does have in everyday life. This can be clearly seen in the use of deconstruction in the field of organization theory. Joanne Martin (1990), for example, uses a single paragraph from a speech to make far-ranging assertions about the suppression of feminism in an organization and organizations in general without any attempt to demonstrate the assertions empirically. Deconstruction thus licenses generalization independent of empirical evidence, making it impossible to evaluate the logic and coherence of the argument.

Second, Cooper's view that the will to organize originates in an inherent ambivalence in language is reductionist. Clearly, as Gellner (1979) states, social reality is complex and there are many factors that lead to organizational activities. Postmodernism's idealization of language ignores, for example, the influences of economic scarcity, geographical conditions, and political resources such as money and people. Even some animal groups organize for hunting and/or safety. Certainly they are not motivated by existential ambivalences in language.

Third, Stephen Linstead does not ask the question why semantic closure is needed as a "heuristic device" in human life. If he did, he would realize that communities as well as organizations require the "inertial force" of tradition to hold together in a given form over time (Shils 1981, 25). Without this force, trust and depth of experience would become difficult to say the least. In any case, Linstead's acceptance of semantic closure for learning but rejection of it as a way of life is contradictory, because learning assumes a way of life. Thus, here too, the presumption of a world of openness cannot be a world at all.

Fourth, Cooper's characterization of cultural authority as a "violent hierarchy" is obviously a condemnation of authority. The condemnation is based on the assumption that language is "undecidable" and thus any hierarchy is repressive. Repression is seen unfavorably because some meanings are "privileged" while others are denied expression. This argument is misleading because without repression, no meaning is possible. Linstead (1993b, 111), for example, wants to reconceptualize the oppositional nature of culture as a "mutually supportive pivotal point around which meaning turns." This will perhaps have no detrimental effect on organizations, since its practical absurdity will be ignored by everyone except academics. In the area of business ethics, however, Linstead and Grafton-Small's (1992, 341) goal of reconceptualizing cultural opposition as "cohabitation," "joining," and "both/and" is more dangerous because it attacks precisely the dividing line between right and wrong. It is an attack on moral authority and the capacity of organizations to define and enforce moral limits. Limits exist not fundamentally to oppress the weak, but to define the good. Deconstructionists, by pushing the democratization of meaning to the extreme because of their inability to distinguish between power and authority, forget the lesson of the French Revolution: democracy requires limits, too. This can also be seen in collegial organization, which, without a moral consensus, can easily break down to destructive levels of envy and self-interest (Hirschhorn 1993).

Deconstructionist thinking is characterized by a lack of memory. It forgets the social nature of man/woman; that is, it forgets that man/woman develops inside a community and cannot exist outside of it. Even the hermit is a social being. Indeed, unstable communities are dangerous. The great increase in suicide since the middle of the eighteenth century, for example, has been explained by a breakdown in the moral community in which individuals find a purposeful life (Masaryk 1881; Durkheim 1897). The deconstructionist "search for instabilities" obviously does not address this problem.

The problem of memory originates at the center of the deconstruction project, the notion of *differance* (Cooper and Burrell 1988). *Differance* posits that all discourse is self-referential; that is, terms contain their own opposites, refusing any singular grasp of their meaning (Cooper and Burrell 1988). Cooper and Burrell (1988, 98) write,

> *Difference* is thus a unity which is at the same time divided from itself, and, since it is that which actually constitutes human discourse (Derrida 1973), it is intrinsic to all social forms. At the very center of discourse, therefore, the human agent is faced with conditions of irreducible indeterminacy and it is this endless and un-stoppable demurrage which postmodern thought explicitly recognizes and places in the vanguard of its endeavors.

By posting discourse as "divided from itself," deconstructionists throw a monkey wrench into the chain of memory.

They also make two important assertions based on their belief in the "irreducible indeterminancy" of discourse. First, facticity has disappeared from the world (Burrell 1993). The singular meaning of a fact cannot exist, because the language used to characterize it cannot have a single meaning. Second, any form of idealism is shown to be false (Linstead 1993a). Ideals are false because the language needed to characterize ideals necessarily implies their opposites.

Deconstructionists explain these surprising assertions by claiming there is an "originary force of 'sameness'" underlying the idea of *differance* (Cooper 1989, 489). Cooper (1989, 489) writes,

> the two opposed meanings . . . actively *defer* each other, the deferred term being postponed for the present, waiting for an opportunity to flow back to the medium from which it was severed. This latter point, especially, brings out the processual character of differance, for underlying the idea of *differance from* (i.e., static difference) is an originary force of 'sameness' (to be distinguished from static identity in which one thing is said to be the same as another) which works in a subterranean and unconscious way to bind differences together . . . .

This "originary force of 'sameness' " is largely based on the Freudian model of the unconscious (Lash 1988). According to Freud's (1933) famous definition of the unconscious, the laws of contradiction do not apply.

In *differance*, alternative meanings "are the same to the extent that a single force passes through them, crosses the boundary between them" (Harland in Cooper 1989, 489). This single force is the "process of metaphorization," where meaning never stabilizes but is processual

(Cooper 1989, 489). To say meaning is processual is to say that it signifies through the movement *between* terms; meaning is not locatable *in* terms. Hence, in *differance* there can be no logic of identity. Mumby and Putnam (1992, 468) write,

> The aim of deconstruction is to problematize the present term and to reclaim the absent one (upon which the present term depends for its meaning). However, as Poovey (1988: 52) indicated, the overall project of deconstruction "is not to reverse binary oppositions but to problematize the very idea of opposition and the notion of identity upon which it depends."

Meaning as a process can be only temporarily delayed and it is the job of *differance* to make sure this primary process is never again mystified and hidden. Metaphorization discredits the ideas of boundary, location, and identity.

I will make four points concerning the notion of *differance*. First, by claiming that the underlying reality of organizational life is an "originary force of 'sameness'," deconstructionists introduce a theory of organization based on resentment. If the essence of organizational life is "sameness" (process, movement), then any decision for or against anything can have no legitimacy. Inevitably organization will lead to resentment. This is clear in Linstead and Grafton-Small's (1992, 345) statement that "'shared meaning' is impossible" because it is "nothing more than the deferral of Difference." If it is truly "nothing more," then "shared meaning" must be illegitimate and thus oppressive. The problem with this position is that the opposite is just as true: *differance* is nothing more than the deferral of shared meaning. By reversing the traditional primacy of cultural form over nihilism, deconstruction changes how we value the *form/nothing* dichotomy, shifting our trust from the former to the latter. This changes our understanding of organizations from wholes potentially worthy of our admiration to dictatorships deserving our resentment. It is a negative and cynical view of human organization.

Second, as Burrell informs us, since terms contain their opposites, facticity cannot exist. The only historical precedent I know for the loss of facticity is social conditions under totalitarianism. Stalin always claimed that Moscow had the only subway system in the world. He made this true in the Soviet Union by killing everyone who had been to Paris or knew about the London subway (Arendt 1950). Just to be sure, he killed anyone whom the first group might have had the opportunity to tell (Arendt 1950). In the end, the fact of other subway systems itself did not exist in the Soviet Union. Without facticity, human autonomy at its barest level evaporates and total dependence and total control are accomplished. Despite its great fear of totalizing systems, deconstructionism, in its political naïveté, destroys facticity as the fundamental support of freedom.

Third, Linstead's claim that since terms contain their opposite, ideals cannot be valid, has some dire consequences for organizations. McCarthy (1993) agrees we should interrogate our ideals, but he points out that without ceasing the interrogation, we cease to be participants. Hence, without common beliefs, collective effort is impossible and without common ideals this effort remains without moral direction. Certainly, ideals require the responsibility to critically evaluate them (Durkheim 1925; Rieff 1985), but without ceasing to criticize at some point, the individual becomes an untrusting fortress incapable of rising beyond its own doubt/self-interest to work with others for the good of all.

Fourth, *differance* assumes that any meaning not temporary is oppressive. Indeed, the method of deconstruction is designed to dismantle meaning continuously by collapsing its boundaries so as to find repressed contents. This orientation negates the role of the past in organizations and, in so doing, undermines the basis of organizational traditions. It assumes not only that there can be no truths worth saving, but that previous generations have nothing to teach us. For how can we learn and remember, if no sooner than we realize something, we become concerned with what it is not?

This demonstrates the fundamentally negative nature of deconstruction and its goal of creating a negative culture. It would create a world of radical contemporaneity where continuity with the past is lost. However, when we forgo learning from the past and maintaining a tradition to house this learning, we lose exactly the depth business ethics requires and the depth that is needed in a world dominated by massive change. For moral authority that changes too fast soon loses all credibility (Durkheim 1925). Organizations require collective effort and thus cannot survive without moral authority to integrate the individual into the group. Deconstructionism, with its program of "ceaseless moving between terms," destroys the links to the past, and with them, the possibility of moral culture.

Deconstruction and Organization Ethnography

Deconstructionism's attack on cultural authority takes an amazing political position: it claims to be neutral. This claim is based on the deconstructive view of language. Linstead (1993b, 97) writes about deconstructive ethnography,

> This ethnographic praxis would demystify social and organizational actions by revealing their inevitable and ever-present internal contradictions without resorting to an externally contrived theoretical or moral standard. It would realize its emancipatory potential through "self-deconstruction."

This is, of course, impossible. Its moral standard is *anti*-authoritarian; it seeks to overturn cultural order and thereby change the distribution of organizational power.

Its anti-authoritarianism stems from the deconstructionist's theory of culture. Culture has a double meaning; it is both a process that creates and a structure that oppresses. This creation/oppression dichotomy is at the root of all its key definitions. Invariably, however, process dominates structure. For example, "holism" is ironically defined as a "diverse differentiated plurality" (Ryan in Linstead 1993b, 115). Or the "essential qualities . . . [of culture are defined as] . . . negation, paradox, and ambiguity" (Linstead 1993a, 60). In deconstructionism, structure is clearly secondary; it plays the role of a straw man that is set up to be knocked down. Hence, deconstructionist organization ethnography is anti-organizational in the sense that organization assumes at least a minimal level of fixed cultural plates to at least generally define jobs and their responsibilities.

The centrality of the assumption concerning process over structure leads deconstructionism inevitably to extreme cultural relativism. Linstead (1993a, 49) writes,

> As the determinancy of meaning by a flow of intentionality from origin to recipient has been called into question, so the constructive effects of the medium of transmission (language, symbol or the mass media) and the creative possibilities of the 'reader' (through 'bricolage') have been emphasized (Linstead and Grafton-Small, 1989). Knowledge becomes relative, dispersed between multiple, fragmented realities: the 'selves' who experience and produce these emerge as more of a social and shifting phenomenon than integral cohesive one.

It is as if symbols can be creatively constructed independent of the social groups who use them in particular ways; and as if readers are not limited by the particular sociohistorical context in which they live. Sociologically, since most of us watch the same movies, shop at the same malls, cheer the same sports, eat the same fast food, and work in similar bureaucracies, we are *not* so different or so creative (Gellner 1979). Hence, the great "process" theme in postmodern thought, which is the backbone of its cultural and moral relativism, is greatly exaggerated.

This can be seen in the deconstructionist imagination of the individual. Linstead (1993a, 59) writes about the "subject,"

> The integrated subject of ego-psychology, depending as it does on its being 'centrable', is no longer tenable. Derrida sees its 'sovereign solitude' as being displaced, existing rather as a 'system of relations between strata' (Derrida, 1978: 226–7). It is a site which emerges as an overcrossing of traces, society, the world, the psyche, other texts, other times. It is a weave, a texture, fragmented but intertwined rather than hierarchical and integrated, a process and a paradox having neither beginning nor end.

A tremendous fragmentation of the self is assumed here. This self would be unthinkable in premodern societies (MacIntyre 1984), and even in, say, Japanese society today due to its commitment to hierarchical orders of collective belief (Rohlen 1974). Thus, deconstructive organization ethnography presupposes the ideology of modern individualism and builds it into its theoretical structure. However, it denies this in its claim of neutrality and demonstrates its incomplete grasp of both societal structure and historical context. Deconstructive organization ethnography, then, is not so much premised on the nature of language and *differance*, as on the breakdown of collective belief that characterizes the present age.

The deconstructionist discussion of power demonstrates the same phenomenon. Linstead (1993a, 61) develops the concept of "sting," claiming that any person accepting a command always maintains a wish to negate it. Tocqueville (1850), however, argues persuasively that the development of resentment between individuals in hierarchical relations is a defining characteristic of the advent of equality under conditions of modern democracy. Clearly, the sting shows the profound and pervasive individualism underlying deconstructionism. Linstead's (1992, 346) statement that the sting is the "most powerful formative influence on 'culture'" shows unequivocally that Process Self sat still long enough to read *The Rights of Man*.

The problem this presents to organization ethnography is that deconstructionism's extreme individualism reduces ethics and culture to politics, and to a tyrannical politics at that. By using a theoretical program designed to endlessly dismantle collective belief structures, deconstruction destroys one of the essential strengths of ethnography, its ability to grasp both the moral tone of a belief system and the way the individual's reaction to that system defines the individual's relation to the organization. Deconstructionism turns all relationships into relationships between strangers. Following Freud, ambivalence, this time posited in language, becomes the key interpretive tool. However, it is exactly the powerful human modalities of belief and faith that get short shrift in this approach. The question of whether particular beliefs and faiths are good or evil is lost because they are all automatically seen as oppressive. Deconstructive organization ethnography has no way to evaluate ethical beliefs, since its individualism freezes its analytic focus on the obvious fact of repression. So business ethics cannot be evaluated as a statement on right and wrong, only as a maneuver for organizational control.

The idea of an enduring organization existing before its current employees and carrying on after them is inconceivable in the deconstructive framework. Its individualism biases the study of organizational culture toward "those who participate" (Linstead and Grafton-Small 1992, 341). There is no way to appreciate the existence of a collective past or collective future. *Differance* must work toward fragmentation. The holism of a hundred-year-old organization that socializes new members into its value system is seen by deconstruction only as the repression of the "other." By imagining tradition only as power, deconstruction devalues the reality of the past and the continuity of organizational culture. By insisting that the essence of all supra-individual forms is in what they repress, we lose the ability to appreciate the life they construct.

Conclusion

Those of us who have tried to teach business ethics to graduate students in management know all too well the tremendous influence that the economic model of ethics—that is, that all economic activities can be justified by the maximization of profits that thereby raises the standard of living for all—exercises not only in the classroom, but in the business and political environment beyond. Among a large proportion of the managerial population, economic expediency has completely replaced morality as the standard for conduct between individuals and between organizations. Little can be said against it, because even the less capable business student knows that his/her society agrees on no other moral standard.

Nor does it matter to point out the impersonality, indifference, and moral minimalism that the economic model of ethics brings in its wake. To the students, the model's harmonious fit with corporate life and individual ambition makes it difficult for us just to gain their acknowledgment that the economic model represents a moral decision, and not the very tissue of reality. Their position is clearly bolstered by the democratic cultures of modern societies, which teach energetic youth from the earliest age that the hand of individual ambition is meant to fit the glove of individual rewards.

Postmodernism, as has been shown, continues this drive of modernism to push the limits of individual liberation to the extreme. The intellectual tactic of *differance* is more of the same. Its purpose is to open up collective structures of meaning in order to question their legitimacy. In so doing, it seeks to undermine social structure and win the freedom of the individual through claiming that process and ceaseless change are the only constant and true (thus legitimate) realities. This desire to celebrate paradox, ambiguity, indefiniteness, and, above all, nihilism, is the guillotine of collective spirit. For as we forgo the static in complete rapture of the dynamic, we lose our capacity to live in enduring moral order. Like the economic individualist, the postmodernist seeks "freedom" from collective constraint. This is why postmodernism attacks organization, but not entrepreneurship.

Postmodernism does not answer the most pressing moral issues of our time: in an age of extreme individualism, how is the individual to be related to organization and how are both related to moral order? In the context of the dominance of the economic model of ethics, deconstruction's concern with logos and the "violent hierarchy" furthers the Antinomian premises of an exaggerated individualism thus contributing to the underlying decline of moral consensus. What is needed, on the contrary, is a counter-enlightenment that resurrects the capacity of individuals, organizations, and societies to commit themselves to collective standards of moral order and thereby reduce the scourge of criticism to a secondary tool of refinement rather than a substitute for moral culture itself.

Collective moral standards are badly needed so that we can once again put morality in the center of social life, ultimately to gain control over business behavior. All we have at this time is law, and clearly the regulating power of law to control business in modern democracies is too limited, too delayed, and too abstract to be the only means of moral order. If we are going to achieve moral regulation of business, morality will have to be carried by the individual willing to sacrifice for noneconomic and nonindividualistic values; that is, the individual must be willing to limit his/her ambitions to a range subservient to communal purpose.

Durkheim was wrong to think this could be done rationally and consciously. By now it should be clear that rationality is too easily transformed into the rationalization of any end. Whether it is the justification of Exxon's handling of the Valdez disaster or Nestlé's arrogant dismissal of the plight of African families, without stable moral standards economic behavior will never meet civilized levels of care beyond the insights of cost-benefit analysis. Noneconomic standards are needed for the evaluation of economic ones.

Of course, questions will be raised concerning what standards and who gets to create them. It seems to me that Habermas is wrong to think a stable consensus can be achieved through democratic process alone. We know democratic consensus is not stable; nor is it always much of a consensus. Every attempt to create new moral standards raises as many questions about legitimacy as it resolves. Regardless, the political process is not the only means of addressing moral questions. Indeed, the self-interest at the base of democracy exposes its obvious limits as a way of securing a stable moral order.

My position is that moral standards already exist and have existed throughout the history of our civilization. It is our responsibility to resurrect these traditions and cultivate the moral teachings in them, updating and refining them to meet our own needs. My answer is not new, although it appears, as mentioned above, to be somewhat forgotten in the debate between modernism and postmodernism in the field of organization theory. What is needed above all else is a moral framework that is superior to economic activity and capable of evaluating and restraining it. The great moral accomplishments of the past can speak to this need. Until the Enlightenment, tradition had a central role in organizing the moral standards of Western civilization for several millennia. Indeed, some organizations do have traditions that carry moral standards from one generation to the next. But these are the exceptions.

This is something that must eventually involve all of society. But it must begin somewhere. It is not going to begin in business, nor are the power interests of government a possible origin. In modern society, I see no other possibility than the universities (although the thought of it makes one recognize the colossal size of the endeavor in the teaching profession alone, with its unbridled individualism and destructive imitations of business organization). The moral leadership must come from the universities. It is here that a broader perspective than profit maximization has a reasonable chance of being considered, and it is here that the intellectual resources are available to re-found a moral tradition that is capable, through the teaching discipline, of gaining adherents in a society that prefers to adhere to nothing.

Notes

1. In this chapter, except for minor references, I will exclude the important influence of Michel Foucault on discussions of organization control inside the discipline of organization theory, having concentrated solely on this influence in other chapters.
2. The word "repression" here and throughout the text is used in the Freudian sense (Freud 1915); that is, culture is seen, as will be shown, as a repressive force. In Freudian terms, the superego is the representative of culture inside the individual. Certain ideas that are unacceptable to the superego (that is, to cultural beliefs) are repressed or denied to individual consciousness. Repression, therefore, is *the* dynamic of culture in the sense that there is a dynamic relationship between the cultural beliefs of a group and the repressed contents in the minds of group members. Change the beliefs of the group and it will result in a changed character structure in individual group members. For a historically relevant example, in the period of the French Revolution, ideas as to the equality of individuals became widespread in French society. This led to repression of desires for hierarchical authority in favor of individual freedoms. A few decades later, this relationship was reversed to its original position as desires for individual freedoms were devalued and forgotten and desire for unity and self-sacrifice became widespread.

8

The Leveling of Organizational Culture: Egalitarianism in Critical Postmodern Organization Theory

Critical postmodern organization theory posits the increasing rationalization of organizational life as a threat to individual choice and well-being. Organizational knowledge is seen as a carrier of power relations that subjugate individuals for organizational purposes. Thus, individual resistance through the cultivation of egalitarian forms of self-knowledge is advocated. In this chapter, I review the arguments and suggestions put forward by critical postmodern organization theorists. I conclude that critical postmodern organization theory's power/knowledge critique destroys the basis of moral culture in its attack on the dehumanizing processes of rationalization. A more balanced approach that limits critical fervor through the appreciation of moral traditions is suggested.

The ubiquity and harshness of modern life has increased the popularity of doctrines that focus the individual on him—or herself, attempting to provide salvation from the apparent madness of collective attachment. Doctrines as diverse as Unitarianism, modern economic theory, and psychoanalysis all seek to put the individual in the driver's seat of his or her experience in the world. It is in this context that this chapter analyzes the doctrine of critical postmodern organization theory[1]. Although critical postmodern organization theory is a relatively new contribution to the discipline of organization theory, and despite the fact that it calls itself *post*modern, it carries on the modern tradition of individualism. Specifically, I show that its central concept of power/knowledge is designed to remove the individual from attachment to shared cultural values. In this sense, this theory shares the basic drawback of all individualistic doctrines that have dominated modern consciousness since the Enlightenment: It suffers from a one-sidedness that impoverishes moral commitment, weakening the basis of human organization.

In reading this chapter, it is important to keep in mind that the focus is on organizational culture. Culture is defined as the system of symbols that organizes the moral demands and the limited releases from these demands that make men/women intelligible and trustworthy to each other. Culture is hierarchical in that moral demands are primary, releases secondary, giving culture clarity and stability over time (Dumont 1980). This is a different focus than, for example, Jaques's (1990) work on hierarchy that focuses on the hierarchical relations between individuals in an organizational structure. My concern with the hierarchical nature of culture stems from the fact that critical postmodern organization theory advocates the dismantling of cultural hierarchy to increase the capacities of individuals to choose their own value positions in the workplace. The postmodern program to dismantle cultural hierarchy has significant implications for both individual development and organizational behavior. This chapter explains and evaluates these implications.

The chapter focuses on the theoretical writings of critical postmodern organization theorists because few empirical studies have been carried out in this body of research (Reed, 1993). The method I use is textual analysis (Van Maanen 1995). Textual analysis seeks to explicate the ideas being promulgated by both grasping the intellectual traditions from which they derive and the organizational, social, and moral practices and values to which they point. In short, textual analysis attempts to understand the vision being put forward and to evaluate it.

I will use empirical studies of organizational culture to ground my analysis in actual organizational realities. These studies are Kunda's (1992) analysis of a large electronics company, referred to as Tech Corporation; Feldman's (1988a; 1989a; 1990) research on a family-dominated electronics company, referred to as Smith Electronics; and Feldman's (1985; 1986a) study of a large telephone company, referred to as Telephone Company. There will also be a description of a university restructuring effort. In this way, the textual analysis will be supplemented, clarified, and empirically supported.

The chapter is divided into two sections and a conclusion. The first section focuses on the postmodern concept of power/knowledge and organizational control. The second section focuses on the concept of power/knowledge and individual resistance. Both sections begin with a presentation of the postmodern position followed by an analysis of this position.

Power/Knowledge and Organizational Control

In Foucault-inspired organization theory, power and knowledge are seen as coterminous (Townley 1993). One begets the other. The basic principle, in Foucault's words (1977, 194), is:

> The individual is no doubt the fictious atom of an 'ideological' representation of society; but he is also a reality fabricated by this specific technology of power that I have called 'discipline'. We must cease once and for all to describe the effects of power in negative terms: it 'excludes', it 'represses', it 'censors', it 'abstracts', it 'masks', it 'conceals'. In fact, power produces; it produces reality; it produces domains of objects and rituals of truth. The individual and the knowledge that may be gained of him belong to this production.

In this view, power is a kind of social production process through which collective meaning is created and maintained. It is created and maintained in knowledge. Knowledge becomes an instrument of power that people use in making sense of the world without fully grasping its implications. Foucault sees this process as a ritual that is collectively enacted. This can be seen clearly at Tech Corporation, where employees had to attend seminars to gain knowledge of the culture that, in effect, acted as a mechanism of normative control (Kunda 1992).

Knowledge is a natural medium for power because before something can be controlled, it first must be known (Townley 1993). Once it is known, it can be manipulated or changed. Perhaps the classic example in management is Frederick W. Taylor's (1911) "scientific" measurement of assembly line workers in order to increase the speed and effectiveness of these workers. Postmodernists point out that knowledge is not objective, as it is made out to be, but is the product of heterogeneous practices of power (Calás and Smircich 1991). Indeed, at Tech, company policies are part of the interpretive battleground, with each group reinterpreting them to its own advantage (Kunda 1992).

This view of knowledge has been applied to many aspects of management and organization theory. Knights and Collinson (1987), for example, apply the power/knowledge framework to the discipline of accounting. They argue that workers are individualized through accounting practices and that this undermines their ability to act collectively. Accounting is successful in this process because it promotes the idea that the worker can achieve financial independence by constituting himself or herself as being materially self-interested. In reality, however, workers cling to these illusions to maintain their dignity in conditions of actual dependence (Knights and Collinson 1987). Alvesson and Deetz, (1996, 205) write,

> The experience of the world is structured through the ways discourses lead one to attend to the world and provide particular unities and divisions. As a person learns to speak these discourses, they more properly speak to him or her in that available discourses position the person in the world in a particular way prior to the individual having any sense of choice. As discourses structure the world they at the same time structure the person's subjectivity, providing him/her with a particular social identity and way of being in the world.

The purpose of the discourse is to fit the individual into a structure. In an example from management, Townley (1993, 538) shows how "the act of inscribing the individual through performance appraisal schemes serves to articulate and develop a management role that becomes institutionalized in structure."

A key to modern power/knowledge regimes, then, is the "ethos of individualism" (Calás and Smircich 1992, 233). This can be seen clearly in the discipline of organization theory. Calás and Smircich (1992: 233) write, "Concepts like competition, achievement motivation, leadership, and even group dynamics are legitimated by a taken-for-granted autonomous, acultural, and ahistorical self." By focusing on the autonomous self, they tend to de-emphasize the relational aspect of organizational behavior, such as conflict, class, and power (Steffy and Grimes 1992). This decontextualization results in the limiting of the self in the workplace because it leaves the effects of power/knowledge discourses unanalyzed. The training seminars at Tech are a good example. By focusing on the individual's own development, they de-emphasize the individual's restrained position in a web of organizational goals, processes, and systems (Kunda 1992).

The reason power/knowledge regimes are so pervasive in social life is that they create "positive benefits"—for example, the profitable control over the flow of goods, finances, and labor (Hoskin and Macve 1986). This is why individuals voluntarily participate in their implementation. Hence, power/knowledge regimes present a dilemma: They are a productive part of social organization, even though they stifle individual choice. For example, total quality management programs increase productivity, but the autonomy they offer actually increases dependence (Willmott 1993).

Foucault's concept of power is designed to address these issues: it is relational (Townley 1994). It focuses on the practices, techniques, and procedures through which we define others and ourselves. In a sense, the concept of power/knowledge takes the individual out of the analysis (Steffy and Grimes 1992). For example, in her study of the evaluation of management competencies, Townley (1994) points out that management competencies are constructed through observational techniques and thus are more given than possessed. The Foucauldian focus is always on how the possibilities for action are structured. Mingers (1992, 108) writes, "Power is not all or nothing, but a complex continuum from influence to violence, from easing to constraining, which channels and guides rather than forces and blocks, structuring the possibilities for action within the network of ongoing social practices."

At Tech, for example, distinct presentational styles were developed to inform, motivate, and organize employees. Disagreement and conflict were always explicitly encouraged. It was stated repeatedly that the company was "open." However, rogue employees who were not satisfied with their token criticism and continued to voice dissent were either cut off by superiors or pressured into submission by peers (Kunda 1992).

In the writings of postmodernists, these social practices are portrayed as totalizing. Deetz (1992, 37), for example, states that "disciplinary power resides in every perception, every judgment, every act." This complete control is accomplished through "unexamined totalizing assumptions" (Knights and Vurdubakis 1994). Clegg (1977, 35) writes,

> Thus, power relations are only the visible tip of a structure of control, rule and domination which maintains its effectiveness not so much through overt action, as through its ability to appear to be *the* natural convention. It is only when taken-for-grantedness fails, routines lapse, and 'problems' appear, that the overt exercise of power is necessary.

Indeed, power/knowledge routines are so implicitly effective that rarely is overt power needed (Deetz 1992). This is seen in the previous Tech example. Dissenting employees usually backed down when the same point that they objected to was simply repeated (Kunda 1992). In other

cases, laughter resulting from jokes was used to discredit the serious-
ness of the dissent.

A key power/knowledge discourse that achieves this level of implicit control is the ideology of modern humanism (Knights and
Willmott 1989). Modern humanism falsely conceives the individual as
separate from society, and this forces the individual back in on himself
or herself by becoming "'tied to their own identity by a conscience or
self-knowledge'" (Foucault in Knights and Willmott 1989, 550). This
process of individualization increases the individual's dependence on
the demands of power/knowledge regimes because it is the only way
to secure a stable identity. Furthermore, because the self/society dichotomy is taken for granted, the individual is unaware of the role
ideology plays in his or her institutionalized dependency.

Tech employees, for example, often complain about pressure on
their "true" self from the "organization self" they have to develop to
succeed in the organization (Kunda 1992). They talk of strategies to
maintain the boundary between the two selves. The postmodern critique of modern humanism points out, however, that this boundary is
an illusion. There is no private self; all selves are social. Hence, the
belief that escape into a private self is possible precludes the person
from cognizing fully the reality of organizational life.

The situation becomes even more exploitative when we consider
that as the individual attempts to meet organizational demands, this
leads to competition between individuals as they all try to achieve
scarce recognition (Knights and Willmott 1989), leaving them sus-
pended in uncertainty and insecurity (Townley 1994). Self-identity
becomes a condition of nihilistic fragmentation as the self chases the
continually changing demands of authority figures (Willmott 1994).
Hence, the liberal humanist ethos turns into a process of subjugation
by transforming work into matters of "personal" fulfillment and "private" identity (Willmott, 1993).

The false self inherent in the illusion of the private self is widely
apparent at Tech. Few employees were ever able to find the right
balance between the two selves (Kunda 1992). On the contrary, it was
common to find that the organizational self swallowed the private self.
This is shown in the pervasiveness of 17-hour days, broken marriages,
and the organizational disease referred to as burnout.

Analysis

By making knowledge and power coterminous, postmodernists collapse the distinction between culture and politics. This collapse represents a confusion between inner and outer, between mind and action (Rieff 1985). In social life, there is always a tension between mind and action, between knowledge and power. To argue that they are coterminous is to say that the implementation of knowledge exactly reflects its meaning. But this is never the case. Knowledge of an external object is always dependent on a complex web of internal (tacit) awareness (Polanyi 1958). This collapse of culture into power is an indirect inheritance from Marx, as Marx was optimistic that ideas could be implemented as planned (Rieff 1985). Ironically, the relation to Marx shows the postmodernists as heirs to modern rationalism, which they strongly reject.

At Tech, collapse of the distinction between culture and politics would lead us to see the corporate culture merely as a control mechanism. Although this culture is indeed a control mechanism, which postmodern theory is useful to help us understand, it is much more than that. It is a creation of the human imagination and as such tells us something about the internal life of Tech employees. For example, the phenomenon of burnout is not simply the result of corporate disregard for employee work capacity but includes the harsh ambition of employees themselves, who manage difficult emotional conflicts by overworking. Divorce, for example, is not simply the result of excessive work, but excessive work is also used to avoid managing marital conflict.

The collapse of the distinction between culture and politics in the concept of power/knowledge also explains the exaggerated emphasis on system-level control in postmodern organization theory. The critique of accounting practices, for example, is one-sided in that it explains the process of individualization only as a result of system-level dependencies. However, workers, like all human beings, have an instinctive concern with their bodily selves (James 1890). Individualization is never simply the result of accounting practices or theories of organization. It is a fact of human existence. By collapsing the distinction between knowledge and power, postmodernists devalue the profound psychological significance of the fact that the mind is yoked to the body and that a natural concern of the mind is the well-being of the body. By reifying culture through the power/knowledge monad, accounting, organization theory, personnel psychology, and so forth, are assumed to exercise a level of control (and responsibility) that ignores the individual's instinctive capacities to experience his or her own sentiments and to accept or reject them.

Few employees at Tech, for example, are so brainwashed that the organizational ideology becomes their central system of beliefs (Kunda 1992). In fact, the majority of employees are quite alert to the boundary between the organizational ideology and their inner sense of themselves. They know when they feign these beliefs, and some are quite proud of how sincere they can make themselves appear. They go to all this trouble precisely in the pursuit of individual rewards. Postmodernism exaggerates the role culture plays in this selfishness and in so doing misses the alternative explanation that selfishness can result precisely from a lack of culture (Freud 1908).

The power/knowledge monad also one-sidedly explains discipline only from the point of view of organizational control, that is, "inscribing the individual." But discipline is also essential for cooperation (Barnard 1938; Durkheim 1933). For multiple individuals to achieve a common purpose, each individual must be disciplined to integrate his or her actions with the actions of others. This integration involves more than control; it also involves morality because collective purpose requires higher level moral commitments such as justice (Aristotle 1971). Discipline is an attribute of civilization (Mill 1836). By politicizing discipline through its complete incorporation into the concept of power/knowledge, its moral aspect is lost. This is a clear example of postmodernism's implicit individualism because power/knowledge is seen as opposed to the solitary individual. Thus, despite this theory's rejection of the self-society dichotomy of modern humanism, we see the value of the autonomous individual motivating the postmodern critique of organizational control.

At Tech, most individuals tried to fit into the organizational community neither because they were brainwashed nor only because they were rewarded but because they had a natural need to please others and to bond (Kunda 1992; compare Trist and Bamforth 1951). Getting along with others was required in the complex division of labor; it was also a reward in and of itself for many employees. Their relationships at Tech were the continuation of affectionate relations that many employees had valued all their lives. Discipline, the internalization of moral restraint, is a necessary part of maintaining affectionate bonds. Postmodernism's reduction of discipline to a mechanism of control also implies a level of individual autonomy that would require a surpassing of the individual's socialization in the family, the moral institution par excellence (Sullivan 1950).

By collapsing the distinction between politics and culture, critical postmodern organization theory misunderstands discipline merely as a form of control in a second way: it devalues the historical dimension of culture. By seeing knowledge only as a form of power, the past is ignored because the concept of power primarily explains culture as a current system of domination. However, culture is a historical phenomenon. Continuity through time is the basis for cultural stability; that is, the coherent meaning of beliefs and values (Dilthey 1886). Hence, organizational discipline seen from a cultural perspective involves an element of tradition. Tradition is not merely a matter of current control but is the outcome of the labor of previous generations that actively participated in continuing and modifying the inherited stock of knowledge (Shils 1981). The culture of service at the Telephone Company, for example, was not just a form of power to maximize the productivity of workers; it was also a way of life that many people found meaningful when they worked and after they retired (Feldman 1986). Culture, unlike power, involves sharing meaning with those who lived and worked in the past. This is important because it shows the trans–temporal nature of much organizational experience. In the concept of power/knowledge, this trans–temporal element is lost.

A related problem can be seen in the postmodern analysis of self-discipline as a vehicle to increase dependency, because self-discipline plays an essential role in ensuring autonomy. Without self-discipline, organizational control would be even greater. The argument that self-discipline increases dependency is only partly true because self-discipline also functions to replace organizational control by synthesizing control and autonomy in a new way. This is demonstrated in "flextime," for example, where organizational autonomy leads to individual autonomy in that workers are able to leave work early after meeting organizational goals (Capowski 1996). Self-discipline thus has a double effect: It increases dependency as the individual pursues organizational goals, but it also increases autonomy; by transferring responsibility for action to the individual, it opens up a space for initiative and thus for the refiguring of individual and organizational routines. In this way, it becomes a means to limit organizational control. Hence, self-discipline can act to keep both individual and organization in mutual check.

Power/Knowledge and Individual Resistance

Despite a strong tendency to imagine culture as a dominating system of control, postmodernists do allow the individual some personal resources. "The exercise of power brings into being resistance to power, and indeed power as a relation implies some space of freedom against which it is exercised" (Mingers 1992, 108). Willmott (1994, 114) writes,

> It is perhaps necessary to stress that Foucault does not ascribe to human beings an essential desire to either become free or to resist the authority of power/knowledge relations. Instead, he argues that the authority and continuity of such relations is fundamentally and irremediably precarious because human agency is open and mercurial. 'The intransigence of freedom' resides at the center of every power/knowledge relationship because the openness of human agency is at once a condition for the development of such a relationship and an inherently unstable basis for its renewal and continuation. However, precisely because freedom is understood by Foucault to be at the heart of every power relationship, his conception of freedom is undiscriminating: all power/knowledge relations are potential seducers of human agency; all are equally vulnerable to 'the recalcitrance of the will'; all are to be viewed with equal suspicion.

Indeed, "subjects . . . .are active in both positioning themselves within [power/knowledge] relations and committing themselves to particular subject positions" (Knights and Vurdubakis 1994, 184). Intervention—through participation—is possible, and thus the postmodern conception of power is paradoxical. Even though it is assumed that "there is no position exterior to power-knowledge relations," it is still seen as possible to resist these relations (Knights and Vurdubakis 1994, 169).[2] At Tech, for example, it was part of the organizational ideology that if one did not like the work situation, one was responsible to change it (Kunda 1992). By accepting the power/knowledge system, managers and engineers positioned themselves to change parts of it.

One explanation for the paradoxical conception of power is that power/knowledge relations develop for "socio-historical reasons . . . [and are not a] . . . seamless web" but compete with and contradict each other (Knights and Vurdubakis 1994, 177-8). Their configuration is contingent and precarious. Apparently, the individual can take advantage of conflicts between power/knowledge regimes as a conscious strategy of resistance. Nonetheless, in the critical postmodern organization theory literature, the emphasis is on the exploitative relations that power/knowledge regimes create (Deetz 1992). Indeed, the call to action emanating from this literature is to oppose power/knowledge discourses so that true autonomy can blossom. Engineers at Smith Electronics, for example, routinely used marketing rationales to win funding for technological projects from finance managers (Feldman 1989a). In this case, however, the win was short lived because before long marketing rationales, too, had to show financial results.

The origin of the oppressive potential of power/knowledge regimes that critical postmodern organization theorists emphasize is "in the increasing rationalization of social conduct" (Steffy and Grimes 1992, 190). Indeed, for postmodernists, the tendency of power/knowledge schemes to classify and categorize—"the insatiable drive toward greater clarification" (Townley 1993, 539)—is the defining characteristic of modernity. Critical postmodern organization theorists thus advocate an attitude of permanent questioning to critically reflect on the legitimacy of power/knowledge discourses (Townley 1994). By permanent questioning, postmodernists mean "knowledge must be deconstructed for emancipation" (Knights and Collinson 1987, 475). Alvesson and Deetz (1996, 210) write,

> The role of postmodern research is very different from more traditional roles assigned to social science. It primarily serves to attempt to open up the indeterminancy that modern social science, everyday conceptions, routines, and practices have closed off. The result is a kind of anti-positive knowledge (Knights, 1992).

For example, Townley (1993) argues that permanent questioning is required to establish equality for women in patriarchal organizational cultures. The questioning must be continuous lest a matriarchal power/knowledge system merely replaces the patriarchal one. The point is that by keeping up the play of cultural indeterminacy, established culture can be removed as a bulwark of inequality.

Opening up the indeterminacy means resisting established structures of knowledge. Calás and Smircich (1991, 579), for example, argue that any dominant knowledge is "nothing more than a play of differences." Knowledge, for them, always involves the suppression of someone's voice. Because postmodernists assume all knowledge is power laden, they distrust all commitments to knowledge. Their position is an extreme form of epistemological relativism. Alvesson and Deetz (1996, 209–10) write,

> Most postmodernists treat the external as a kind of excess or 'otherness' which serves as a resource for formations and also prevents language systems from becoming closed and purely imaginary. While the referent has no specific character it always exceeds the objects made of it, and thus reminds one of the limited nature of all systems of representation and their fundamental indeterminacy (Cooper, 1989). The presence of 'otherness' in the indeterminacy provides a moment to show the domination present in any system, to open it up, and to break the sealed self-referentiality of some textual systems.

Hence, meaning is seen as expressed through textual systems that are self-referential. This leads postmodernists to conclude semantic boundaries are arbitrary (Martin and Frost 1996). There is no reason why they cannot be altered simply by changing the relations between signs. Indeed, it is morally imperative that they are so altered in order to free suppressed voices, real and potential (Calás and Smircich 1991). For example, at the Telephone Company there was an informal rule against asking what salaries other workers receive (Feldman 1985). In postmodern terms, this rule is a mere symbol in a system of symbols that has nothing more than an arbitrary legitimacy based on its own self-reference. Furthermore, this legitimacy not only conceals the interests of some participants but also acts as a power mechanism to advance these interests. Hence, the principle of equality morally justifies questioning these rules.

It follows that the way we organize is arbitrary and that we always have the legitimate right to rebel against our organizations (Townley 1994). Townley, (1994, 146) writes,

> From the recognition that there is no 'essential, natural or inevitable way of grouping or classifying people' or things comes the freedom to rebel against ways in which we are already defined, categorized and classified (Rajchman, 1985: 62). Clearly, disciplinary power has real effects which constrain us, but it is possible to resist the ways people have been identified, classified and constituted as individuals: 'at every moment, step by step, one must confront what one is doing . . . what one is' (Foucault, 1984c: 374). Foucault offers a 'politics of revolt', a 'constant "civil disobedience" within our constituted experience' (Rajchman, 1985).

But it is an odd or at least novel kind of revolt that is being advocated.

"[W]e need to remain skeptical at one and the same time precisely of those rights that we support . . . if only to avoid the kind of self-subjugation or project identification which stifles critical judgement" (Knights and Vurdubakis 1994: 191). Hence, postmodernists cannot advocate a "new form of life . . . [but only] . . . unpredictable and specific criticism" (Townley 1994, 146).[3] At bottom, postmodernists see employee identification as the problem. It is a rigid psychological mechanism that stifles the growth of the autonomous (rational) worker. At Smith Electronics, for example, the president was so closely identified with the founder that most employees felt it was impossible to tell their opinions apart (Feldman 1990). When the founder had a stroke and was hospitalized, the president was unable to run the company on his own.

The solution to the rigidities of identification is to remain in a critical poise, never accepting any truth or belief as final. This, of course, creates other problems. There is an "absence of a clear 'positive' message" (Alvesson and Willmott 1992, 9). Indeed, as Knights and Vurdubakis (1994) point out, by remaining in a critical position, genuine political agency is impossible. Willmott (1994, 115) writes,

> In effect, Foucault paints himself, and his devotees, into a corner. Since there is a refusal to clarify the normative criteria for distinguishing more or less acceptable forms of power, the Foucauldian struggle against subjection is not only restless but fundamentally capricious, individualistic and ultimately nihilistic (Berman, 1993). Foucault calls for 'new forms of subjectivity through the refusal of the kind of individuality which has been imposed upon us for several centuries' (Foucault 1982a: 16, quoted in Knights 1990: 323). But aside from the incitement to (recurrent) transgression, he offers no lead on how any new, de-subjected form of subjectivity is to be realized.

As was noted, some employees at Tech pursued nothing more than their own self-interest, using company ideology as a screen to manipulate others for their own ends. Some critical postmodernists seek a third path, what Willmott (1994) calls "de-subjection," rejecting both psychological identification and nihilistic individualism.

The de-subjected self would be accomplished by opening up individual identity to potential competing identities. Identity as a fixed coherent unity is considered an illusion and is to be rejected (Willmott 1994). Instead, uncertainty, indeterminacy, contingency, and drift are to be embraced. Hence, the de-subjected "self" is self-rejecting. All identifications are seen as rigidifying. Willmott (1994, 116) refers to this as a "democratic self-organization." He claims it will be a positive force in organizations because it will stimulate flexibility and innovation. At the Telephone Company, for example, there was a high-level manager known for his capacity to play many different roles (Feldman 1985). It was said that he directed plays at a local college. At work, he rejected the company culture of service and was able to significantly increase innovation in his organization.

Analysis

The power/knowledge-resistance dualism is based on the postmodern assumption that the essence of modern life is the increasing rationalization of social conduct. Once this assumption is accepted, modern organizations are seen as impersonal and oppressive. This characterization is similar to the Weberian bureaucracy thesis, except in the postmodern view rationalization is taking place in the cultural system instead of in the organizational structure. In addition, Weber's (1946) insistence that the leader is in control of the system has been replaced with the insistence that the cultural system is an autonomous force with its own purpose, that is, to discipline social bodies. For example, at Smith Electronics, Mr. Smith, the company founder and CEO, was subjected to the same forces of cultural repression as everyone else. In this case, the cultural repression had to do with an obsessive concern with technological perfection at the expense of human relations, both among employees and toward customers (Feldman 1988a).

The importance of the power/knowledge framework is best demonstrated, for example, in its application to management disciplines such as accounting, human resource management, and advertising. The framework highlights the impersonal and rationalizing tendencies of these systems. However, this is what the Weberian theory of bureaucracy already has done quite well (Crozier 1964; Jackall 1988). Perhaps the forcefulness of the power/knowledge framework is to emphasize the unavoidable connection between power and knowledge in practice, that is, to remind us of the ever-recurring tendency of ideas to become the pawns of power interests.

The problem with writers working in this area, however, is that they tend to overshoot the analysis of the effects of specific rational systems in specific contexts and assume that the essence of modern organizational life is power/knowledge oppression. All organizations begin to look like Orwell's (1949) world of *1984*. Critical postmodern organization theory easily passes beyond social science analysis into an anti-ideology ideology. This can be seen in the notion of resistance, which assumes an autonomous individual whose key characteristic is a natural capacity to resist organizational control. It is significant that this notion of the resisting individual is abstract, free of any particular cultural context.[4] It is a very different assumption than that found in my discussion of self-discipline in the previous section, because I posit a mutual relation between individual autonomy and organizational control. Indeed, the assumption of the abstract individual not only enables the postmodernists to justify the transformation of culture into oppressive power/knowledge but also to recommend the anti-ideology practice of permanent criticism.

In regard to the postmodern assumption that power/knowledge systems are autonomous, it is true, for example, that Mr. Smith is subject to the same forces of cultural repression as are his employees. He is subject to the same forces of repression, however, because he is the origin of these forces (Feldman 1988a). The culture at Smith Electronics is not an autonomous self-rationalizing system. It is a human creation, the result of human choices and of the unconscious motivations behind them. Some individuals do resist Mr. Smith and the culture that developed around him, but not because of some natural autonomy. On the contrary, entrepreneurial managers who could not fit into the Smith culture clashed with Smith over specific ideals that were inconsistent with their own socially constructed beliefs (Feldman 1988a). If power/knowledge systems were all self-rationalizing, then all our organizations would be very similar, which obviously they are not.

Postmodern organizational theorists themselves point out that permanent criticism undermines both political participation and cultural attachment. Indeed, it creates a negative culture in which all commitments are distrusted. This represents a nihilistic rejection of the transmission of moral knowledge from our inherited culture. Postmodern organizational theorists seem to believe that they can criticize this heritage and have it too, as if faith and belief are not based in the emotional depths of human character (Rieff 1959). This rationalistic fantasy is at the heart of postmodern cultural critique. It not only points out postmodernism's necessary existence as a subculture, dependent on the established order of modern society, but also the futility of its wish to create a culture based on criticism.

At the Telephone Company, for example, a new CEO was brought in who highly prized participation. His vice presidents, however, had spent the previous 30 years under authoritarian leaders. At first they just criticized the CEO, but before long they were criticizing everything, including each other (Feldman 1986a). The result was pervasive, debilitating conflict. Criticism is an important management tool, but the impulse to criticize must be restrained lest it destroy goodwill between individuals crippling their capacity to trust and cooperate with each other. When criticism becomes the dominant behavior in relations between managers, the culture is not long to survive. It is a delicate question how much criticism any culture can tolerate.

Postmodernists not only rely on the same abstract individualism that they criticize in mainstream organization theory, but it also leads them to the same place: moral relativism. For example, when Calás and Smircich (1991) argue that knowledge is nothing more than the play of differences and that it always suppresses someone's voice, they are assuming that dominant knowledge has no historical legitimacy and that the potential voice in suppressed differences is equally valid to all existing traditions. This demonstrates the postmodern bias toward contemporaneity. Indeed, the "selves" they are trying to protect in some cases do not exist as persons. They are little more than logical potentialities arrived at through a negation of the dominant knowledge configuration. Thus, their analysis is motivated not only by a self freed from history, but one defined by nothing more than the postmodern disposition to question all restrictions, even potential restrictions. This is the logical consequence of the "politics of revolt": absolute moral relativism.

As we have seen in the Telephone Company example, when continuity with established tradition (even an unsavory tradition, as we have in this case) is disrupted, the result is psychological disorientation and organizational conflict (Feldman 1986a). The postmodern wish to live in the pure present in order to avoid being subjected to dominant knowledge inevitably engenders a breakdown in the moral regulation of interpersonal relations. At the Telephone Company, once the new CEO did not enforce the old culture, the result was not a period of interpersonal bliss freed from the burden of the past but the manifestation of long repressed aggression, exaggerated self-importance, and envy (Feldman 1986a). Without the restraining power of cultural legitimacy, all human impulses are manifested, not just the noble ones.

Another aspect of the ahistorical character of the politics of revolt is the theory of meaning on which it is based. All meaning is understood as being expressed through self-referential textual systems. In other words, meaning is created through the relationship between signifiers. This is a synchronic or structural formulation. The historical dimension is not considered. Once the historical dimension is removed, meaning is reduced to a historical accident. It thus appears to be unjustifiable. This is why postmodernists are so keen on revolt: They see not only a tremendous potential being bound up in any particular organizational cultural arrangement, but a moral issue in that it is bound up unjustifiably.

There is a problem with this position. It assumes that potential activity is more valuable than past accomplishments. This seems unlikely because it requires present workers to be more insightful than *all* previous workers. Instead of mastering past knowledge and improving them, the emphasis is on deconstructing past knowledge and departing from them. What is lost in this approach is the work of previous generations in refining and improving organizational knowledge through the cultivation of traditions. Indeed, it is impossible to imagine modern organizations being effective (or just) without the traditions of financial, human resource management, legal, and marketing knowledge, for example. It appears that the strengthening of weaker traditions (or parts of traditions) that promote justice is a more reasonable approach to remedying some of the problems postmodern theorists rightfully point out than is opening up the indeterminacy that will loosen our already ambivalent grasp on the difference between right and wrong.

In an academic organization, for example, the dean, attempting to deal with the low productivity of tenured faculty, redesigned the school personnel policies. "Research" was renamed "discovery;" "service" was said to have an element of "scholarship." Despite an intensive effort to define the new terms, the result was widespread confusion as to the standards for promotion, with each department interpreting the new policies to advance their own interests. When the dean assumed the organizational culture was a mere system of signs that he could rationally redesign at will, he underestimated the psychological and political forces that would be unleashed, the potential for manipulation by current power holders, and the infinite capacity of individuals to rationalize and justify the most self-serving of actions. Tradition is important in organizations because it provides the ideals through which the self, by addressing what previous others have found important, is guided toward participating in collective purpose.

On the subject of the democratic self, it is worth comparing the postmodernist claim that a coherent self is an illusion with the view that the self necessarily develops a hierarchical order. The idea of the hierarchical self is based on man and woman's social existence. From the long period of socialization where first the infant and then later the child is educated into the cultural beliefs of his or her family and community, to the adult applying the same moral judgments to his or her own self that he or she applies to others, a hierarchical moral ordering is unavoidable in human life (James 1890; Mead 1934; Sullivan 1950). The postmodern claim that there are so many discourses that psychological fragmentation is inevitable demonstrates an ahistorical conception of culture, underestimating cultural continuity and exaggerating cultural change. For example, the American anxiety about appearing inferior that Tocqueville (1850) witnessed in the 1830s is still common in modern organizations (Kanter 1977). In any case, if postmodernists are right, it would be impossible to initiate new members into a culture because one culture would not exist.

It is interesting to note that the democratic self based on self-rejection must assume an abstract self of selves without which it would be impossible to accept or reject any experience at all. In other words, Willmott is forced to assume the autonomous, abstract self of humanism that he strongly rejects. Let's assume, for the sake of a simple example, an individual with two distinct selves, one of Japanese disposition, the other American. Furthermore, let's assume that this bundle of selves is a purchasing manager working in the United States and is offered a "gift" from a supplier. How would this "individual" be able to identify this "gift" as a "bribe"? (In Japan, a gift is seen as a common cultural courtesy, whereas in the United States it is seen as a bribe and is illegal.) The only way possible would be if the two selves were synthesized by yet a higher self. However, this higher self of selves, which is separate from the two cultural selves, assumes exactly the self-society dichotomy that the democratic self was created to replace. Indeed, this self-awareness stripped of any particular cultural values bears an uncanny resemblance to the naked ego of eighteenth century romanticism, which (it should be remembered) was the proto-type for the unchecked egoism of the past 200 years.

Conclusion

> *"The ideal in this polyglot world, where reason can receive only local and temporal expression, is to understand all languages and to speak but one, so as to unite . . . comprehension with propriety."*
> —George Santayana (1905, 185)

Critical postmodern organization theory is a reaction to and an out-growth of modern rationalism. As such, it is inseparable from it. This can be seen in the solution to critical postmodern organization theory's updated version of bureaucratic rationality, power/knowledge. Because power/knowledge discourses such as accounting or human resource management mummify individuality, critical postmodernists advocate the development of a democratic version of the self. The key charac- teristic of the democratic self is that it eludes bureaucratic rationality by eluding all cultural boundaries. In other words, nihilism is used as a weapon against overly narrow organizational rationalities. This is a major theme in critical postmodern organization theory: irrational ra-tionality is replaced with rational irrationalism. Hence, critical postmodern organization theory simply reverses modern social organi-zation. It is hard to imagine that nihilistic individualism is an improve-ment over dehumanizing rationality. Indeed, one begets the other. In any case, critical postmodern organization theory is throwing out the baby with the bath water by reducing all knowledge to power. This is a cynical rejection of our moral and intellectual inheritance.

The value of equality is at the basis of the critical postmodernist project. Equality is a foundational value of Western civilization. Its application to organizations has positive benefits because it encour-ages organizations to operate in harmony with the broader society. It is also an important positive influence in that it draws attention to and works against gross unfairness in the treatment of specific groups and individuals.

In critical postmodern organization theory, however, equality is promoted too far because it is taken beyond power relations between people to cultural relations between values. The inevitable result is the destruction of cultural values. In organizations, the process of permanent criticism adds impetus to the already declining commitment to professional integrity because the shared values on which integrity must be based are disconfirmed. For behavioral scientists, the weakening of shared values should be a concern because it undermines the psychological and social stability that enables organizations to become effective and humane places to live and work.

Critical postmodern organization theory seeks to be free of the burden of the past. Since Descartes, this goal has been the central characteristic of modern rationalism. It sees the past in negative terms as an unfair and oppressive inheritance. Although this perception has some truth in it, it is misleading. The past, as we find it transmitted through organizational cultures, is also a wealth of positive moral and social values. I have never been in an organization whose memory was filled only with stories of oppression and inequality. On the contrary, stories of sacrifice, caring, assistance, and loyalty abound. It is crucial that these positive values and the traditions that carry them are recognized as a positive force in developing moral culture in organizations.

Like all forms of rationalism, critical postmodern organization theory seeks to make up its mind about what values to follow in each case, after carefully searching for repressed voices. However, even then it fears attachment, lest domination again arise out of any new commitment. Like a jilted lover, critical postmodernism is unable to love out of fear of being forlorn yet again. Hence, it agitates for permanent criticism, endless movement. The centrality of criticism is no principle on which to maintain a culture, no shared attachment on which to build a moral vision. Continuity with the past is but the one source for organizational stability and moral depth.

It is mostly an impossible job to sort out the political forces at work in an organization from the deeper, less changing base of shared values. Political players manipulate ideas and ideals. It takes extended analysis to discover underlying values and attachments. To be sure, these underlying values can also be problematic compared to values of efficiency and professional integrity and may require change efforts. In any case, the distinction between political and cultural systems is required if an effort is to be made to work toward establishing a culture of integrity based on positive historical tendencies in the work group. In the concept of power/knowledge, this distinction is lost and along with it not only the ability to recognize the positive historical basis of moral organization but also the commitment to develop this basis into an enduring moral culture.

Notes

1. This chapter analyzes the influence the work of Michel Foucault has had on the conception of individual-organization relations in the field of organization theory. Foucault's work is just a part of what has become known as postmodernism (Cooper and Burrell 1988), and postmodernism is just a part of a broader critical tradition (Alvesson and Deetz 1996). Hence, Foucault's influence has affected writers from diverse backgrounds who are quite different from each other except for their interest in Foucault. I will refer to the body of literature I am reviewing as *critical postmodern organization theory* because Foucault's influence gives the critical tradition certain postmodern characteristics such as a wish to keep open the indeterminate backdrop surrounding all cultural meaning.
2. Knights and Willmott (1989) are not always consistent. They state that there is no position outside power/knowledge relations but then argue that "human action is fundamentally free as long as there are possibilities outside of those given by power" (1989, 553). Another contradiction appears in "power does not deny freedom, it directs it" (1989, 553) because direction implies constraint.
3. This is an important difference between postmodern organization theory and radical (Marxist) organization theory. Because postmodernists believe power/knowledge relations are omnipresent, they merely advocate local resistance. Marx, of course, advocated system-wide change.
4. The assumption of the abstract individual free of any particular cultural text was created by eighteenth century romanticists, for example, Rousseau's (1755) "noble savage." It is one of the roots of secular individualism (Lukes 1973), modern egoism (Tocqueville 1850), and modern fanaticism (Polanyi 1958).

9

Conclusion:
Sanctuaries Against the Modern World

The central assumption of this book is that the study of culture is concerned with the nature of moral commitment, choices about good and bad, right and wrong. I maintain that since it is concerned with moral issues, the study of culture should teach moral lessons. It is in this context that I examine organization theorists as a *culture class* in the field of management, in contradistinction to *social class*. Social class refers to the managers and leaders of organizations, in a word, to practitioners. Organization theorists, on the other hand, specialize in formulating the ideas, concepts, and moral perspectives that practitioners use to consider, revise, and direct their actions. This book is primarily a study of the work of the managerial culture class, that is, an investigation into the moral assumptions and implications of its products.

In the study of the cultural elites in the area of organizational culture, I found three primary "moral" commitments. These are commitments to rationalism, individualism, and democracy. These three moral commitments characterize in complex variations, transitions, and combinations moral theorizing in the study of organizational culture. All three of these moral commitments are modern in the sense that they are independent of any hierarchically ordered system of beliefs. Of course, each of the three is a system of belief in itself, but only in a special sense: they are based on the premise that traditional authority must be weakened or destroyed. They are anti-tradition traditions. "Modern" thus implies a rejection of the authority of the past. The organization theorists examined in this book all share the modern grandiose desire to totally create and control themselves. Despite decades of organizational "change" efforts, however, organization theorists have not been happy with the outcome. From Barnard to the postmodernists they all believe that changes in the nature of modern society—for example, increasing pluralism, competition, impersonalization, and rationalization—have put the moral quality of our lives in jeopardy. Thus in their work, both explicitly and implicitly, they seek to create moral sanctuaries against the modern world.

Chester Barnard perceives a threat in the 1930s from democratic socialism and attempts to reestablish social and moral control through the belief in the rational superiority of the executive. By the end of the century, however, we have all become sensitized to the limits of rationality. Diane Vaughan, for example, perceives a threat from the overwhelming complexity of modern organizations. True to the neo-rationalism inherent in the "new institutionalism," she warns that we cannot be rational enough, and concludes that we cannot avoid organizational disaster. Along with Barnard and Vaughan, critical organization theorists share a belief in rationality as the central instrument to understand and improve modern society, but, differing from Barnard and Vaughan, they believe the problem is a lack of true democracy. They seek to rationalize political communication to increase individual rationality and rational participation in democratic decision-making.

Melville Dalton sees the moral problem in modern organizations as a residue from premodern moral systems that irrationally restrict individual creativity and organizational action. Like Barnard, he seeks to rationalize organizational morality through the superior rationality of the superior executive; though, for Dalton competition replaces morality as the ultimate organizing principle because there are multiple superior executives. Dalton is a forefather of the democratic ethic in critical organization theory since he is the first to discuss cultural and moral rigidity as an obstacle to individual rationality.

"Postmodern" organization theorists follow Dalton in the sense that they too see belief as a form of organizational control. They add to Dalton's concern for individual creativity (though they do not share the stress he puts on organizational effectiveness) the concern for individual freedom. Dalton attempts to show that the political intrigues of large-scale business organization in the 1950s are acts of individual freedom, whereas in the 1980s and 1990s, the postmodernists focus on the homogenizing power of organizational "culture" and rationality. Postmodernists seek their sanctuary against the modern world in undermining rational systems, not merely advocating and justifying informal organization à la Dalton. It appears that Dalton's insights are more balanced and important because the superior level of detailed data he worked with enabled him to keep his images of individual and organization in a more realistic tension. Postmodernism has come close to destroying the idea of the individual by reducing person to personality, that is, by claiming the person is nothing more than the sum of its social parts. It shows little interest in the idea of individual moral responsibility or what used to be called the soul.

Despite important differences, all the organization theorists studied in this book seek to change the moral quality of modern organizations rationally. They all seek to create, none seek to conserve. Hence, the cultural elites in the study of organizational culture encourage the already established drive towards continuous change (compare Kanter 1983). This message is influential not only with the creative-destruction crowd of capitalistic competitors, but affects the views of public and nonprofit managers as well. This is, in my opinion, a reason unique to organization studies for the lack of consensus in the area of management ethics: ethics cannot be fully incorporated into a paradigm based on change. Ethics, to be respected, must be stable. The ideology of endless change in modern organizations and the endless questioning by modern critical culture devalue the respect for the past that makes ethical commitments viable.

However, all rational frameworks for decision-making are encased in traditions. To the extent decision-makers really do approach "continuous change" (that is, independent of any tradition), their thinking must be shallow and trivial because they have no way to evaluate the quality of their decisions. Decision-making requires a traditional component because tradition maintains what is believed to be important and good in social organization. For example, the simultaneous rise of capitalism and decline in the tradition of charity led to an insensitivity to human suffering in competitive arenas (Dickens 1854). My position is different than the positions studied in this book because I believe (and have argued throughout the book) that the past is an important part of the present, indeed, the essential part for maintaining ethical values through time. We must cultivate the past in the present as a means to evaluate—and in some cases condemn—the immediacy of our wants no matter how "rational" (that is, rewarding or efficient) they appear.

There is a revolutionary impulse implicit in modern organization theory's commitment to continuous change. This impulse affects, for the most part, the cultural realm, not the political or social. It seeks to weaken culture to free the individual from shared cognitive controls (Vaughan) or oppressive systems of power/knowledge (critical and postmodern organization theorists). Culture is either not rational enough or too rational, undermining the autonomy of the individual. The revolt against culture focuses on what it sees as mind control; it does not focus on behavior or even the exercise of power by one person or group over another. Culture, in a variety of formulations, is the central problem of modern organization theory. It draws angst-driven criticism from both rationalists and relativists.

Since Barnard's rejection of Christianity as inadequate for the moral needs of an industrial society, there has been a steady movement towards release from cultural controls in the writings of organization theorists. Only with deconstructionism has the logical end been reached: All cultural boundaries are to be destroyed through the release of the repressed opposite hidden in all symbolic forms. This whole movement is an example of what Michael Polanyi (1958) has called "moral inversion:" The value of the individual is set above any criteria for deciding good and evil. Thus, morality becomes synonymous with the removal of restriction from the individual, which, in effect, channels all moral energy into personal and collective action, leading the way to fanaticism. In Vaughan, for example, the ideal is the removal of shared unconscious cognition; individual conscious choice is represented as superior. Implicit in this ideal is the assumption of a natural rationality that inevitably goes astray through the establishment of collective thought patterns; that is, rationality is unable to exercise its presumed inherent tendency to seek the good.

The organization theorists studied in this book in effect act as secular moral guides. Dalton, for example, in his critique of moral traditions is clearly trying to create a moral justification for intra-organizational competition. In Dalton's case, his moral authority stems from his *artistic* ability. He creates images that influence the way organizations are understood and evaluated. His image of the leader as "social lion," for example, who uses the "informal system" to out-compete rivals through inexplicable superiority at managing "uncertainty," implies a justification for secrecy, manipulation, and power. In this style of moral preceptorship, Dalton is not trying to lead us to a moral framework, but away from all fixed moralities. Despite his use of natural metaphors—for example, leader as "lion"—Dalton's vision takes us away from all systems to a world of multiple and alternative realities. He seeks to uproot us, suggesting instead we exchange our fixed inwardness for unfixed externalizations, the better to create or at least adapt to new possibilities.

Another form of moral guide found in organization theory is the *political revolutionary*. Critical and postmodern organization theorists, following Marxism and before that the French revolutionary tradition, seek to change the distribution of power by altering the individual's relationship to the organization culture. As was noted in regard to critical organization theory, the central goal is to increase the rational awareness of the individual to improve his/her effective participation in democratic decision-making. The basic value motivating this framework is equality. Postmodernists, though sharing equality as a foundational value, distrust the slippery slope of "rationality," thus advocate the more defensive posture of permanent criticism. In either case, both critical and postmodern organization theorists take on the role of the political revolutionary, criticizing the oppressive conditions of modern organizations and advocating methods to achieve a better world.

The common root in these attempts at moral preceptorship, artistic and political, is an effort to provide spiritual leadership without established commitments to moral values. Only by killing all the gods, we are told, can a temple be built. This can be seen most clearly in a third type of spiritual guide found in the organization theory literature: the *scientist* as spiritual leader. Diane Vaughan is an example. She argues that morals had nothing to do with the *Challenger* launch disaster because macro–organizational forces controlled the "cognitive maps" of the individuals involved. The solution she seeks, to the extent she feels a solution can be found, is to lessen tacit constraints on decision-making, that is, increase the range of conscious choice. Vaughan recommends no moral guidelines, only more choices, that is, power. Thus, the world implied in her work is a world of rational control, where "good" decisions will be achieved purely by the maximization of consciousness. This is spiritual leadership without morality.

Historically, postmodernism is a reaction against scientific rationalism. To the postmodernist, science and technology have developed into systems of total control. Postmodernism seeks to create alternative realities to protect the individual's freedom from the overwhelming forces of scientific rationalization. The "democratic self" discussed in Chapter 8 is an example. It seeks to escape the enveloping power/ knowledge system by keeping equally distant from all beliefs. It attempts to create a private space. Postmodernism tries to enliven an existence that has been removed from nature by science, while simultaneously sharing with science a refusal to make lasting moral commitments. In this sense, the scientists (such as Vaughan) and the postmodernists (for example, Willmott) both demand a removal of inwardness and internalization from the human personality. They both see it as a preconscious form of mind control. They may imagine it in different forms and proffer different remedies, but ultimately modernism and postmodernism seek to slay the same dragon.

The innovation that postmodernism brings to modern culture is a systematic effort to externalize and unfix objects of cultural meaning. Calás and Smircich (1991), for example, uncover and expose male sexuality implicit in classical theories of organizational leadership. Their goal is to make visible and thus weaken the capacities of theories of leadership to support male domination in organization studies. Ultimately their analytic journey is only negative; they do not arrive at a new community. This is spiritual guidance for the autonomous individual, training in the deconstruction of community. The externalizations—male sexuality in this case—are always left isolated, disconnected from any socially acceptable or "natural" system of meaning. The moral demand system is left broken and inoperative.

In the writings of all the organization theorists studied in this book, there is a tendency to focus on macro structures to justify moral arguments. Their approach to moral issues is always impersonal. This can be seen in Vaughan's emphasis on "institutional forces," and in critical and postmodern organization theory's emphasis on "power/knowledge systems." Ironically, this use of abstractions to explain behavior actually strengthens modern individualism because it implies a need for the individual to resist irrational systems of collective control. The underlying theme or moral principle is always the same: The individual is caught in and misled by the (unavoidable) collective cocoon. By always framing the collective in negative terms, the system of moral demand is inevitably devalued. This is a central criticism in my study of organization theory: Ethics is reduced to politics and seen as an oppressive force to be resisted. Motivating this worldview is the unconscious insistence on the intellectual and moral superiority of the "natural" individual.

The criticism of *macro–ideational* structures is a logical development from earlier criticism of macro–organizational structures, that is, bureaucracy, à la Gouldner (1954), Crozier, (1964), Kanter (1977), etc. What is new in the criticism of ideational structures is seen most clearly in critical organization theorists: They seek to break the tension between inner and outer life. Benson (1977), for example, utilizing the Marxist dialectic between social production and reproduction, argues that commitments to ideals function to entrench the status quo and block organizational change. He argues for a continuous process of organizational reconstruction to realize human potentialities. This process of continuous reconstruction undermines the idealization of moral belief essential to stabilize commitment. Hence, the tension between an ideal (internal) world and the world of practice is lost. This is the ultimate meaning of all modern moralities; beliefs are maintained in the intimacy of means and the illusoriness of ends. Both an ethics of responsibility and an ethics of conscience are rejected as being oppressive. An ethics of action is proclaimed instead.

Without the tension between inner and outer life, the role of ethics in organizations is significantly weakened. This is the end result of the Protestant preference for achieving grace through action. Though originally motivated by deeply held religious beliefs, the rationalization of action eventually turned against ideals as obstacles to further rationalization. This is the reason for the collapse of ethics into politics in organization theory: When all thought is understood only in terms of its effect on action, the capacity to tell the difference between right and wrong is blunted as moral criteria merge with questions of utility. Ethics start to look like interests. Only by maintaining a tension between ideals and actions can we clearly use the former to evaluate the latter.

Without a tension between inner ideals and outer action putting limits on choice, the specifically modern problem of nihilism arises. When public moral codes are no longer an internalized part of the individual, the individual develops an excessive autonomy from moral values. These values become merely public, thus are easily ignored or manipulated. There is little to discourage the mind from entertaining any thought, little to stop the mind from suggesting any action. In this situation, the life of the individual becomes too private. Some attachment to collective ideals is essential to reinforce and stabilize moral character, bringing the individual into the middle road of civility between egoism and totalitarianism.

Is the belief in the modern tradition of "enlightened self–interest" such a middle road of civility? Can it maintain a workable tension between inner ideals and outer life? I think not because it relies too heavily on self-interest. It presumes a natural morality and takes our moral heritage for granted. Our sense of indebtedness to those who came before us is put to sleep. The individualist tends to assume that his/her ethics is his/her own accomplishment rather than the gift of his/her culture. This results in the loss of the sense of responsibility that is needed to maintain and apply ethics in the face of many countervailing forces. Most notably the (highly plastic) countervailing force of self-interest easily becomes our sole concern. Moral responsibilities that are not productive of our own goals are ignored.

The key question that must be asked of the new theories of culture is: Can they go beyond mere negativity and establish a fresh imbalance of controls and releases? Or do they just release? Deconstructionism, in its goal of dismantling the boundary between meaning and what it represses, is by definition a vehicle of failed controls. From Barnard to Dalton to critical and postmodern organization theorists, a new imbalance is never developed. After Barnard, the new theories are all one-way tickets to release, assuming that once oppressive controls are destroyed man/woman will exist in a state of innocence.

If we study the cultural dynamics that led to these programs for release, we learn that control or release cannot operate without each other. Indeed, it is precisely the overly strong controls of an earlier culture that led to the present remissive overreactions. For example, in the 1960s long held prejudices (for example, segregation) against African Americans led to demands for releases (for example, equal opportunities) from these controls. In some ways these releases were misused and had detrimental effects, as in the case of lower expectations for the performance of African American workers (Steele 1990). Hence, one-sided theories of release do not reflect historical realities nor do they offer a workable scheme for cultural organization. Cultural change is disorienting enough for the individual even when it is for the better—for example, sexual harassment laws—but continuous culture change is a cure worse than the disease.

The question remains what is the appropriate imbalance between controls and releases? As this book demonstrates, recent developments in the cultural study of organizations are one-sided in the direction of release. Simple controls are mentioned while elaborate releases are discussed in detail. For example, Barbara Townley (1994) briefly mentions respecting others as a requirement for organizational ethics, but spends the bulk of her effort recommending the means to resist power. It is common to find ethics downgraded from a system of moral proscriptions to recommendations for self-development. This assumes that the individual does not need guidance in making moral commitments. But moral commitments are anything but self-evident. In modern society, the individual is caught between a social environment bursting at the seams with information and contradictory advice and his/her own contradictory internal life. In this context, knowing and doing the right thing is extremely challenging. Morality is self-evident only in a clear and dominant culture. This we have not.

The field of organization theory is a reflection of the same forces that characterize modern society as a whole. It was created in modern society in close affiliation to science; thus it shares the same limitation, that is, an inability to arrive at a system of moral belief. From Barnard's rationalism to postmodern irrationalism, the field of organization theory represents a continuous "moral" development. It starts with Barnard's right of the executive to create his/her own moral values and ends with postmodernism's demand to reject all values because, being created by man/woman, none has any special right to be privileged. The Protestant cultural revolution has come full circle: Modern culture has evolved from Luther's revolt against institutional rationalization in the search for religious purity to Newton's scientific search for god in the laws of nature to Comte's scientific design of society to the search for self in the modern (psychological) era to the postmodern attack on rationalism. With religion and science rejected, the "self" descends into a state of interminable search.

To rid our selves of the mindlessness of endless search is not the only reason for the importance of moral commitments. Through commitments one gathers up all the loose ends of one's life in an organization that establishes priorities and restraints. In this way, our action as well as our character become purposeful and consistent. Only through these compromises can we make life meaningful and thus worth living. And only through these sacrifices can we gain a standard by which to establish self-respect. For we gain self-respect only through a respect for not-self.

The process of making a moral commitment implies the process of idealization because only in ideals do we find truth. The ebb and flow of everyday life leads only to the conflicting diversity of experience. By defining the good, ideals limit action, making it possible for people to live and work together. Without a consensus of shared ideals even disagreement is impossible. A consensus is achieved by an overlapping of various beliefs. It is brought about slowly over time through compromise as people attend to collective problems. For these beliefs to maintain our best efforts, they must be cultivated in traditions changing yet linking common themes (for example, "Honesty is the best policy" with "business ethics") through time. Only through tradition, reflected upon and revised from accumulated experience, can we guard against the outbreak of evil ideologies that turn the process of idealization into a vehicle of destruction. Moral traditions act as ballast against both individual greed and organized aggression. Without them, we are feeble in judgement and vulnerable to self-delusion.

References

Allinson, R. 1998. The cog in the machine manifesto: The banality and the inevitability of evil. *Business Ethics Quarterly* 8 (4):743-56.

Alvesson, M., and Willmott, H. 1992a. *Critical management studies*. London: Sage.

———. 1992b. Critical theory and management studies. In *Critical management studies*, edited by M. Alvesson and H. Willmott. London: Sage.

———. 1992c. On the idea of emancipation in management and organization studies. *Academy of Management Review* 17 (3):432-64.

Alvesson, M., and Deetz, S. 1996. Critical theory and postmodernism: Approaches to organizational studies. In *Handbook of organizational studies*, edited by S. Clegg, C. Hardy, and W. Nord. London: Sage.

Arendt, H. 1968. *Between past and future*. New York: Penguin Books.

———. 1950. *The origins of totalitarianism*. New York: Meridian Books.

Argyris, C. 1957. *Personality and organization*. New York: Harper.

Aristotle. 1982. *Nicomachean ethics*. Translated by H. Rackham. Cambridge, Mass.: Harvard University Press.

———. 1971. *The politics of Aristotle*. Translated by Ernest Barker. Oxford: Oxford University Press.

———. 1968. *Poetics*. Translated by Gerald F. Else. Oxford: Clarendon.

Asch, S.E. 1955. Opinions and social pressure. *Scientific American* 193 (5):14–22.

———. 1951. Effects of group pressure upon the modification and distortion of judgments. In *Groups, leadership, and men*, edited by H. Guetzkow. Pittsburgh: Carnegie Press.

Augustine. 1984. *The city of God*. Translated by Henry Bettenson. London: Penguin Books.

Badaracco, J., and Webb, A. 1995. Business ethics: A view from the trenches. *California Management Review* 37 (2):8–28.

Barnard, C. 1938. *The functions of the executive*. Cambridge, Mass.: Harvard University Press.

Baum, H. 1993. Organizational politics against organizational culture: A psychoanalytic perspective. In *The psychodynamics of organizations*, edited by L. Hirschhorn and C. Barnett. Philadelphia: Temple University Press.

Bauman, Z. 1989. *Modernity and the Holocaust*. Ithaca, N.Y.: Cornell University Press.

Bell, D. 1976. *The cultural contradictions of capitalism*. New York: Basic Books.

Benhabib, S. 1992. *Situating the self*. New York: Routledge.

Benson, J. 1977. Organizations: A dialectical view. *Administrative Science Quarterly* 22 (1):1–22.

Boyatzis, R. 1995. *Innovation in professional education.* San Francisco: Jossey-Bass.

Brody, M. 1986. NASA's challenge: Ending isolation at the top. *Fortune,* May 12.

Burke, E. [1795] 1967. *The philosophy of Edmund Burke.* Ann Arbor, Mich.: University of Michigan Press.

Burrell, G. 1994. Modernism, postmodernism and organizational analysis 4: The contribution of Jürgen Habermas. *Organization Studies* 15 (1):1–45.

———. 1993. Eco and the bunnyman. In *Postmodernism and organization,* edited by J. Hassard and M. Parker. London: Sage.

———. 1988. Modernism, post modernism and organizational analysis 2: The contribution of Michel Foucault. *Organization Studies* 9 (2):221-35.

Calás, M., and Smircich, L. 1992. Using the 'f' word: Feminist theories and the social consequences of organizational research. In *Gendering organizational analysis,* edited by A. Mills and P. Tancred. London: Sage.

———. 1991. Voicing seduction to silence leadership. *Organization Studies* 12 (4):567–602.

Capowski, G. 1996. The joy of flex. *Management Review* 85 (3):12–18.

Carr, A. 1968. Is business bluffing ethical? *Harvard Business Review* 46 (1):11–18.

Carter, P. 1995. Writing the wrongs. *Organization Studies* 16 (4):573-5.

Chapman, G. 1967. *Edmund Burke: The practical imagination.* Cambridge, Mass.: Harvard University Press.

Clegg, S. 1995a. Parker's Mood. *Organization Studies* 16 (4):565-70.

———. 1994. Social theory for the study of organization: Weber and Foucault. *Organization* 1 (1):149-78.

———. 1977. Power, organization theory, Marx and critique. In *Critical issues in organizations,* edited by S. Clegg and D. Dunkerley. London: Routledge.

Clegg, S., and Dunkerley, D. 1977. Introduction: Critical issues in organizations. In *Critical issues in organizations,* edited by S. Clegg and D. Dunkerley. London: Routledge.

Cochran, T. 1972. *Business in American life.* New York: McGraw-Hill.

Collins, R. 1981. On the micro-foundation of macro-sociology. *American Journal of Sociology* 86 (5):984–1014.

Cooley, C.H. [1922] 1983. *Human nature and the social order.* New Brunswick, N.J.: Transaction.

Cooper, R. 1989. Modernism, post modernism and organizational analysis 3: The contribution of Jacques Derrida. *Organization Studies* 10 (4):479–502.

Cooper, R., and Burrell, G. 1988. Modernism, postmodernism and organizational analysis: An introduction. *Organization Studies* 9 (1):91–112.

Crozier, M. 1964. *The bureaucratic phenomenon.* Chicago: University of Chicago Press.

Dalton, M. 1959. *Men who manage.* New York: Wiley.

Deetz, S. 1995. Character, corporate responsibility, and the dialogic in the postmodern context. *Organization* 2 (2):217-25.

———. 1992. Disciplinary power in the modern corporation. In *Critical management studies,* edited by M. Alvesson and H. Willmott. London: Sage.

Deetz, S., and Mumby, D. 1990. Power, discourse and the workplace: Reclaiming the critical tradition in communication studies in organization. In *Communication yearbook 13,* edited by J. Anderson. Newbury Park, Calif.: Sage.

Diamond, M. 1991. Stresses of group membership: Balancing the needs for independence and belonging. In *Organization on the couch: Clinical perspectives on organizational behavior and change,* edited by M. Kets de Vries. San Francisco: Jossey-Bass.

Dickens, C. [1854] 1966. *Hard times*. New York: Heritage Press.

Diesing, P. 1971. *Patterns of discovery in the social sciences*. New Brunswick, N.J.: Transaction.

Dilthey, W. [1886] 1989. Introduction to the human sciences. In *W. Dilthey: Selected writings*, edited and translated by H. P. Rickman. Princeton, N.J.: Princeton University Press.

———. [1883] 1986. *Dilthey*. Cambridge: Cambridge University Press.

Douglas, M. 1990. Converging on autonomy: Anthropology and institutional economics. In *Organization theory: From Chester Barnard to the present and beyond*, edited by O. Williamson. New York: Oxford University Press.

du Gay, P. 1994. Colossal immodesties and hopeful monsters. *Organization* 1 (1):125-48.

Dumont, L. 1986. *Essays on individualism*. Chicago: University of Chicago Press.

———. 1980. *Homo hierarchicus*. Chicago: University of Chicago Press.

Durkheim, E. 1957. *Professional ethics and civic morals*. Translated by Cornelia Brookfield. New York: Routledge.

———. 1933. *The division of labor in society*. Translated by George Simpson. New York: Free Press.

———. [1925] 1973. *Moral education*. Translated by Everett K. Wilson and Herman Schnurer. New York: Free Press.

———. [1915] 1965. *The elementary forms of the religious life*. Translated by Joseph Ward Swain. New York: Free Press.

———. [1897] 1951. *Suicide*. Translated by John A. Spaulding and George Simpson. New York: Free Press.

Eliot, T.S. 1932. *The sacred wood*. London: Methuen.

Elmes, M., and Barry, D. 1999. Deliverance, denial, and the death zone: A study of narcissism and regression in the May 1996 Everest climbing disaster. *Journal of Applied Behavioral Science* 35 (2):163-87.

Elshtain, J. 1995. *Democracy on trial*. Chicago: University of Chicago Press.

Featherstone, M. 1988. In pursuit of the postmodern: An introduction. *Theory, Culture, and Society* 5 (2–3):195–215.

Feldman, S.P. 1990. Stories as cultural creativity: On the relation between symbolism and politics in organizational change. *Human Relations* 43 (9):809-28.

———. 1989a. The broken wheel: The inseparability of autonomy and control in innovation within organizations. *Journal of Management Studies* 26 (2):83–102.

———. 1989b. The idealization of technology: Power relations in an engineering department. *Human Relations* 42 (7):575-92.

———. 1988a. How organizational culture can affect innovation. *Organizational Dynamics* 17 (1):57–68.

———. 1988b. Secrecy, information, and politics: An essay on organizational decision making. *Human Relations* 41 (1):73–90.

———. 1986a. Culture, charisma and the ceo: An essay on the meaning of high office. *Human Relations* 39 (3):214-28.

———. 1986b. Management in context: An essay on the relevance of culture to the understanding of organizational change. *Journal of Management Studies* 23 (6):587–607.

———. 1986c. *The culture of monopoly management*. New York: Garland Publishing.

———. 1985. Culture and conformity: An essay on individual adaptation in centralized bureaucracy. *Human Relations* 38 (4):341-56.

Forester, J. 1992. Critical ethnography: On fieldwork in a Habermasian way. In *Critical management studies*, edited by M. Alvesson and H. Willmott. London: Sage.

Foucault, M. 1980. *Power/knowledge*. Translated by Colin Gordon. New York: Pantheon.

———. 1977. *Discipline and punish*. Translated by Alan Sheridan. New York: Vintage.

Freud, A. [1936] 1974. *The ego and mechanisms of defense*. New York: International Universities Press.

Freud, S. 1938 1963. *Jokes and their relation to the unconscious*. Translated by James Strachey. New York: Random House.

———. [1933] 1965. *New introductory lectures in psychoanalysis*. Translated by James Strachey. New York: Norton.

———. [1930] 1961. *Civilization and its discontents*. Translated by James Strachey. New York: Norton.

———. [1921] 1960. *Group psychology and the analysis of the ego*. Translated and edited by James Strachey. New York: Bantam Books.

———. [1916] 1949. Some character-types met with in psycho-analytic work. In *The collected papers of Sigmund Freud*. Vol. 4. Translated and edited by Ernest Jones. London: Hogarth.

———. [1915] 1963. Repression. Translated and edited by Ernest Jones. In *General psychological theory*, ed. P. Rieff. New York: Collier Books.

———. [1913] 1950. *Totem and taboo: Some points of agreement between the mental lives of savages and neurotics*. Translated by James Strachey. New York: Norton.

———. [1910] 1957. The antithetical meaning of primal words. In *The complete psychological works of Sigmund Freud*. Vol. 11. Translated by James Strachey. London: Hogarth.

———. [1908] 1949. 'Civilized' sexual morality and modern nervousness. In *The collected papers of Sigmund Freud*. Vol. 2. Translated and edited by Ernest Jones. London: Hogarth.

———. [1901] 1953. *The psychopathology of everyday life*. Translated by James Strachey. New York: Norton.

Friedman, M. 1970. The social responsibility of business is to increase its profits. *Sunday New York Times Magazine*, September 13.

Geertz, C. 1973. *The interpretations of cultures*. New York: Basic Books.

Gellner, E. 1992. *Postmodernism, reason, and religion*. New York: Routledge.

———. 1992. *Reason and culture*. London: Blackwell.

———. 1979. The social roots of egalitarianism. *Dialectics and Humanism* 6 (4):27–43.

Gephart, R.P. 1984. Making sense of organizationally based environmental disasters. *Journal of Management* 10 (2):205-25.

Gergen, K. 1992. Organization theory in the postmodern era. In *Rethinking organization*, edited by M. Reed and M. Hughes. London: Sage.

Gigch, J. van, Borghino, J., LeMoigne, J., Logan, A. and Vervilos, V. (1988). A metasystematic view of a disaster: Example of the space shuttle *Challenger*. *Human Systems Management* 7 (3):251–64.

Godfrey, P. 1994. 'The functions of the executive' and 'The republic': Exploring the Platonic roots of Chester Barnard. *International Journal of Public Administration* 17 (6):1071–91.

Goffman, E. 1967. *Interaction ritual*. New York: Pantheon.

Golembiewski, R., and Kuhnert, K. 1994. Barnard on authority and zone of indifference: Toward perspectives on the decline of managerialism. *International Journal of Public Administration* 17 (16):1195-238.

Gouldner, A. 1954. *Patterns of industrial bureaucracy*. New York: Free Press.

Habermas, J. 1994. *The past as future*. Translated by Max Pensky. Lincoln, Neb.: University of Nebraska Press.

———. 1984. *The theory of communicative action, Vol. I: Reason and the rationalization of society*. Translated by Thomas McCarthy. Cambridge: Polity Press.

———. 1979. *Communication and the evolution of society*. Translated by Thomas McCarthy. Boston: Beacon Press.

———. 1971. *Toward a rational society: Student protest, science, and politics*. Translated by Jeremy Shapiro. London: Heinemann.

Heller, A. 1993. Existentialism, alienation, postmodernism: Cultural movements as vehicles of change in the patterns of everyday life. In *A postmodern reader,* edited by J. Natol and L. Hutcheon. Albany, N.Y.: State University of New York Press.

Hennis, W. 1988. *Max Weber: Essays in reconstruction*. Boston: Allen and Unwin.

Hertzberg, D., and Cohen, L. 1992. Scandal is fading away for Solomon, but not for trader Paul Mozer. *Wall Street Journal*, August 7.

Heydebrand, W. 1977. Organizational contradictions in public bureaucracies: Toward a Marxian theory of organizations. *The Sociological Quarterly* 18 (Winter):83–107.

Hirschhorn, L. 1993. Professionals, authority, and group life: A case study of a law firm. In *The psychodynamics of organizations,* edited by L. Hirschhorn and C. Barnett. Philadelphia: Temple University Press.

Hirschhorn, L., and Young, D. 1993. The psychodynamics of safety: A case study of an oil refinery. In *The psychodynamics of organizations,* edited by L. Hirschhorn and C. Barnett. Philadelphia: Temple University Press.

Hobbes, T. [1651] 1985. *Leviathan*. New York: Penguin.

Homans, P. 1989. *The ability to mourn*. Chicago: University of Chicago Press.

Hoskin, K., and Macve, R. 1986. Accounting and the examination: A genealogy of disciplinary power. *Accounting, Organizations, and Society* 11 (2):105-36.

Hynes, T., and Prasad, P. 1997. Patterns of 'mock bureaucracy' in mining disasters: An analysis of the Westray coal mine explosion. *Journal of Management Studies* 34 (4):601-22.

Jackall, R. 1988. *Moral mazes: The world of corporate managers*. New York: Oxford University Press.

Jackson, N. 1995. To write, or not to right? *Organization Studies* 16 (4):571-3.

James, W. [1890] 1950. *Principles of psychology*. New York: Dover.

Jameson, F. 1984. Foreword to *The postmodern condition* by J. Lyotard. Minneapolis: University of Minnesota Press.

———. 1984. Postmodernism or the cultural logic of late capitalism. *New Left Review* 146:53–93.

Janis, I. 1972. *Victims of groupthink*. Boston: Houghton-Mifflin.

Jaques, E. 1990. In praise of hierarchy. *Harvard Business Review* 68 (1):127-33.

———. 1951. *The changing culture of a factory*. London: Tavistock Publications.

Jermier, J. 1985. When the sleeper wakes: A short story extending themes in radical organization theory. *Journal of Management* 11 (2):67–80.

Jung, C. 1959. *The collected works of C.G. Jung*. Translated by R.F.C. Hull. Princeton, N.J.: Princeton University Press.

Kafka, F. [1919] 1971. In the penal colony. In *Kafka: The complete stories,* edited and translated by N. Glatzer. New York: Schocken Books.

Kanter, R. 1983. *The change masters*. New York: Simon and Schuster.

———. 1977. *Men and women of the corporation*. New York: Basic Books.

Kaufmann, W. 1974. *Nietzsche: Philosopher, psychologist, anti-Christ.* 4ᵗʰ Ed. Princeton, N.J.: Princeton University Press.

Kellner, D. 1988. Postmodernism as social theory: Some challenges and problems. *Theory, Culture, and Society* 5 (2–3):239–69.

Kets de Vries, M. 1991. On becoming a CEO: Transference and addictiveness of power. In *Organizations on the couch: Clinical perspectives on organizational behavior and change,* edited by M. Kets de Vries. San Francisco: Jossey-Bass.

Kilduff, M. 1993. Deconstructing organizations. *Academy of Management Review* 18 (1):13–31.

Knights, D., and Collinson, D. 1987. Disciplining the shopfloor: A comparison of the disciplinary effects of managerial psychology and financial accounting. *Accounting, Organizations, and Society* 12 (5):457-77.

Knights, D., and Vurdubakis, T. 1994. Foucault, power, resistance, and all that. In *Resistance and power in organizations,* edited by J. Jermier, D. Knights, and W. Nord. New York: Routledge.

Knights, D., and Willmott, H. 1989. Power and subjectivity at work: From degradation to subjugation in social relations. *Sociology* 23 (4):535-58.

Kunda, G. 1992. *Engineering culture.* Philadelphia: Temple University Press.

Larson, M. 1977. *The rise of professionalism.* Berkeley, Calif.: University of California Press.

Lasch, C. 1984. *The minimal self.* New York: Norton.

———. 1979. *The culture of narcissism.* New York: Warner Books.

Lash, S. 1988. Discourse or figure? Postmodernism as a 'regime of signification.' *Theory, Culture, and Society* 5 (2–3):311-36.

Levine, S. 1955. Management and industrial relations in postwar Japan. *Far Eastern Quarterly* 15 (1):57–75.

Linstead, S. 1993a. Deconstruction in the study of organization. In *Postmodernism and organizations,* edited by J. Hassard and M. Parker. London: Sage.

———. 1993b. From postmodern anthropology to deconstructive ethnography. *Human Relations* 46 (1):97–120.

Linstead, S., and Grafton-Small, R. 1992. On reading organizational culture. *Organization Studies* 13 (3):331-55.

Lukes, S. 1973. *Individualism.* London: Blackwell.

Lyotard, J. 1984. *The postmodern condition.* Manchester: Manchester University Press.

Maanen, J. Van. 1995. Style as theory. *Organization Science* 6 (1):133–43.

———. 1988. *Tales of the field.* Chicago: University of Chicago Press.

Machiavelli, N. [1532] 1952). *The prince.* Translated by Luigi Ricci, revised by E. R. P. Vincent. New York: Mentor Books.

MacIntyre, A. 1988. *Whose justice? Whose rationality?* Notre Dame, Ind.: University of Notre Dame Press.

———. 1984. *After virtue.* Notre Dame, Ind.: University of Notre Dame Press.

Marsden, R., and Townley, B. 1995. Power and postmodernity: Reflections on the pleasure dome. *Electronic Journal of Radical Organization Theory.* November. (http://tui.mngt.waikato.ac.nz/leader/journal/ejrct.htm).

Martin, J. 1990. Deconstructing organizational taboos: The suppression of gender conflict in organizations. *Organization science* 1 (4):339-59.

Martin, J., and Frost, P. 1996. The organizational culture war games: A struggle for intellectual dominance. In *Handbook of organization studies,* edited by S. Clegg, C. Hardy, and W. Nord. Thousand Oaks, Calif.: Sage.

Marx, K. [1844] 1964. *Karl Marx: Early writings.* Translated and edited by T. B. Bottomore. New York: McGraw-Hill.

Marx, R., Stubbart, C., Traub, V., and Cavanaugh, M. 1987. The NASA space shuttle disaster: A case study. *Journal of Management Case Studies* 3 (4):300-18.

Masaryk, T. 1994. *Constructive sociological theory.* Edited by A. Woolfolk and J. Imber. New Brunswick, N.J.: Transaction.

———. [1881] 1994. The development of the modern suicide tendency. In *Constructive sociological theory,* edited by A. Woolfolk and J. Imber. New Brunswick: Transaction Publishers.

McCarthy, T. 1993. *Ideals and illusions.* Cambridge, Mass.: MIT Press.

McCoy, C., and Fritsch, P. 1996. Exxon defends its 'novel' approach to reducing Valdez punitive damages. *Wall Street Journal,* June 14.

McSwite, O.C. 1995. Humanism and pseudo-critique: The danger of missing the postmodern moment. *Organization* 2 (2): 233-40.

Mead, G. H. [1934] 1962. *Mind, self, and society.* Chicago: University of Chicago.

Melville, H. [1853] 1990. *Bartleby and Benito Cereno.* Edited by S. Applebaum. New York: Dover.

[1851] 1991. *Moby-Dick, or the whale.* New York: Vintage Books.

Milgram, S. 1963. Behavioral study of obedience. *Journal of Abnormal and Social Psychology* 67 (4):23-36.

Mill, J.S. [1838] 1962. Bentham. In *Essays on politics and culture,* edited by G. Himmelfarb. New York: Doubleday.

———. [1836] 1962. Civilization. In *Essays on politics and culture,* edited by G. Himmelfarb. New York: Doubleday.

———. [1831] 1962. The spirit of the age. In *Essays on politics and culture,* edited by G. Himmelfarb. New York: Doubleday.

Mingers, J. 1992. Technical, practical, and critical OR—past, present, and future. In *Critical management studies,* edited by M. Alvesson and H. Willmott. London: Sage.

Minkes, A.L. 1988. The presidential commission on the space shuttle *Challenger* accident: A management perspective. *International Journal of Technology Management* 3 (5):579-86.

Mintzberg, H. 1983. *Power in and around organizations.* Englewood Cliffs, N.J.: Prentice Hall.

Mitchell, T., and Scott, W. 1985. The universal Barnard: His micro theories of organizational behavior. *Public Administration Review* 9 (3):239-59.

Morgan, G. 1992. Marketing discourse and practice: Towards a critical analysis. In *Critical management studies,* edited by M. Alvesson and H. Willmott. London: Sage.

Mumby, D., and Putnam, L. 1992. The politics of emotion: A feminist reading of bounded rationality. *Academy of Management Review* 17 (3):465-86.

Nietzsche, F. [1887] 1974. *The gay science.* Translated by Walter Kaufmann. New York: Vintage Books.

———. [1886] 1966. *Beyond good and evil.* Translated by Walter Kaufmann. New York: Vintage Books.

Nord, W., and Jeremier, J. 1992. Critical social science for managers? Promising and perverse possibilities. In *Critical management studies,* edited by M. Alvesson and H. Willmott. London: Sage.

O'Neill, J. 1988. Religion and postmodernism: The Durkheimian bond in Bell and Jameson. *Theory, Culture, and Society* 5 (2–3):493-508.

Orwell, G. 1949. *1984.* New York: Harcourt, Brace.

Parker, M. 1995a. Angry young man has egoistic tantrum. *Organizational Studies* 16 (4):575-7.

———. 1995b. Critique in the name of what? Postmodernism and critical approaches to organization. *Organization Studies* 16 (4):553-64.

———. 1992. Post-modern organizations or postmodern organization theory. *Organization Studies* 13 (1):1–17.

Perrow, C. 1984. *Normal accidents.* New York: Basic Books.

———. 1972. *Complex organization.* Glenview, Ill.: Scott, Foresman.

Pettigrew, A. 1985. *The awakening giant.* Oxford: Basil Blackwell.

Pfeffer, J. 1981. *Power in organizations.* Marshall, Mass.: Pitman Press.

Pincoffs, E. 1986. *Quandaries and virtues: Against reductivisim in ethics.* Lawrence, Kans.: University Press of Kansas.

Plato. 1980. *The laws of Plato.* Translated by Thomas L. Pangle. Chicago: University of Chicago Press.

———. 1968. *The republic of Plato.* Translated by Allan Bloom. New York: Basic Books.

Polanyi, M. 1969. *Knowing and being.* Chicago: University of Chicago Press.

———. 1966. *The tacit dimension.* New York: Doubleday.

———. 1959. *The study of man.* Chicago: University of Chicago Press.

———. 1958. *Personal knowledge.* Chicago: University of Chicago Press.

Powell, W., and DiMaggio, P. 1991. *The new institutionalism in organizational analysis.* Chicago: University of Chicago Press.

Power, M. 1990. Modernism, postmodernism, and organization. In *The theory and philosophy of organizations,* edited by J. Hassard and D. Pym. London: Routledge.

Power, M., and Laughlin, R. 1992. Critical theory and accounting. In *Critical management studies,* edited by M. Alvesson and H. Willmott. London: Sage Publications.

Pye, A. 1994. Walking and talking Chester I. Barnard. *International Journal of Public Administration* 17 (6):1125–56.

Reed, M. 1993. Organizations and modernity: Continuity and discontinuity in organization theory. In *Postmodernism and organization,* edited by J. Hassard and M. Parker. London: Sage.

Rieff, P. 1991. The newer noises of war in the second culture camp: Notes on Professor Burt's legal fictions. *Yale Journal of Law and Humanities* 3 (2):315-88.

———. 1990. *The feeling intellect.* Chicago: University of Chicago Press.

———. 1987. *The triumph of the therapeutic.* Chicago: University of Chicago Press.

———. 1985. *Fellow teachers: Of culture and its second death.* Chicago: University of Chicago Press.

———. 1981. By what authority: Post-Freudian reflections on the repressive in modern culture. In *The problem of authority in America,* edited by J. Diggins and M. Kann. Philadelphia: Temple University Press.

———. 1979. *Freud: The mind of the moralist.* Chicago: University of Chicago Press.

———. 1954. Freud's contribution to political philosophy. Ph.D. diss. University of Chicago. Ann Arbor, Mich.: UMI Dissertation Services.

———. 1953. History, psychoanalysis, and the social sciences. *Ethics* 63 (2):107–20.

Riesman, D. 1950. *The lonely crowd.* New Haven, Conn.: Yale University Press.

Roberts, K. 1997. The launch of STS–5IL. *Administrative Science Quarterly* 42 (2):405-10.

Rohlen, T. 1974. *For harmony and strength.* Berkeley, Calif.: University of California Press.

Rousseau, J. [1755] 1992. *Discourse on the origin of inequality.* Translated by Donald A. Cross. Indianapolis, Ind.: Hackett.

Santayana, G. [1905] 1936. The life of reason. In *The philosophy of Santayana,* edited by Irwin Edman. New York: Random House.

Schein, E. 1992. *Organizational culture and leadership.* San Francisco: Jossey-Bass.

Schluchter, W. 1981. *The rise of western rationalism.* Berkeley, Calif.: University of California Press.

Schumpeter, J. 1934. *The theory of economic development.* New York: Oxford University Press.

Schwartz, H. 1990. *Narcissistic emotion and corporate decay: The theory of the organizational ideal.* New York: New York University Press.

Scott, W. 1982. Barnard on the nature of elitist responsibility. *Public Administration Review* 42 (3):197–201.

Scott, W. 1992. *Chester I. Barnard and the guardians of the managerial state.* Lawrence, Kans.: University Press of Kansas.

Scott, W., and Mitchell, T. 1989. The universal Barnard: His meta concepts of leadership in the administrative state. *Public Administration Quarterly* 13 (3):295–320.

Selznick, P. 1992. *The moral commonwealth.* Berkeley, Calif.: University of California Press.

Shils, E. 1981. *Tradition.* Chicago: University of Chicago Press.

Simon, H. 1945. *Administrative behavior.* New York: Free Press.

Smith, C., Child, J., and Rowlison, M. 1990. *Reshaping work.* Cambridge: Cambridge University Press.

Smith, E. 1994. Chester Barnard's concept of responsibility. *International Journal of Public Administration* 17 (6):1157–74.

Stauth, G., and Turner, B. 1988. Nostalgia, postmodernism, and the critique of mass culture. *Theory, Culture, and Society* 5 (2–3):509-26.

Steele, S. 1990. *The content of our character.* New York: St. Martin's Press.

Steffy, B., and Grimes, A. 1992. Personnel/organization psychology: A Critique of the discipline. In *Critical management studies,* edited by M. Alvesson and H. Willmott. London: Sage.

Stewart, D. 1989. Barnard as a framework for authority and control. *Public Productivity Review* 12 (4):413–21.

Stivers, R. 1994. *The culture of cynicism.* Cambridge, Mass.: Blackwell.

Strother, G. 1976. The moral codes of executives: A Watergate-inspired look at Barnard's theory of executive responsibility. *Academy of Management Review* 23 (2):13–22.

Sullivan, H. S. 1950. The illusion of personal individuality. *Psychiatry* 13 (1):317–32.

Tawney, R.H. [1926] 1962. *Religion and the rise of capitalism.* Gloucester, Mass.: Peter Smith.

Taylor, C. 1989. *Sources of the self.* Cambridge, Mass.: Harvard University Press.

———. 1984. Foucault on freedom and truth. *Political Theory* 12 (2):152-83.

Taylor, F. 1911. *Scientific management.* New York: Harper and Brothers.

Thompson, P. 1993. Postmodernism: Fatal distraction. In *Postmodernism and organization,* edited by J. Hassard and M. Parker. London: Sage.

Tocqueville, A. [1850] 1969. *Democracy in America.* Translated by George Lawrence. Garden City, N.J.: Doubleday.

Townley, B. 1994. *Reframing human resource management.* London: Sage.

———. 1993. Foucault, power/knowledge, and its relevance for human resource management. *Academy of Management Review* 18 (3):518-45.

Trevino, L., and Nelson, K. 1995. *Managing business ethics.* New York: Wiley.

Trist, E., and Bamforth, K. 1951. Some social and psychological consequences of the Longwall method of coal-getting. *Human Relations* 4, 3–38.

Troeltsch, E. 1992. *The social teaching of the Christian churches.* Translated by Olive Wyon. Louisville, Ky.: Westminster John Knox Press.

Turner, B.A. 1976. The organizational and interorganizational development of disasters. *Administrative Science Quarterly* 21 (3):378-97.

Turquet, P.M. 1974. Leadership: The individual and the group. In *Analysis of groups,* edited by G. Gibbard, J. Hartman, and R. Mann. San Francisco: Jossey-Bass.

Vaughan, D. 1996. *The Challenger launch decision: Risky technology, culture, and deviance at NASA.* Chicago: University of Chicago Press.

Veblen, T. 1948. Christian morals and the competitive system. In *The portable Veblen,* edited by M. Lerner. New York: Viking Press.

Weber, M. 1946. *From Max Weber.* Edited and translated by H. Gerth and C.W. Mills. London: Routledge and Kegan Paul.

———. [1922] 1963. *The sociology of religion.* Translated by Ephraim Fischoff. Boston: Beacon Press.

———. [1918] 1946. Politics as a vocation. In *From Max Weber,* edited and translated by H. Gerth and C.W. Mills. London: Routledge.

———. [1918] 1946. Science as a vocation. In *From Max Weber,* edited and translated by H. Gerth and C.W. Mills. London: Routledge.

———. [1915] 1946. Religious rejections of the world and their directions. In *From Max Weber,* edited and translated by H. Gerth and C.W. Mills. London: Routledge.

———. [1904-5] 1958. *The Protestant ethic and the spirit of capitalism.* Translated by Talcott Parsons. New York: Scribners.

Weick, K.E. 1993. The collapse of sensemaking in organizations: The Mann Gulch disaster. *Administrative Science Quarterly* 38 (4):628-52.

Weick, K. 1997. Book review of *The Challenge launch decision* by Diane Vaughan. *Administrative Science Quarterly* 42 (2):395–401.

Wells, L. 1963. The limits of formal authority: Barnard revisited. *Public Administration Review* 23 (2):161–6.

Whyte, W. 1956. *The organization man.* New York: Simon and Schuster.

Williamson, O. 1985. *The economic institutions of capitalism.* New York: Free Press.

Willmott, H. 1994. Bringing agency back into organizational analysis: Responding to the crisis of postmodernity. In *Toward a new theory of organization,* edited by J. Hassard and M. Parker. London: Routledge.

———. 1993. Strength is ignorance; slavery is freedom: Managing culture in modern organizations. *Journal of Management Studies* 30 (4):515-52.

Winnicott, D.W. 1971. *Playing and reality.* London: Tavistock.

Winsor, D.A. 1988. Communication failures contributing to the *Challenger* accident: An example for technical communicators. *IEEE Transactions on Professional Communications* 31 (3):101-7.

Wolf, W. 1994. Understanding Chester I. Barnard. *International Journal of Public Administration* 17 (6):1035–69.

Wolfe, T. 1987. *Bonfire of the vanities.* New York: Farrar, Straus & Giroux.

Wolin, S. 1960. *Politics and vision.* Boston: Little, Brown

Wrong, D. 1994. *The problem of order.* New York: Free Press.

Index

Printed in the United States
by Baker & Taylor Publisher Services